GOOD *&* EVIL ACTIONS

GOOD & EVIL ACTIONS

A Journey through Saint Thomas Aquinas

STEVEN J. JENSEN

The Catholic University of America Press
Washington, D.C.

Copyright © 2010
The Catholic University of America Press
All rights reserved

The paper used in this publication meets the minimum
requirements of American National Standards for Information
Science—Permanence of Paper for Printed Library Materials,
ANSI Z39.48-1984.

∞

Library of Congress Cataloging-in-Publication Data
Jensen, Steven J., 1964–
Good and evil actions : a journey through Saint Thomas Aquinas /
Steven J. Jensen.
p. cm.
Includes bibliographical references and index.
ISBN 978-0-8132-1727-7 (paperback : alk. paper)
1. Good and evil.   2. Thomas, Aquinas, Saint, 1225?–1274.
3. Good and evil—History of doctrines—Middle Ages,
600–1500.   I. Title.
BJ1401.J46 2010
171'.2092—dc22
2009036241

For my parents

Parentibus non potest secundum aequalitatem

recompensari quod eis debetur.

(II-II, 80, 1)

CONTENTS

FOREWORD

It is inescapably true that we should do good and avoid evil, but how are we to know the difference between them? Whenever St. Thomas faces this question, he quotes the Psalmist in the Vulgate (Ps. 4, 6): Quis ostendit nobis bona? The answer is: Signatum est super nos lumen vultus tui, Domine. Who will show us what is good? The light of the countenance is sealed upon us, O Lord. That is, by a participation in the divine wisdom, men have a natural capacity to discern good and evil.

One becomes a good person by performing good deeds; a primary task of moral philosophy, accordingly, is getting clear on the nature of the human act. Human acts are acts that humans perform, of course, and it is important to begin with such resounding truisms. But difficulties arise and one learns to appreciate Thomas Aquinas's distinction between the human act and the act of a man. Not every activity truly ascribed to a man counts as a human act, the mark of the latter being that it is deliberate and voluntary. Inhaling and exhaling, dreaming, and the like thus do not count as human acts. One must know what he is doing and freely do it in order for the act to be human. Thus one is drawn into a consideration of the constituents of the human act, the contributions of reason on the one hand and of will on the other. There is the inner act as well as the external action and moral appraisal of the one or the other poses different though related questions. The constituents of the complete human act enable us to appraise imperfect actions that do not reach their term and yet form part of our moral history.

So it is that students of St. Thomas have long since learned the complexity that awaits them in following initial leads of fundamental certainty. Along the way, a host of problems arise, more or less central, and little schools are formed. Each of the constituents of the human act raises issues of its own. Notably, the notion of the intention of the agent calls for lengthy reflection. In short, an ample menu of difficulties confronts the student who wants both to be guided by St. Thomas and to learn from the efforts of others. This presents a problem of method. Should one simply identify the problem areas, take them up one by one, and then present one's own interpretation?

Comes now Steven Jensen who has chosen a far more promising and difficult method: he will seek to make emerge from the discussion of the difficulties, artfully arranged, the authentic doctrine of Thomas Aquinas. The advantages of this method are manifest, but it puts great demands on the reader as it did on the writer. Familiarity with the chief rival positions is of little moment if one is not at the same time aware of the developing dialectic which gives rise to them. Jensen undertakes both to acquaint us with the best that has been hitherto said, why it has been said, and, often, why it is insufficient.

The present book, then, is a remarkable compendium of the status quaestionis of a large number of prickly issues associated with Thomas Aquinas's theory of human action, a fair look at proposed solutions, and finally Jensen's own best thought on the matter. In the course of doing this, he confronts positions put forward by friends of his, always, as Aristotle learned vis-à-vis Plato, the severest test. Whether persuaded or not, none of his interlocutors could consider him hasty or unfair.

Over the past half century, much has been written about Thomas's moral philosophy. This has doubled the scholar's task, since he must both immerse himself in the original texts and give a fair hearing to what his predecessors have made of those texts. I doubt that anyone has done this more thoroughly and impressively than Steven Jensen, and I for one am grateful to him.

Ralph McInerny

ACKNOWLEDGMENTS

I would like to thank all those who have helped with this book. Those deserving special mention include James Stromberg and Ralph McInerny, who provided the foundation and inspiration, Stephen Brock, whose insights have guided me over the years, Thomas Osborne, Thomas Hurley, Richard Cain, and Thomas Cavanaugh, all of whom provided helpful comments and suggestions, Barbara Stirling, who found the ideal artwork for the cover, Jessica Jacobs, for assistance with the index, my wife, Christine, for her constant support, and my children, who endured my many hours of seclusion.

GOOD & EVIL ACTIONS

INTRODUCTION

In 1954 Elizabeth Anscombe coined the term "consequentialism" to designate those moral theories that reduce the moral value of any action to its effects or consequences, leaving no moral significance to the act itself.[1] Although she thought consequentialism morally bankrupt, and patently so, she claimed the philosophical explanation of its inadequacy was lacking, and given the current philosophical resources, a reasoned account was likely to remain unavailable. She herself did much to provide the philosophical tools for the wanted explanation when in 1957 she launched the field of action theory with the publication of *Intention*.[2] If actions themselves, and not merely their consequences, provide moral content, then we must in some manner understand the action itself.

Anscombe noted that an action can have many descriptions, but it is intended only under some of these descriptions. The act of pumping water to a household might also be an act of poisoning its inhabitants, but if the agent is unaware that the water is poisoned, then he intends the action only under the first description and not under the second. Anscombe's analysis became commonplace, being further developed by thinkers such as Donald David-

1. G. E. M. Anscombe, "Modern Moral Philosophy," *Philosophy* 33 (1958): 1–19.
2. G. E. M. Anscombe, *Intention*, 2nd ed. (Ithaca, N.Y.: Cornell University Press, 1963).

son.[3] These developments in secular philosophy, however, did little to identify the moral import of the act itself. If a single action has many descriptions, then it seemed to thinkers such as Jonathan Bennett that we could not even separate out the act from its effects.[4] If Jones kills Smith, then his action might be described as pulling a trigger, firing a gun, killing a man, making a noise, and so on. If his action is simply pulling the trigger, then the death of Smith is a consequence. Certainly, the action of "pulling a trigger" has no inherent moral significance; only the consequence of death matters. Unless there is some way to determine that the "act itself" includes the death, and so must be a killing, then only the consequences of an action must hold moral import.

Anscombe's emphasis upon intention corresponded to a strain within Thomistic moral philosophy in which intention had come to play a central role, even a comprehensive role, largely through what is called the principle of double effect. It seemed intention could be used to separate those descriptions that belong to the action itself and those that should be relegated to the consequences of the action. In the typical example of self-defense, for instance, it was claimed that the defender need not intend to kill her assailant; she need intend only to stop the attack. Although her action can be described as "killing the assailant," this description and the death it implies are actually only consequences of her action, since they fall outside intention. All too often this emphasis upon intention took center stage, leaving the action itself in a minor supporting role. The debate shifted from the task of separating an action and its consequences to the task of separating intention from what is outside intention.

As Anscombe had noted, there was much at stake. Non-Thomist philosophers took note and then took aim. Many attacked the idea

3. See Donald Davidson, *Essays on Actions and Events* (Oxford: Clarendon Press, 1980).

4. Jonathan Bennett, *The Act Itself* (Oxford: Clarendon Press, 1995).

that a useful distinction could be drawn between intention and what is outside intention. As long as a consequence of an action was foreseen, claimed some, then it was intended; only ignorance allowed something to remain outside intention. After nearly thirty years of debate, however, when the dust had settled it became clear that even non-Thomist philosophers had to acknowledge that foreseen consequences need not be intended.

This acknowledgment did little to resolve the dispute among Thomists themselves, who disagreed over where to draw the line between intention and what falls outside intention. One particular case, the so-called craniotomy case, dominated the discussion, taking on nearly iconic stature even though it was already practically obsolete when it was introduced at the very beginning of the debate by H. L. A. Hart.[5] Its importance for the analysis of the act itself remains today, and it plays a fittingly focal role in this book. If a doctor must crush the head of a baby *in utero* in order to end a life-threatening labor, then does the consequent death of the baby fall within the intention of the doctor or outside her intention? Thomist and non-Thomist philosophers alike weighed in on either side, some claiming that the death must be intended and others claiming that it can fall outside intention.

More than others, Germain Grisez and his followers Joseph Boyle and John Finnis stressed the importance of intention, sometimes seemingly to the exclusion of the physical characteristics of the act itself.[6] They emphasized that intention and the moral character of actions did not depend upon the causal structure of the physical action. In a move to distance themselves from what came to be called "physicalism" they also eschewed the importance of teleology, or human nature, for the moral evaluation of actions.

5. See H. L. A. Hart, "Intention and Punishment," *Oxford Review* 5 (1967): 5–22.
6. See, for instance, John Finnis, Germain Grisez, and Joseph Boyle, "'Direct' and 'Indirect': A Reply to Critics of Our Action Theory," *The Thomist* 65 (2001): 1–44.

The morality they presented seemed rather disembodied. In place of physical actions, they provided mental intentions. Rather than human goods depending upon our human physical nature, they presented human goods immediately grasped by a practical reason that could do without teleology. Martin Rhonheimer followed with similar views, although he tempered both of these claims by stressing a material element that enters into our actions and our moral judgments.[7]

A reaction against Finnis and Grisez set in, claiming that moral evaluations must return to teleology and to the physical nature of the action. The act of crushing the baby's head appeared, by its physical nature, to be an act of killing, and if one's theory of intention reached some other conclusion, then it must have gone awry somewhere or other. It must have gone wrong, it seems, in the rejection of teleology. Steven Long claimed that the physical act has its own teleological structure, which intention must respect.[8] Kevin Flannery claimed that intention is shaped by human practices, which serve a kind of teleological role.[9] In these teleological structures one hoped to find the act itself, that important moral unit set apart from the effects of an action, that key to the rejection of consequentialism alluded to so many years previously by Elizabeth Anscombe.

Thomas Aquinas certainly seems to have thought that there was some "act itself" that could be identified and separated from what he called its circumstances. But how does this separation between the act and its circumstance come about? Examination of

7. See, for instance, Martin Rhonheimer, *Natural Law and Practical Reason: A Thomist View of Moral Autonomy* (New York: Fordham University Press, 2000).

8. See Steven Long, *The Teleological Grammar of the Moral Act* (Naples, Fla.: Sapientia Press, 2007).

9. See Kevin Flannery, *Acts Amid Precepts: The Aristotelian Logical Structure of Thomas Aquinas's Moral Theory* (Washington, D.C.: The Catholic University of America Press, 2001).

the physical nature of the action hardly seems promising. Jones's action of pulling the trigger is also an act of firing a gun, killing a man, making a noise, waking the neighbors, staining the carpet, and so on. As Jonathan Bennett suggests, any line drawn between act and circumstance seems arbitrary. Is the act itself an act of making a noise, while the death is only a consequence? Or is the killing what is essential to the act itself, and the noise is circumstantial? Aquinas thought that actions are ordered realities, essentially directed to some form or end, even as heating is directed to the end of heat and killing to the end of death; physical actions, however, appear to involve a string of otherwise unrelated effects.

It is little wonder, then, that Finnis and Grisez should disregard the physical structures of actions, finding in these structures a kind of trap, a lure that might lead us to attribute moral characteristics to merely physical realities. Much better, it seems, to find moral character in the spiritual realities underlying the physical act, in the agent's intention and in reason's perception of eternal moral truths. Aquinas himself is unequivocal: an action takes its order and moral species from what is intended.

On the other hand, it hardly seems true to our physical nature to suppose that a doctor can so "direct" her intention, such that an act of crushing a baby's head is not also an act of killing the baby. It is equally unsurprising, then, that some should react against Finnis and Grisez, finding within the physical action itself an essential nature and order. An act of crushing a baby's head *just is* an act of killing.

The analysis of the moral species within Aquinas confounds the most resolute, justifying the book length arguments and distinctions of authors such as Joseph Pilsner.[10] Nevertheless, at its core lies a very simple idea. The moral character of actions depends upon two orders: what an action *is* directed to and what an action

10. See Joseph Pilsner, *The Specification of Human Actions in St. Thomas Aquinas* (Oxford: Oxford University Press, 2006).

should be directed to. The act of killing an innocent human being *is directed* to his death; it *should be directed* to his good. An act of sexual intercourse *should be directed* to the good of the offspring, but an act of fornication *is actually directed* elsewhere. When the actual direction conforms to what should be, then the action is morally good; when the direction is opposed to what should be, then it is morally evil.

The difficulty is in clarifying the nature of these two orders. To what is the doctor's action actually ordered? To the baby's death or merely to resizing the baby's head? Is a lethal act of defense actually ordered to the death of the assailant or merely to stopping the attack? Must sexual intercourse be directed to the good of offspring? What gives it its "should be" order? Unfortunately, this difficulty of spelling out the two orders is all too often compounded by a simple error: the two orders are not kept distinct but rather jumbled together and confused, so that one is mistaken for the other.

Careful attention to the two orders reveals that the first, the order that an action actually takes on, depends fundamentally upon intention. An action is ordered to that which the agent intends. If the doctor intends to kill the baby, then her action is directed to his death. Such intentional direction, however, depends upon the physical causes of an action. Our intentions are not constructed in the clouds, but use as their tools or materials the actual causes in the world around us. Discovering the connection between these two—between intention and the causal structures of actions—is no simple task; by itself, it has occupied almost the entire debate concerning the moral species of actions. I propose that it is a mistake to introduce teleology into the order an action does have, a mistake that rightly deserves the name of "physicalism."

In contrast, the "should be" order of an action depends not upon intention but upon teleology. For this second order, the causal structures of actions are also important; the very meaning of "causal structure," however, takes on entirely new significance, so much so that the causal structures that enter into and influence intention cannot be classed with those that reveal the direction an action should take; no more does a deck of cards belong to the same class as the deck of a ship. The causal structures that enter intention can be entirely incidental relations depending upon oddities of the circumstances at hand. The causal structures of teleology, on the other hand, belong essentially to the nature of an action.

This book is roughly divided into a consideration of these two orders. The first three chapters are devoted to uncovering the direction that actions actually take on. The fourth chapter begins an inquiry into the order that actions should have. The fifth chapter focuses upon some difficulties of applying the first order, the actual direction, to what has been discovered concerning the second order, the direction an action should have. Chapters 6 and 7 complete the analysis of the second order. The overall structure is simple enough. Nevertheless, the reader begins in the thick of the debate and remains there until chapter 7. The reader is allowed to taste the confusion incurred by confounding the two orders. The separation of the two orders will be arrived at through the heat of dialectic.

1 | HUMAN ACTIONS

SECTION 1.1. *The Problem*

Traditionally, Catholic moralists have drawn a sharp distinction between two similar cases in medical ethics. In the craniotomy case, the head of the fetus is too large to pass through the woman's pelvis, so that natural labor will not result in delivery but will continue indefinitely, probably resulting in the death of both the mother and the child. With the current medical technology of C-sections, the situation poses no difficulty, but a century ago there was no sure way to save the life of the mother without killing the fetus. Standard procedure amongst non-Catholic doctors was to perform a craniotomy on the fetus, crushing his head, so that his body might then pass through the mother's pelvis. When petitioned on the issue, however, the Vatican replied that this procedure was unacceptable;[1] Catholic doctors were then faced with the unpleasant choice of allowing both the unborn child and the mother to die. The only alternative, so it seemed, was killing one person in order to save the life of another.[2] While the first choice was painful, the second was morally abhorrent.

1. Or rather, that it was unsafe to teach that it was acceptable. John Finnis et al. ("Direct and Indirect," 1–44, at 26–27) argue that the Church has not taught that the craniotomy is immoral, but that it could not be taught to be licit. On the other hand, Kevin Flannery argues that it cannot be taught because it is in fact not morally acceptable; see "What Is Included in a Means to an End?" *Gregorianum* 74 (1993): 499–513, at 508–10.

2. The discussions throughout this book will operate under the assumption

In the hysterectomy case, on the other hand, a pregnant woman is found to have cancer of the uterus, standard treatment of which may include a hysterectomy, which will result in the death of the fetus. Yet in this case, according to the standard Catholic view, the doctor may perform the hysterectomy because she does not kill the baby. She merely removes the womb with the result that the baby dies.

The two cases are similar in many respects. In both, the continued pregnancy poses a threat to the life of the mother; in both, the baby will almost certainly die; in both, a procedure may be performed that saves the life of the mother but in which the baby dies sooner than would naturally occur. Despite these similarities two contrary ethical conclusions are reached. The craniotomy is considered killing the baby in order to save the life of the mother, while the hysterectomy is considered saving of the life of the mother with the result that the baby dies. The two cases are distinguished through the action that the doctor performs. In the craniotomy case, she performs an act of killing a baby; in the hysterectomy case, she performs an act of removing a diseased organ, with the result that a baby dies. While killing an innocent human being is never permissible, removing diseased organs is not only permissible but also praiseworthy.

1.1.1. Hairsplitting Casuistry

Such reasoning, some protest, exhibits the worst of casuistry. This minute hairsplitting has nothing to do with the lives involved; it is a game of mental gymnastics designed to justify the conclusions we have already reached. In whatever manner we describe the actions involved, the same upshot results. In both instances a baby dies and a woman is saved. No line can be drawn separating the craniotomy from the hysterectomy. We need only look at the results of both actions to see that they are morally equivalent. This

---

that an unborn child is a human person, deserving of equal respect with other human beings.

objection seems to suppose that any attempt to distinguish different kinds of actions, as opposed to the consequences of actions, is
abusive casuistry, and *ipso facto,* morally irrelevant; all that matters,
morally speaking, are the consequences of an action.

Casuistry may be irrelevant to the consequentialist, but if we
reject consequentialism with its reductive calculations, then somehow what we do must matter. Consider a soldier whose wartime
mission is to destroy a certain bridge over which the enemy troops
will soon cross in their path of slaughter and destruction. He has
laid the explosives and has just removed himself sufficiently to detonate them. But as he is about to depress the plunger he notices a lone
pedestrian beginning to cross the bridge, a young child of about
five years. At the same time he sees the enemy troops approaching
the bridge. If he waits for the slow child to cross the bridge a large
portion of the enemy will have crossed. He decides to detonate the
explosives. Has he killed the child? Certainly he has done something that resulted in her death, but it seems plausible to say that
he did not most properly kill her. What he did was destroy a bridge,
with the result that the child died.

In contrast, consider another soldier in a similar situation, but
suppose that his detonator fails. One means remains to set off the
explosives, for another detonator is upon the bridge, but the soldier
cannot count on his wary enemy setting it off. The child is currently
standing over the spot where the soldier knows the detonator to be,
so he takes aim with his rifle and shoots the child, who falls upon
the detonator, setting off the explosives. Although the two cases
have the same upshot, namely, the child dies and the bridge is destroyed, it seems that in the second case the soldier kills the child
in order to destroy the bridge. In the first case, on the other hand,
it seems plausible to suppose that the soldier destroys the bridge,
with the result that the child died.

A consequentialist may care little how we identify the soldiers'
actions, for in either event a child dies and a bridge is destroyed.
But if we reject consequentialism, then it may make all the differ-

ence whether the soldiers kill the child or destroy the bridge. The sort of soldier who would go about killing an innocent child has distinguished himself from the soldier who would never set himself to kill a child, even if sometimes he might destroy a bridge, recognizing that a child will die.

Even if casuistry has been abused, then, its task remains important. The commandant says, "You shall not kill" not, "You shall not produce death." We must distinguish, therefore, between instances of killing and instances of merely producing death. This task is made especially demanding—and therefore easily open to abuse—because we tend to identify actions in terms of their effects. The act of killing, for instance, is identified through the effect of death, and the act of growing is identified through increased size. Since a single action has multiple effects, it will also have many descriptions. In the craniotomy case, for example, the doctor's action may be described as moving forceps, crushing a skull, ending labor, killing a baby, and saving the mother, for by a single action she brings about all of these effects. Through what has been called the accordion effect we may describe an action to include some effects but not others, and we usually have the option of expanding our description to include yet later effects. The description "crushing a skull" does not reach to the effect of death, but we can choose to redescribe the action as "killing a baby" and so expand the action to include the effect of death. The boundaries of actions, then, appear more fluid than fixed. If we describe the doctor's action as "reducing the size of the head," then the death of the baby is an effect of her action; then, the craniotomy case begins to look more like the hysterectomy case, for the doctor performs an action that in itself is without objection, reducing the size of the head, even though it has lethal consequences. Nothing prevents us, however, from also describing the doctor's action as "killing the baby." Under the latter description, but not the former, the doctor has broken the commandment.

A major task of casuistry, then, is to identify what is truly done, to pick out from amongst the many possible descriptions of an action, the "real" description, or the most proper or appropriate description. For the craniotomy and the hysterectomy cases the doctor's action may certainly be described as "killing a baby," but the question before us concerns what the doctor is most properly going about doing. Is she most properly killing a baby? Or is she, in the craniotomy case, most properly reducing the size of the head, with the consequence that the baby dies? In the hysterectomy case, is she most properly removing a diseased organ, while killing the baby is merely an extended or secondary description of what she does? How we describe actions, it turns out, may be of the utmost importance.

1.1.2. Many or One

Our focus is upon Aquinas's treatment of the question, whose discussion of the unity and multiplicity of actions brings clarity to the problem. He is concerned to determine whether a human action is only one action or many. The answer, he says, depends upon what is meant by unity and diversity.

> Something can be a multitude in one respect but a unity in some other respect. Indeed, every multitude is in some sense one, as Dionysus says. Still, some multitudes are simply speaking many but one only in some respect and others are simply one but a multitude only in some respect.
>
> Anything that is one in substance is simply one and a multitude only in some respect. For example, in the category of substance, the complete substance, which is made of its parts (either integral or essential) is simply one.
>
> On the other hand, those which differ in substance and are united in some property are simply speaking many but one only in some respect. For example, many people are one nation, and many stones are one pile, for these things are one only through composition or order.[3]

3. *Summa theologiae* I-II, 17, 4. "Nihil prohibet aliqua esse secundum quid multa et secundum quid unum. Quinimmo omnia multa sunt secundum aliquid

A pile of old clothes, scraps of wood, and other miscellanies, may be called one heap or pile, but the unity of the heap is superficial. There are really many things that just happen to be in one place. On the other hand, a baby has many parts, such as legs, arms, and head, but she is truly one thing that has many parts. She is a multitude only in a qualified sense. In short, sometimes many things have a certain unity about them and sometimes what is simply one thing has a certain multiplicity about it.

Another kind of diversity, besides the multiplication of parts, applies more immediately to our problem. A single cat has many features or properties from which he may be described in many different ways, for example, as a black cat, a fat cat, or a furry cat. Aquinas portrays a similar picture of actions. He distinguishes between the substance of an action and its properties, which he calls its circumstances.[4]

> The name of circumstance is taken from our understanding of place and applied to human actions. Something is said to stand around [*circumstare*] a place when it is extrinsic to the thing but touches it, or at least is close to it. Therefore, any conditions that are outside the substance of an act, but still touch the act in some way, are called circumstances. Since what is outside the substance of a thing

---

unum, ut Dionysus dicit ult. cap. *De Div. Nom.* Est tamen differentia attendenda in hoc, quod quaedam sunt simpliciter multa et secundum quid unum, quaedam vero e converso. . . . Et ideo quaecumque sunt unum secundum substantiam, sunt unum simpliciter et multa secundum quid. Sicut totum in genere substantiae, compositum ex suis partibus vel integralibus vel essentialibus, est unum simpliciter. . . . Quae vero sunt diversa secundum substantiam et unum secundum accidens, sunt diversa simpliciter et unum secundum quid; sicut multi homines sunt unus populus, et multi lapides sunt unus acervus; quae est unitas compositiones aut ordinis." Henceforth, references to the *Summa theologiae* will be simply by roman numerals, indicating part, and Arabic numerals, indicating question and article.

4. For an excellent summary of the nature of circumstances, as well as the role they play in the specification of actions, see Pilsner, *Specification*, 172–98.

but pertains to that thing, is called a property of it, the circumstances of human acts are called their properties.[5]

If we describe the doctor's action as "what she did at one o'clock" or "what she did in the operating room" we recognize that we are not getting at the essence of what she did but merely giving circumstantial descriptions. The question before us, then, is not, "How may we describe the doctor's action, as a killing or as the removal of an organ?" but, "What did the doctor most essentially do?" Did she most essentially remove a diseased organ, with the death of the baby being merely a property or circumstance, or did she most essentially kill the baby? We are after not simply descriptions of actions, which are unquestionably diverse and multiple; we are after what Thomas calls the species or substance of actions. Our search is not merely of "academic" interest; it is not mere hairsplitting. It lies at the divide between consequentialism and those ethical views that find some importance in what a person does, not merely in what he effects.

1.1.3. Resizing Heads, Killing, and Murder

As with most important questions, the answer to our problem is not simple. If we turn to Aquinas, we find an abundance of statements concerning the species of human actions, many of them seemingly in conflict with one another. As Stephen Brock notes, "Aquinas's treatment of the specification of actions is complex, sometimes downright bewildering."[6] Joseph Pilsner has done much to lift the confusion by identifying the many meanings of the relevant terms

5. I-II, 7, 1. "Et inde est quod nomen circumstantiae ab his quae in loco sunt, derivatur ad actus humanos. Dicitur autem in localibus aliquid circumstare, quod est quidem extrinsecum a re, tamen attingit ipsum, vel appropinquat ei secundum locum. Et ideo quaecumque conditiones sunt extra substantiam actus, et tamen attingunt aliquo modo actum humanum, circumstantiae dicuntur. Quod autem est extra substantiam rei ad rem ipsam pertinens, accidens eius dicitur. Unde circumstantiae actuum humanorum accidentia eorum dicenda sunt."

6. Stephen Brock, *Action and Conduct: Thomas Aquinas and the Theory of Action* (Edinburgh: T. & T. Clark, 1998), 198.

within Aquinas and by removing any appearance of contradiction.[7] Nevertheless, the multiple attempts to unite these diverse terms into a coherent account have left the application of these terms obscure. The followers of Aquinas give us a plethora of views, sometimes differing from one another by the most subtle of details.

The craniotomy case may serve as a microcosm of the dispute. I have suggested that Catholic ethicists identify the craniotomy as a killing and therefore as morally reprehensible. Such indeed is the traditional position, but it is not the only view expressed by those following the thought of Thomas Aquinas. As indicated earlier, for instance, some thinkers draw a tight parallel with the hysterectomy case, suggesting that the doctor's action might be seen as "reducing the size of the baby's head," with the death of the baby being a consequence or circumstance of her action. Joseph Boyle writes,

> On the face of it, it is not the *killing* which removes the threat; the means here appears to be the craniotomy itself insofar as it alters the dimension of the skull *in order* to allow labor to proceed.[8]

Still others note that the essence of human actions is not merely physical but involves some moral component. If we wish to discover what the doctor did most essentially, it does not suffice to say that she "killed the baby," for we thereby provide only a physical description of her action. "Killing" is one thing; "murder" is another. It is not enough, then, to determine that the craniotomy is a killing of the baby; we must yet determine whether that killing is murder. Some would claim that killing an innocent human being *just is* murder, and therefore killing the baby, who is certainly innocent, is murder; in contrast, the view called Proportionalism claims that the moral judgment concerning murder cannot be based simply upon such nonmoral features as innocence; it involves a rather

7. Pilsner, *Specification*.
8. Joseph Boyle, "Double Effect and a Certain Type of Embryotomy," *Irish Theological Quarterly* 44 (1977): 303–18, at 309. See also Finnis et al., "Direct and Indirect," 21–31.

complex assessment, including both physical features and psychological features, such as the agent's intention.

We find, then, three prominent views concerning the craniotomy. Some claim that the doctor most properly reduces the size of the baby's head, and only in a secondary sense does she kill the baby. Others claim that the doctor does kill the baby properly speaking. Still others claim that naturally speaking she does kill the baby, but that morally speaking she might not murder the baby. Clearly, the anatomy of a craniotomy is no simple matter.

1.1.4. Physicalism and Abelardianism

These diverse analyses of the craniotomy are founded upon more general views about how to identify actions. Although the views are dizzying in their multiplicity, they can be gathered together under two broad approaches. A nearly universal approach identifies the species of actions by way of the agent's intention. On this view, what the doctor does depends upon what she intends. If she intends to reduce the size of the skull, but not to kill the baby, then most properly she does not kill the baby but only resizes the head. On the other hand, if she does intend to kill the baby, then her action is most properly a killing.

The debate often shifts from the action performed by the doctor to her intention. Rather than ask what the doctor did, the disputants discuss what the doctor intended. Did she intend merely to reduce the size of the head or did she intend to kill? Some will claim that she need merely intend to reduce the size of the skull, for to achieve her goal of ending the pregnancy and so save the mother, the death of the baby is in no way instrumental; she need only reduce the size of the head. Others will claim that she cannot avoid intending to kill the baby. The recourse to intention, then, does not resolve the dispute, but merely changes the arena of debate.

A much less common approach emphasizes not the agent's intention but the physical features of the action itself, especially the material or subject upon which the agent acts. Upon examining the act of crushing a skull, for instance, we find an intimate connection between this action and the death of the victim; the two cannot be pulled apart. Even before we know the doctor's intention, we can conclude, merely from the physical features of the action, that the action must be a killing.

On account of its emphasis upon the physical aspects of an action, the latter view has been called physicalism,[9] while the former view has sometimes been called Abelardianism, because of its emphasis upon intention, shared with the medieval philosopher Abelard. We can clarify the difference between these two approaches by use of Aquinas's distinction between the exterior and interior actions, two components that Thomas finds in every human action. My act of driving to the symphony, for example, includes both the choice to drive and the actual physical activity of driving. We should take care to note that the terms "exterior" and "interior" do not refer to the body but to the will: the interior act is interior to the will, while the exterior act is exterior to the will. The exterior action, therefore, need not always be bodily exterior, but can be something entirely mental. When someone reminisces upon his past, there is still the interior act of choosing to reminisce and the exterior action of actually reminiscing.

Physicalism, then, is the view that the exterior action has its own moral species, not derived from the act of will. Abelardianism is the view that by itself the exterior action must receive its moral character from the interior act of will. Physicalism focuses upon the exterior activity of the craniotomy, trying to determine whether it has the nature of a killing. Abelardianism claims that no feature of the craniotomy can by itself make it a killing; in itself the act is in-

9. The term "physicalism" refers to two aspects of an ethical account of human actions. On the one hand, it refers to what I have described, namely, the identification of an action based upon certain physical features of that action; on the other hand, it refers to a view that claims the moral goods or norms of human life can be discovered in the ends of nature (see sections 6.1, 6.2, and 6.3). The two views need not be joined, despite their single name.

determinate, ready to receive determination from the agent's intention. Neither view should be taken as a precise position, but each should be taken as a collection of tendencies. Therefore, whether any particular thinker belongs entirely to one position or another cannot be determined, nor is it our concern. Certainly, thinkers such as John Finnis and Germain Grisez have expressed views that feature Abelardian tenets; on the other hand, thinkers such as Steven Long, Jean Porter, and Kevin Flannery have defended positions that have some appearance of physicalism. The categories of physicalism and Abelardianism serve as convenient dialectical types, not as fixed positions into which I am trying to fit individual thinkers.

A third position, which can be readily identified with particular thinkers, should not be forgotten. Proportionalism has elements of Abelardianism and physicalism. Its distinctiveness, for our concern, is its emphasis upon the difference between the natural and moral species, with its insistence that the latter must incorporate a moral judgment. The moral species of "murder," for instance, cannot be determined simply from the physical act of killing an innocent human being, as physicalism might suggest, or even simply from *willing* to kill an innocent human being, as Abelardianism might suggest, but it must include a moral judgment, such as "the *wrongful* killing of a human being."

1.1.5. What Lies Before Us

Our task is to understand Aquinas's account of the moral species of human actions. In light of his teaching, we hope better to understand cases such as the craniotomy and hysterectomy. We will focus upon what have come to be called transient or transitive actions, that is, normal physical actions such as killing or handing over money, rather than so-called immanent actions, that is, mental actions such as thinking or desiring. Although much of Aquinas's moral discussion focuses upon the latter, for instance, in his discussion of virtues and vices associated with various emotional desires, nevertheless, the current debate has focused upon the former.

The argument will be presented in dialectical fashion, as a conflict between the prominent positions of Abelardianism, physicalism, and Proportionalism. From the conflict, Aquinas's view will emerge. Necessarily, however, it will emerge piecemeal and in fits and starts. A bird's-eye view will arise only gradually, with the resolution of various conflicts. What is taken up at one point will be developed to fruition only later on. Therefore, I beg the reader's patience. Apparent conclusions should not be presumed to be final, but may await further clarification. Apparent rejections of various positions may prove to be only partial; the same positions might later be accepted in modified form. All views within the dialectic attain to some truth; it is only a matter of hitting upon that truth. I am much indebted to those on all sides of the debate who have uncovered the rich truths that I hope to weave together into that eloquent tapestry of Aquinas's thought. Some will wish to know, ahead of time, whether I am, as they say, on the side of the angels. Others will suppose, because I reject some elements of various interpretations, that I must be on the side of the demons. I prefer to postpone any declaration, keeping in mind that a view, or an element of it, can be rejected in part and need not thereby be rejected entirely.

Since most of the discussion directly or loosely connected with the thought of Thomas has emphasized intention, we will commence with a consideration of the role it plays in the specification of human actions. Intention will occupy our enquiry for the remainder of this chapter and for the next.

SECTION 1.2. *Per Se Actions*

Why should intention be so important for the specification of human actions? Because actions might be viewed as an emanation arising from the agent and going out to some subject or patient. The act of fire heating water is like an emanation of heat from the fire into the water. The character of this emanation depends upon its originating source in the fire. Similarly, human actions take their character from their source, and an important source for human actions is intention. This section (1.2) will spell out how actions have a definite character that arises from their originating source.

1.2.1. Multiple Descriptions

It is now commonplace to note that a single action can have many descriptions, for example, as Jones fires the gun, he kills Smith, but he also makes a noise, and after Smith's blood flows onto the floor we can say that Jones stains the carpet. Contemporary action theory does not distinguish between two possible explanations of this truth. On the one hand, we might have what is simply speaking a single action that has an incidental multiplicity from which the many descriptions are derived. Even as a cat can have many descriptions because of its many properties, for example, being black and fat, so a single action can have many descriptions because of its many circumstances. If Jones kills Smith in the study at 12:15 a.m. then we may describe his action in different ways: "Jones killed Smith"; "Jones killed Smith in the study"; and "Jones killed Smith at 12:15 a.m."

On the other hand, we might have simply speaking many actions that happen to be united through some property. Even as a collection of miscellaneous items can be united into one heap or pile through the property of place, so many actions might be called one through their relationship to a single property. The acts of "making a noise" and "staining the carpet" might be called one action because they both arise from the same movements of Jones.

The many descriptions of actions derive in part from the diverse effects that an action produces. Jones's action produces Smith's death, a noise, and a stain on the carpet, so it may be described as "killing Smith," "making a noise," and "staining the carpet." Its many other effects generate further descriptions still. In some sense, of course, we have one action with many descriptions. But in what sense? Is the action one only as a heap is one or is it one like the cat? Aquinas holds the latter. Jones did one thing, but this one action has many circumstances or properties that give rise to multiple descriptions. If he is correct, then there should be some way to pick out, from the multiple descriptions of an action, the "real" description, which identifies the essence or substance of the action. Such a principle of unity lies at the source or origin of human actions.

1.2.2. The Importance of Origin

Actions are constituted by their origin. Contemporary action theory recognizes as much when it distinguishes mere events—such as an arm rising—from human actions—such as Jones's raising his arm. The two differ in their origin. Human actions are events that originate in human deliberation and will. An event together with its origin constitutes an action.

The Angelic Doctor distinguishes actions more generally, whether they be human actions or not, from mere events by adding to the event its origin.[10] A cat killing a mouse includes the event of the mouse dying but adds the cat that gave rise to the death. If we take the event of water warming and add to it the fire that caused it to heat, then we have the action of fire heating water. As Aristotle notes, every event includes some subject that changes and some new state that it attains, even as the mouse is a subject that takes on death and the water takes on heat.[11] Actions add a third element, namely, the origin of the change coming to be in the subject.[12] The mouse's dying is merely an event because it involves only a subject undergoing some change, but the cat's killing the mouse identifies the origin of the change.

10. Brock (*Action and Conduct*, 7–48) argues that "action" in this more general sense is used analogically.

11. *Physics*, bk. I, chap. 7, 189b30–191a23.

12. I, 41, 1, ad 2. "Et ideo actio secundum primam nominis impositionem importat originem motus."

While events might be said to remain within a subject, actions go between two realities. Dying is a change occurring in the mouse, but killing goes out from the cat to the mouse. These two realities, the cat and the mouse, are called, in Thomistic terminology, the agent (whether human or otherwise) and the patient, the one that acts and the one that is acted upon. The cat acts upon the mouse and so is called the agent. The water is acted upon by the fire, so it is called the patient. Any action, then, has at least three important constituents: an agent that acts, a patient that is acted upon, and some change that is brought about in the patient by the agent.[13]

A human action, then, is a *human* agent originating some change in a patient. This statement is not so straightforward as it first appears, for we originate many things in a manner not so human.[14] Sometimes we act as a human being—*qua* human—and sometimes we act simply as matter, or simply as an animal. According to Thomas, we act *qua* human, performing a truly human act and not merely what he calls an act of man, when we act insofar as we are human, when we act deliberately and voluntarily.[15] The will and intention, then, are at the root and origin of our actions.

1.2.3. Per Se Causes

Through a single origination an agent may bring about many changes in a patient, for example, when fire heats wax, it not only brings about the change of heat but also the change of melting, so

---

13. Aquinas distinguishes between transitive and immanent actions, which are more properly called operations. Transitive actions are physical activities such as heating or killing, while immanent actions are mental activities such as thinking. Immanent actions do not actually bring about some change in a subject, but they are still directed to some subject or object, for example, we might think about a tree, although we do not thereby change the tree. As Brock notes in *Action and Conduct* (7–47), these different senses of action are analogical.

14. Ralph McInerny has a good treatment of this distinction in *Aquinas on Human Action: A Theory of Practice* (Washington, D.C.: The Catholic University of America Press, 1992), 3–24.

15. I-II, 1, 1.

we describe its action both as heating and melting. According to Aquinas, however, these diverse effects are not on an equal footing, for some come from the cause *per se,* or through itself, and others come from it *per accidens,* or through another. The heat comes to the wax from the fire itself, but the softness comes only by way of the heat. The fire's causality is not some indefinite origination from which a string of effects arises incidentally; it is the origination of heat, from which other effects follow.

In the *De malo* Aquinas notes the marks of a *per se* cause, two of which concern us: it intends its effect, and it is similar to its effect.[16] The second mark, which is the more straightforward of the two, may be exemplified through the diverse effects of a fiery furnace upon wet clay and upon a block of wax: the clay becomes hot, the wax becomes hot, the clay hardens, and the wax melts.[17] The first two effects are *per se* while the latter two are *per accidens.* The fire is itself hot, and through its own heat it makes the clay and wax hot as well. But the fire is neither hard nor soft, although it causes the clay to become hard and the wax to become soft. While the fire heats directly, through its own heat, it may be said to harden and to soften indirectly—through the heat it has caused in the clay and the wax.

The similarity between cause and effect need not be absolute. When Smith builds a shed he is not absolutely similar to it, but he does possess a likeness of the shed, and through this likeness he acts, for in building the shed Smith has some conception of what the shed will be like—we might say that he has a blueprint in his mind—and it is by means of this idea that Smith builds the shed.[18]

---

16. *De malo,* 1, 3 (Leonine ed., vol. 23, 14–15, 139–74).

17. A good account of this aspect of *per se* causes may be found in Richard Connell, *Nature's Causes,* Revisioning Philosophy, vol. 21 (New York: P. Lang, 1995), 132–36 (from which the example is taken); also see Brock, *Action and Conduct,* 106–10.

18. This "intellectual" likeness is expressed in *Summa contra Gentiles* III, 2, no. 5 (Leonine ed., vol. 14, 6).

Similarity is not enough for a *per se* cause. Jones, too, had some idea of Smith's shed, but Jones was not the *per se* cause of the shed; indeed, he was not a cause at all. What Jones lacked, and Smith had, was intention. Smith had a firm intention to build the shed, while Jones merely had an idea of what it was like. This mark of a *per se* cause, that it must intend its effect, may seem a little odd when applied to causes such as fire, but Aquinas has this application in mind, for later in the same article we find Thomas saying that fire is the *per se* cause of fire (as when fire spreads) but the *per accidens* cause of the destruction (or evaporation) of water. Clearly, therefore, when he says that every *per se* cause must intend its effect, he must be using some broad meaning of the word "intend" that could apply to fire as well as Jones. "Intention" refers not only to some psychological state involving deliberation, but as its etymology would indicate it refers to any tendency into something. "Intend" simply means "to tend into."

A cause must possess some characteristic, which it then causes in the patient. But the possession of a characteristic is not enough. A cause must also tend to pass it on; it must "intend" an effect; it must not be merely inert but must move to pass on the characteristic.[19] Going back to the furnace, we can see that fire does tend to make things hot, but it does not tend to make things hard or soft. Rather, by making clay hot it thereby makes it hard, and by making wax hot it thereby makes it soft.

1.2.4. The Substance of Actions

A single action or origination, then, can bring about many effects, but some of them might be *per se* and others *per accidens*, for example, by the single origination of heat, fire also brings about softness. While the fire does two different things, it has only one action. The string of effects appears to be incidentally united as long

19. See Brock (*Action and Conduct,* 114–18) for a good account of inclinations or impulses as necessary for action.

as we consider them only as events following upon one another. But if we consider these effects insofar as they arise from the agent, then some arise directly and *per se* while others follow indirectly. The fire originates heat, and thereby it originates a string of other effects.

The heating and the melting are not actions in the same sense. While the fire does indeed heat—for possessing heat, it moves to bring about heat in the wax—it does not most properly melt. The softness does not originate directly from the fire but is merely a consequence of the heat. From the fire comes heat, and from the heat in the wax comes the softness. If we imagine an action after the fashion of a substance with properties, even as a cat is black, fat, and so on, then the substance of the fire's action is simply heating while it has the action of melting as a property. One action, then, can be the property of another.

Aquinas makes this point by including "what was done" amongst the circumstances of an action. Although "what was done" sounds like the action itself rather than its circumstance, Aquinas gives an example in order to clarify what he means when he lists it as a circumstance.

> "What was done" refers to something separate from the substance of the act. When someone washes a man by pouring water over him, "washing" is not a circumstance of the act of washing. But by washing a man, he might make him cold or hot, healthy or sick, and these actions are circumstances of washing.[20]

Warming someone, cooling him, or healing him, then, can be circumstances of washing him.

Similarly, making a noise can be a circumstance of killing a man. While Jones did do many things—he killed, he made a noise,

20. I-II, 7, 3, ad 3. "Similiter etiam ex parte eius quod est quid; nam quod aliquis perfundens aliquem aqua, abluat ipsum, non est circumstantia ablutionis; sed quod abluendo infrigidet vel calefaciat, et sanet vel noceat, hoc est circumstantia."

and he stained the carpet—he did so through only one action. Only one emanation arose from Jones and went out to a patient, but riding piggyback on this single emanation—like properties upon a substance—were other actions, which must be counted as circumstances rather than as the substance of the action itself. The problem of the craniotomy and hysterectomy can be analyzed in a similar manner. The doctors' actions have many descriptions, but some of these descriptions depict the substance of the action, while others are merely properties or circumstances. In performing the hysterectomy, the doctor both removes a diseased organ and kills a baby, but what she does *per se*, in the substance of her action, is remove the organ, while the killing of the baby is merely a property that rides upon the initial emanation of her action.

1.2.5. The Importance of Intention

How do we know which is the substance and which the circumstance? How do we know that the fire truly heated and melted only circumstantially? How do we know that the doctor, in substance, removed the uterus but killed only as a circumstance? For the answer to these questions Abelardianism directs us to intention. An agent does most properly what it intends to do.

We saw that the fire both heats and melts, but that properly it only heats, for the fire "intends" to heat but not to melt. Similarly, we will know what Jones properly did—the substance of his action—through his intention. Jones killed *per se* and made a noise only *per accidens* because he intended to kill but not to make a noise. He moved to bring about Smith's death but not to break the silence. Like the melting of the wax, the noise followed upon the primary activity, which was killing.

The same could be said of Smith as he pounds nails in order to make his shed. He pounds nails and he makes a noise, but he intends only to pound nails. He is not moving to bring about a noise. The noise, as it were, rides piggyback upon the pounding of nails, which alone is the emanation arising directly from Smith. If we ask

Smith what he is doing, we would certainly protest if he replied, "I am making a noise." We would grant, of course, that in some sense he is making a noise, but we were looking for something more essential; we were looking for what he is primarily about, what he is setting out to do.

On one day, however, a flock of crows settles in Smith's back yard, and he immediately begins to pound nails vigorously, hoping to scare off the crows. On that day Smith truly intends to make a noise; it is something he moves to bring about, not merely something that follows upon his action. On that day, then, we might say that Smith makes a noise *per se;* on other days, he does so only *per accidens.*

Countless texts of Aquinas indicate that the substance of an action depends on intention, for Thomas repeatedly says that the species of human actions is taken from what is intended. Here are samples.

> Moral acts receive their species from what is intended, not however, from what is outside intention, since this is *per accidens.*[21]

> A sin has two elements: the act itself and its disorder, which is a failing from the order of reason and the divine law. The species of sin is not taken from the disorder, which is outside the intention of the sinner.[22]

We have been brought to the position of Abelardianism. Human actions take their species from the agent's intention. In the craniotomy case, then, the doctor did what she intended to do. If she intended to reduce the size of the head, only foreseeing the

21. II-II, 64, 7. "Morales autem actus recipiunt speciem secundum id quod intenditur, non autem ab eo quod est praeter intentionem, cum sit per accidens."

22. I-II, 72, 8. "Cum in peccato sint duo, scilicet ipse actus et inordinatio eius, prout receditur ab ordine rationis et legis divinae; species peccati attenditur non ex parte inordinationis, quae est praeter intentionem peccantis, ut supra dictum est." Also see I-II, 72, 5; II-II, 43, 3; II-II, 70, 4, ad 1; II-II, 109, 2, ad 2; II-II, 110, 1; II-II, 150, 2.

death of the baby, then she resized *per se* but killed only circumstantially and *per accidens*, but if she intended to kill, then she killed in the very essence and species of her action. In the next section (1.3), however, physicalism will search for some other defining feature of exterior actions, besides intention. If actions are certain emanations arising from the agent, then an exterior action might have an end of its own, what Aquinas calls the *finis operis*, which does not derive from the agent's intention but from some other originating source, such as a natural inclination. The craniotomy, for instance, might be directed to the death of the baby through its very nature, whatever the doctor intends. As such, exterior actions might have a character that does not depend upon the agent's intention.

SECTION 1.3. *Finis Operis*

Despite the specifying role of intention, physicalism can claim that exterior actions have a species of their own, apart from the agent's intention. In the domain of *per se* actions, after all, Aquinas uses the term "intention" more broadly than the English term allows. If fire can intend heat, then why cannot the exterior action have an intention and an endpoint of its own, independently of the will? Physicalism acknowledges that intention is central to the substance of an action but underscores what has already been noted (section 1.2.3), that the meaning of intention is itself ambiguous. In English it refers exclusively to some sort of mental act or something associated with a mental act, but in Aquinas's Latin it refers to any impulse or tendency to some end, whether that impulse is conscious or not. Fire can intend as well as human beings.

St. Thomas himself distinguishes between the *finis operis* and the *finis operantis*, between the end of the action and the end of the one acting. The *finis operantis* is the reason or motive for which the agent acts, while the *finis operis* is the end of the exterior activity itself. When a builder builds a house, the *finis operis* is the very house constructed, while the *finis operantis* is the use that the builder seeks from it.[23] Similarly, the *finis operis* of the act of killing is the death of the victim, and from this end the action takes its species. Jones's action of killing is specified by the endpoint of death, the end of the exterior action. Similarly, the craniotomy might have an end of its own, independent of the doctor's intention, so that her action will take its species—of killing, or resizing, or saving a life— not from her subjective intention but from the *finis operis*, the end of the very exterior action. As Steven Long says, "intention regards the raw material of our actions, which are not pure logical entities, but have a natural character."[24]

1.3.1. The Finis Operis Gives Species

The specifying role of the *finis operis* is not difficult to discover in Aquinas. In his treatment of the vice of lust, for instance, Thomas distinguishes between a disorder of desire, that is, of the *finis operantis*, and a disorder of the exterior action itself, which derives from its own proper end.

> Sometimes, together with the disordered desire, is a disorder of the very exterior action according to itself, as happens in every use of the reproductive organs outside the act of marriage. That all such acts are disordered according to themselves is apparent because all human acts are said to be disordered when they are not proportioned to the proper end. For example, eating is disordered if it is not proportioned to the health of the body, to which the act of eating is ordered as to an end. Since the end of using the reproductive organs is the generation and education of offspring, every use of these organs that is not proportioned to the generation of offspring, and to their due education, is of itself disordered, for example, every

23. *II Sent.*, d. 1, q. 2, a. 1 (Mandonnet, vol. 2, 45). References to the *Sentences* are taken from *Scriptum super Sententiis magistri Petri Lombardi*, ed. P. Mandonnet and M. F. Moos (Paris: P. Lethielleux, 1929–1947).

24. Steven Long, "A Brief Disquisition Regarding the Nature of the Object of the Moral Act according to St. Thomas Aquinas," *The Thomist* 67 (2003): 45–71, at 48.

act of these organs outside the union of male and female is manifestly unfit for the generation of children.[25]

The end of eating, says Thomas, is the health of the body, and the end of sexual activity is the generation of offspring. Clearly, he cannot be referring to the *finis operantis,* for people often eat without seeking the health of the body and they often have intercourse without aiming to have a child. The exterior actions themselves, then, must be ordered to these ends, independently of the will. Furthermore, the disorder of these exterior actions arises from a lack of proportion to this *finis operis.* What, then, of Aquinas's principle that the *per se* order of an action arises from intention? Nature itself must provide the intention. Just as fire intends heat, so the power of reproduction is ordered to generation of new life, that is, it tends toward new life.

The sin of lying provides another example of the *finis operis* giving species. Thomas identifies a proper object of the exterior action, distinct from the end of the will, that gives species to our acts of speech.

> Moral acts take their species from two things, namely, from the object and from the end. The end is the object of the will, which is the first mover for moral actions; but the power moved by the will has its own object, which is the proximate object of voluntary acts and is related to the act of willing the end as material to form. The virtue

25. *De malo,* 15, 1 (Leonine ed., vol. 23, 270, 124–41). "Quandoque uero cum inordinatione concupiscentie est etiam inordinatio ipsius actus exterioris secundum se ipsum; sicut contingit in omni usu genitalium membrorum preter matrimonialem actum. Et quod omnis talis actus sit inordinatus secundum se ipsum apparet ex hoc quod omnis actus humanus dicitur esse inordinatus qui non est proportionatus debito fini; sicut comestio est inordinata, si non proportionetur corporis salubritati` ad quam ordinatur sicut ad finem. Finis autem usus genitalium membrorum est generatio et educatio prolis; et ideo omnis usus predictorum membrorum qui non est proportionatus generationi prolis et debitae eius educationi, est secundum se inordinatus. Quicumque autem actus predictorum membrorum est preter commixtionem maris et feminae manifestum est quod non est accommodus generationi prolis."

of truth, and consequently the opposite vices, consists in manifestation, which is made through some sign. . . . But the proper object
of a manifestation or enunciation is truth and falsity.[26]

1.3.2. Natural Teleology and Human Practice

Physicalism, then, claims that exterior actions have their own end,
the *finis operis,* through which they receive species. Eating is ordered to health, sexual intercourse is ordered to generation, and
speech is ordered to truth or falsity. But from where do actions get
these ends? Physicalism suggests two possible sources for the order
of actions: first, the *finis operis* might arise from some natural inclination or inherent teleology; second, it might arise from some human convention or practice.

The first possibility is realized most clearly in the sexual act. In
the article quoted above, the third objection claims that fornication need not be a sin, because it can be done for some good end,
such as generating offspring to worship God. In other words, the
action can have a good *finis operantis;* it can be directed to a good
end *by the will.* In his response, Aquinas notes that the action itself
has an end, from its nature, distinct from whatever good end the
agent might intend.

> The end of the act itself is ordered according to its very nature, even
> though the intention of the agent might be for a good end, which is
> not sufficient to excuse the act, as is plain in one who steals intend-
> ing to give to charity.[27]

---

26. II-II, 110, 1. "Actus moralis ex duobus speciem sortitur, scilicet ex obiecto,
et ex fine. Nam finis est obiectum voluntatis, quae est primum movens in moralibus actibus. Potentia autem a voluntate mota habet suum obiectum, quod est
proximum obiectum voluntarii actus, et se habet in actu voluntatis ad finem sicut materiale ad formale, ut ex supra dictis patet. Dictum est autem quod virtus
veritatis, et per consequens opposita vitia, in manifestatione consistit, quae fit
per aliqua signa. . . . Obiectum autem proprium manifestationis sive enunciatio-
nis est verum vel falsum."

27. *De malo,* 15, 1, ad 3 (Leonine ed., vol. 23, 271, 217–21). "Finis etiam ipsius

This end of nature shows up again in the very next reply. Indeed, he speaks of the end "intended" by nature. "Every voluntary emission of semen is illicit unless it is suitable for the end intended by nature."[28]

Plainly, then, Thomas thought that exterior sexual activity has an end from its very nature, independent of the will. What of other exterior actions? Do they also have a *finis operis* derived from nature? While Aquinas is less explicit concerning other actions, he does provide some hints that they too have a natural endpoint. Steven Long and Jean Porter, for instance, have suggested that the act of killing in self-defense has a kind of natural connection with the end of preserving one's life (see also section 6.4).[29] The article on lying, quoted above, indicates that the act of speaking is directed to truth or falsity.

Physicalism might also suggest that the *finis operis* is determined by human practice or convention. We might suppose, for instance, that speaking is directed to truth or falsity by human convention; after all, language itself is a kind of convention. Similarly, Kevin Flannery has suggested that the act of self-defense is defined in part through human laws and conventions that permit self-defense.[30] Flannery even claims that, "a morally significant distinction between [the hysterectomy and craniotomy] can be drawn if we first identify medicine as a discipline that excludes the craniotomy procedure but includes the hysterectomy procedure."[31] The

---

actus secundum suam naturam est inordinatus licet ex intentione agentis possit esse finis bonus, qui non sufficit ad excusationem actus, ut patet in eo qui furatur intendens eleemosinam dare."

28. *De malo*, 15, 1, ad 4 (Leonine ed., vol. 23, 271, 225–27). "Et ideo omnis uoluntaria emissio seminis est illicita, nisi secundum conuenientiam ad finem a natura intentum."

29. Long, "Brief Disquisition," 61; Long, *Teleological Grammar*, 49; Jean Porter, *Nature as Reason: A Thomistic Theory of the Natural Law* (Grand Rapids, Mich.: Eerdmans, 2005), 297.

30. Flannery, *Acts Amid Precepts*, 176–92.

31. Flannery, *Acts Amid Precepts*, 183.

very practice of medicine determines the order of these actions, or as he puts it, the practice provides a fixed path.

1.3.3. Inadequacies

If exterior actions take their species from the *finis operis*, and if the *finis operis* is determined by nature and perhaps by human practice, then what are we to make of the craniotomy case? Unfortunately, the answer is far from clear. Nature especially seems of little help, for there seems no natural act of a craniotomy as there is some natural sexual act. Long thinks that killing is properly ordered to self-defense, while the craniotomy is not properly ordered to save the life of the mother.[32] Unfortunately, he provides little guidance for identifying the proper order of actions; we are left to our own intuitions of the natural orders of actions, which is to say that the account has not helped us to identify the species of actions.

Human practice is of slightly greater assistance. For instance, we can say of the hysterectomy case, that there is a standard human practice of removing a cancerous womb in order to halt the spread of the disease, and that this practice defines the end of the action; the death of the baby, then, is not the endpoint of the action, but is a consequence or side effect. Human practice, however, provides less guidance for the craniotomy case. Someone might argue that there is a human practice of crushing skulls in order to end labor, but someone else might argue that there is no practice of crushing skulls.[33] These discussions might all too easily degrade into counter intuitions concerning the *per se* order that an action has. As Flannery himself acknowledges, "The difficulty will always be in determining which kind of acts constitute fixed paths."[34]

32. Long, *Teleological Grammar*, 102–4.

33. Flannery thinks there is no such practice, because according to human nature doctors seek health (*Acts Amid Precepts*, 190–91), and any good medical practice aims at the good of the object, which is the patient, in this instance the baby (184). Unfortunately, his account smuggles in notions of good human practices and human nature that are left unexplained.

34. Flannery, *Acts Amid Precepts*, 193.

1.3.4. Physicalism

Despite these inadequacies, physicalism does provide an alternative to Abelardianism. Perhaps the details must be worked out, but the emphasis upon intention found within Aquinas does not of itself settle the matter in favor of Abelardianism, since the term "intention" is ambiguous. "Intention" might refer to an interior act of will, which Abelardianism emphasizes as the specifying element of actions; it might also refer to an impulse of nature to some endpoint, which physicalism claims is the *finis operis* and the specifying feature of exterior actions.

Another distinction is needed to resolve these two apparently conflicting sources of the species of human actions. Aquinas distinguishes between the natural species of human actions and the moral species. The moral species applies to human actions precisely insofar as they are human. The natural species applies to human actions in abstraction from their voluntary or human character. Since actions are human precisely insofar as they are deliberate and voluntary, the moral species will depend upon reason and will. Any end that an action has from some other source, for instance, from some exterior power, will apply more to the natural species than to the moral. In the next section (1.4), then, we will see that the search for the moral species of human actions will return our focus to the will and intention.

SECTION 1.4. *Natural and Moral Species*

A fundamental aversion to physicalism arises from the intuition that mere physical activity cannot possibly be morally good or evil. Moral good and evil are aspects of the will and its activity, not of bodily activity. Aquinas himself distinguishes between the moral species of an action and the natural species. For instance, one and the same sexual activity is adultery according to its moral species but merely sexual intercourse according to its natural species. The moral species depends upon an action's relation to reason and the will. Mere physical activity, as it arises from some natural power or teleology, can at most provide natural species.

The marital act and adultery differ in species insofar as they are compared to reason but not insofar as they are compared to the power of generation. For compared to reason they have effects differing in species, since one deserves praise and reward while the other deserves blame and punishment, but compared to the power of generation there is one effect according to species.[35]

The mistake of physicalism that so many want to avoid is to identify the natural physical act with a moral species. Hence, the emphasis upon the will. One can pull the stick too far in the opposite direction, however, and relegate the moral species entirely to the will. The interior act of will, someone might say, is the moral species, and the exterior action is merely natural. The exterior action is left with no moral character; it is moral only by association with the will.

Aquinas's view is far more subtle. A single action has both moral and natural species, for instance, the same conjugal act has both a natural species and a moral species. How are they distinguished? By comparison, says Aquinas, to some power, either the external power of generation or the power of reason. If we consider sexual activity only in relation to the external power of generation, with its endpoint of new offspring, we have only the natural species. The same activity—and not simply the act of will that gives rise to it— takes on a moral species when compared to reason.

---

35. I-II, 18, 5, Ad 3. "Actus coniugalis et adulterium, secundum quod comparantur ad rationem, differunt specie, et habent effectus specie differentes, quia unum eorum meretur laudem et praemium, aliud vituperium et poenam. Sed secundum quod comparantur ad potentiam generativam, non differunt specie. Et sic habent unum effectum secundum speciem." See also De malo, 2, 4 (Leonine ed., vol. 23, 40, 196–220); IV Sent., d.16, q. 3, a.1B, ad 2 (Mandonnet, vol. 4, 796).

1.4.1. A Single Act with Multiple Species

We have seen (section 1.2) that an action takes its substance or species from the form or agency that gives rise to it, as the act of fire is substantially an act of heating rather than melting. Human actions are complicated, however, because they have multiple origins, thereby giving rise to multiple species. One and the same sexual activity, for example, arises both from the external power of generation and from the interior power of will. This dual origination, however, is not haphazard but involves an order of one to another. The will serves as the primary agency that moves the external power—a kind of secondary agent or instrument—to its activity. The multiplicity of agents gives rise to diverse species, but the order of agents assures the unity of action. One and the same action, then, has diverse species.

Aquinas makes the latter point, that ordered agents give rise to a single action, by way of analogy with an agent using an instrument.

> Within a human act we find that the act of a lower power is like the material of the act of a higher power, even as the action of a primary cause is formal with respect to the action of the instrument it moves. For a lower power acts only through the higher power that moves it to act. It follows that the command and the act commanded are one human act, like a whole, but this one act is a multitude through its parts.[36]

When an author uses a pen to write, she is the primary cause that directs the pen to write; she forms the act of the pen to write words. By itself the pen cannot write words, but must have its activity formed by some primary cause. Similarly, if someone places

---

36. I-II, 17, 4. "In actibus humanis, actus inferioris potentiae materialiter se habet ad actum superioris, inquantum inferior potentia agit in virtute superioris moventis ipsam; sicut enim et actus moventis primi formaliter se habet ad actum instrumenti. Unde patet quod imperium et actus imperatus sunt unus actus humanus, sicut quoddam totum est unum, sed est secundum partes multa."

a block of wax over a fire with the express intention of melting the wax, then he directs the activity already inherent in the fire onto the wax. The act of the fire, which by itself is simply a *per se* act of heating and an act of melting only *per accidens,* is formed by the primary agent to become a *per se* act of melting.

The Angelic Doctor concludes that the primary agent and the instrument share a single action. Between the author and the pen there is only one act of writing, since the author writes by way of the pen. The pen's writing is not something over and beyond the author's writing; it is the very same act of writing. The author's act and the pen's act are formal and material parts of a single act. There is but a single act that may be attributed to the pen as executing and the author as the source. As Aquinas favorably quotes Aristotle, "The act of the one that moves and of the one moved is the same act."[37] One and the same change has both the pen and the author as its *per se* cause, so one and the same action is the action of both the pen and the author.

It follows that our actions extend beyond our bodies. Although we might speak of a basic or primary action, which is the act simply of our body, ultimately our actions flow outside our bodies.[38] The author, for instance, might be said basically to move the pen (or perhaps more basically, to move her hand), but she may also be said to write. By using her body to move the pen, she directs the pen to write, and so she is the originator, the agent, of the written words. Similarly, Jones most basically pulls the trigger, but by pulling the trigger, he fires the gun, and by firing the gun he propels the bullet into Smith's chest, and thereby he kills Smith.

37. Quoted in I-II, 17, 4, ad 1.
38. Davidson (*Actions and Events,* 89) says that we never do more than move our bodies. In contrast, Brock (*Action and Conduct,* 85–86) argues that actions extend from the agent into the patient.

1.4.2. Exterior Acts of Will

Ultimately, Thomas wishes to apply this analysis of primary agents and their instruments to the interior action, which is a kind of primary agent, and the exterior action, which is like the act of the instrument. Just as the author forms the action of the pen, so that the pen actually writes, similarly the will forms the action of the external power, directing it to some moral endpoint. It follows that, just as the act of the author extends beyond her body into the pen, so the act of the will extends to include the exterior act as well.[39] Just as the single act of writing is attributed both to the pen and to the author, similarly, the single act of killing is attributed both to Jones's body and to Jones's will, the body as executing and the will as originating. The act of the will does not stop with itself; it continues in the bodily activity that it commands. Thomas expresses the idea as follows:

> We should [first] consider acts that are voluntary because they are elicited by the will, belonging immediately to the existence of the will; [next] we should consider those acts which are voluntary because they are commanded by the will, which belong to the will by way of other powers.[40]

Acts of the will include both those elicited by the will and those commanded by the will. Those elicited by the will belong immediately to the will and are what we have called interior acts. Those acts commanded by the will, what we have called exterior acts, belong to the will only mediately; they belong immediately to the external power. When Jones kills Smith, we readily suppose that his act of will is his choice or intention to kill Smith. And indeed it is.

---

39. The point is made by Brock, *Action and Conduct,* 176–91; see also Rhonheimer, *Natural Law,* 418.

40. I-II, 6, introduction. "Secundo, [considerandum est] de actibus qui sunt voluntarii quasi ab ipsa voluntate eliciti, ut immediate ipsius voluntatis existentes; tertio, de actibus qui sunt voluntarii quasi a voluntate imperati, qui sunt ipsius voluntatis mediantibus aliis potentiis." See also I-II, 8, introduction.

But his act of will is more than the intention; it includes the exterior act of killing as well. His choice is an act of will immediately, as an act elicited by the will; the exterior act of killing is an act of will mediately, as an act commanded by the will.

1.4.3. Two Species

The single act of writing belongs both to the pen and to the author. Although the pen in no way forms letters of its own accord, it does provide something of its own to the act of writing, namely, the ink and the means of distributing the ink upon paper. We can divide the act of writing, then, into a material element that comes from the pen, namely, the distribution of ink, and a formal element that arises from the author, namely, shaping the ink into letters and words. Each of the agents, the author and the pen, contributes something distinct to the single activity of writing.

The single endpoint of written words, then, has two different formalities. To the pen, it is simply dispensed ink; to the author, it is written words. The endpoint of the pen's action and the endpoint of the author's action, then, are in a manner the same and in a manner different. They are numerically one and the same thing, but they are formally distinct, so that they give rise to two distinct species of actions. Put in terms of the agent's "intention," or tendency, we can say that the pen does not tend to pass on ink in precisely these shapes that we call letters; its action, therefore, is simply an act of distributing ink. The author, on the other hand, intends to form precisely these shapes, and so she writes, properly speaking.

The act of the pen, then, has two distinct species. Insofar as it arises from the pen, it is an act of distributing ink, for the pen has ink and *per se* introduces this ink. Insofar as it arises from the author, it is an act of writing, for the author has the form of written words, which she *per se* introduces in her action.

1.4.4. Natural and Moral Species

Similarly, exterior actions have two species, both a moral species and a natural species. Just as the act of writing arises from a primary agent and from an instrument, each of which contributes its part to the action, so human actions arise both from the primary agency of the will and from the instrumental agency of some external power. The act of adultery, for instance, arises from the will moving and directing the power of reproduction upon this particular person. Just as Smith cannot write without the pen, so Jones cannot carry out the act of adultery just by his will; he needs an exterior action, and an external power, to bring it off. From that portion contributed by the external power of generation, the act takes its natural species of sexual intercourse.[41]

Just as the single effect of written words, through its two distinct formalities, is one thing to the pen and another thing to the author, so the single endpoint involved in adultery is one thing to the will or reason and another thing to the power of generation. The power of generation, not possessing the form of good and evil, cannot *per se* introduce this moral form; it is simply directed towards offspring. Insofar as the sexual act is an act of will, however, it must arise from the will, which does possess the forms of good and evil, and can pass these on.

The exterior action can be viewed insofar as it is natural, that is, insofar as it arises from an external power, or it can be viewed insofar as it is moral, that is, insofar as it arises from the will.[42] When viewed as an activity of the power of reproduction, it is nothing more than sexual activity, but when viewed as an act of the will, it is a moral action directed toward some perceived good. As Stephen

41. I-II, 18, 5, ad 3. See also *De malo*, 2, 4 (Leonine ed., vol. 23, 40, 205–15); *IV Sent.*, d. 16, q. 3, a.1B, ad 2 (Mandonnet, vol. 4, 796).

42. Rhonheimer (*Natural Law*, 418) distinguishes between the exterior act (moral species) and the external act (natural species).

Brock sums it up, the difference between the natural and the moral species, "is between species belonging to an act insofar as it proceeds from a physical agent, and species belonging to it insofar as it proceeds from some other kind of agent, e.g., a voluntary agent."[43]

Thomas clearly distinguishes these two manners of considering the emotions, either as they arise simply from the sensitive appetite or as they arise from reason and will.

> The same thing can be said of emotions as was said of actions, namely, that the species of an action or emotion may be considered in two ways: first, insofar as it is in the species of nature, and then the moral good or evil does not pertain to the species of the act or emotion; second, insofar as it pertains to the species of morals, namely, insofar as it shares something of the will and of the judgment of reason.[44]

Actions are human—and therefore moral—precisely insofar as they arise from the will. The end of the action, then, can provide moral species only insofar as it arises from the will.[45] "The 'object' of a human act is always the object of an act of the will."[46] Insofar as actions arise from an external power, they have a natural species. The moral species must always consider the act insofar as it arises from the will.

---

43. Brock, *Action and Conduct*, 198.

44. I-II, 24, 4. "Sicut de actibus dictum est, ita et de passionibus dicendum videtur, quod scilicet species actus vel passionis dupliciter considerari potest. Uno modo, secundum quod est in genere naturae, et sic bonum vel malum morale non pertinet ad speciem actus vel passionis. Alio modo, secundum quod pertinent ad genus moris, prout scilicet participant aliquid de voluntario et de iudicio rationis."

45. I-II, 72, 3. "Finis autem est obiectum voluntatis; ostensum est enim supra quod actus humani habent speciem ex fine."

46. Martin Rhonheimer, "The Perspective of the Acting Person and the Nature of Practical Reason: The 'Object of the Human Act' in Thomistic Anthropology of Action," *Nova et Vetera*, English ed. 2 (2004): 461–516, at 462.

1.4.5. Conclusion

Actions take their species, then, from their origin, from the intention or impulse within the agent that gives rise to them. Fire, possessing heat, tends to pass on heat. Smith, having an idea of a shed, moves to bring about the shed. For human actions, however, this doctrine proves more difficult to apply, since human actions have more than a single origin. On the one hand, human actions arise from reason and will, which implies that they take their species from the intention with which the person acts. If the doctor intends to kill the baby, then her action is, in its substance, an act of killing; if she intends merely to reduce the size of the head, then her action is a cranial reduction. On the other hand, human actions arise from some external power with its own tendency and endpoint, as sexual activity arises from the power of generation, which is directed to new life.

While both of these intentions or impulses will play a role in the species of human actions, for the moment we have seen that the intention of will, which is most proper to human actions as human, has the primacy. If we focus on the exterior action with its external power, then we have only the natural species of human actions; the moral species of the exterior action must be in comparison to the properly human origin of reason and will.

Despite this multiplicity of agency, there is but a single action, for the agents are ordered, one giving rise to the other as primary and secondary causes. A single act of writing can be attributed both to the pen and to the author. Similarly, a single act of sexual activity can be attributed both to the power of generation and to the will. Because the single action arises from multiple sources, it may be considered in diverse species.

One mistake to be avoided, a kind of crude physicalism that no one wishes to endorse, seeks to wrench the exterior action from the will that forms it and still retain the moral character that arises from the formative action of the will. Recognizing the inadequacy of this position, Abelardianism concludes that we will know what the doctor does in the craniotomy only when we know what she intends to do. If she intends to reduce the size of the skull and not to kill, then that is what she does, but if she intends to kill the baby, then her action is an act of killing. We will not find the species of her action simply by looking at the physical activity in itself, but only by looking at the physical activity as it is formed by her intention.

Abelardianism, however, faces difficulties of its own. It is one thing to say that the doctor did what she intended, but it is another to identify her intention. Unfortunately, the nature of intention will prove elusive for Abelardianism, and it must ever do so. Let us turn our attention, then, in chapter 2, to the nature of intention and its object.

2 | INTENTION

We are trying to identify the species of human actions. What belongs essentially to an action is a certain emanation from an agent toward some object. An action has a *per se* order from the agent to the object. What falls outside this order is circumstantial; it does not belong to the essence of the action. The movement or emanation of an action begins within the agent through some impulse or tendency, and this source within the agent provides the essential character of an action. Human actions, precisely as human, arise from reason and will; consequently, the intention of the will plays a central role in the species of human actions. If we wish to know to what the agent is ordered, then we must know what the agent intends.

Unfortunately, it does little good to say that actions are specified through intention unless we can characterize intention itself. The doctor's action is specified by her intention; if she intends to kill, then her action is a killing, but if she intends only to reduce the size of the head, then it is not a killing. But what does she intend? Does she intend merely to save the life of the mother, since this is the goal that she seeks? Does the death of the baby fall outside her intention, since the death is not that by which she achieves her goal? Disputes amongst the followers of Aquinas over the species of actions have focused largely upon such questions.

As we seek to pin down the character of intention, we will begin with general considerations about the nature of its object; is intention concerned only with the end sought or also with the means to achieve this end (section 2.1)? We will then turn our attention to more particular applications, first to the test case of self-defense (section 2.2) and then to some other cases (section 2.3).

SECTION 2.1. *What Is Intended*

Over the past fifty years the diverse views on the precise object of intention have multiplied beyond counting, but for our purposes the views may be reduced to three, a broad expansive view, a lean view, and a middle view. The broad view includes nearly everything foreseen within the scope of intention. The narrow view includes only the end aimed at, excluding both the means chosen to achieve the end and any consequences following upon the end, even those that are foreseen. The middle view includes both the means and the end but excludes side effects or foreseen consequences.

When Jones kills Smith, for instance, the first view holds not only that Jones intends to kill Smith, but also that he intends to make a noise, for he foresees that his action will result in a noise, and he must intend all foreseen consequences. On the second view, Jones might intend the money he hopes to gain from his murder, but he does not intend the means chosen to achieve this end, such as firing the gun or killing Smith, nor does he intend consequences such as the noise. On the third view, Jones intends to kill Smith and he also intends the means of firing the gun, but he does not intend foreseen side effects, such as the noise. We will call these views, respectively, concomitant-intention, end-intention, and means-intention. In recent years, concomitant-intention has been largely discredited.[1] Certainly, no one would maintain that Aquinas de-

1. See, for instance, Michael Bratman, *Intentions, Plans, and Practical Reason* (Cambridge, Mass.: Harvard University Press, 1987), 139–64; Brock, *Action and Conduct,* 200–16; Bennett, *Act Itself,* 96.

fends concomitant-intention. Therefore, we will turn our attention
to the remaining two views (sections 2.1.1 and 2.1.2).

2.1.1. End-Intention

End-intention maintains that we intend the end or goal of our actions but nothing else. We do not intend concomitant effects, nor
do we intend the means chosen to achieve our goals. We intend
only what is truly desired, such as the money Jones wishes to steal
from Smith, and not those actions that get us to it, such as killing
Smith. When applied to the craniotomy case, we may conclude
that the doctor intends to save the mother's life but not to kill the
baby.

In defense of end-intention, Long cites the following text of
Aquinas:[2]

> The movement of the will into the means, insofar as it is ordered to
> the end, is choice, while the movement of the will into the end, in-
> sofar as it is acquired through the means, is called intention.[3]

We must, however, interpret this text with care.[4] Two articles prior
to this text Thomas states that what is a means under one formality can be considered as an end under another formality. A means
may not be the ultimate goal that someone seeks, but it can still be
a proximate or more immediate goal on the way to achieve some-

2. Long, *Teleological Grammar*, 29.
3. I-II, 12, 4, ad 3. "Motus voluntatis fertur in id quod est ad finem, prout ordinatur ad finem, est electio. Motus autem voluntatis qui fertur in finem, secundum quod acquiritur per ea quae sunt ad finem, vocatur intentio." See also I-II,
8, introduction, where Aquinas lists intention as an action that concerns the end,
and I-II, 13, introduction, where he lists choice as concerning the means (as does
I-II, 13, 3); I-II, 13, 4; and especially see *Summa contra Gentiles* III, 6, no. 9 (Leonine ed., vol. 14, 15), where Aquinas states that intention does not concern the
means.
4. For a more complete refutation of this interpretation see Joseph Boyle,
"*Praeter Intentionem* in Aquinas," *The Thomist* 42 (1978): 649–65. Also see John
Finnis, "Object and Intention in Moral Judgments according to Aquinas," *The
Thomist* 55 (1991): 1–27, at 10–14; Finnis et al., "Direct and Indirect," 17.

thing else. Jones certainly perceives killing Smith as a means to get money, but at the same time he has settled upon killing Smith as a more immediate goal, which he achieves by other means, such as firing a gun. Is killing Smith, then, a means or an end? It is a means to get money, but it is the end for which Jones fires the gun. The above text indicates that the killing cannot be intended under the first formality, as a means to get money, but can it be intended under the second? Aquinas says it can.

> Intention refers to the end insofar as it is the term of the movement of the will. In a movement, however, a term may be taken in two ways, either as the ultimate term, which is rested in and which is the term of the whole movement, or as some mediate term, which is the beginning of one part of the movement and the end or term of another part. For example, in the movement which goes from A to C by way of B, C is the ultimate term, while B is a term but not ultimate. Intention may bear upon both of these sorts of terms, so that while it is always of the end, it need not always concern the ultimate end.[5]

In the very next article he gives an application.

> Intention is not only of the ultimate end, as was said, but also of the mediate end. Someone may, however, intend both the proximate end and the ultimate end at the same time. For example, at the same time someone may intend both to prepare medicine and to regain his health.[6]

5. I-II, 12, 2. "Intentio respicit finem secundum quod est terminus motus voluntatis. In motu autem potest accipi terminus dupliciter, uno modo, ipse terminus ultimus, in quo quiescitur, qui est terminus totius motus; alio modo, aliquod medium, quod est principium unius partis motus, et finis vel terminus alterius. Sicut in motu quo itur de a in c per b, c est terminus ultimus, b autem est terminus, sed non ultimus. Et utriusque potest esse intentio. Unde etsi semper sit finis, non tamen oportet quod semper sit ultimi finis."

6. I-II, 12, 3. "Est enim intentio non solum finis ultimi, ut dictum est, sed etiam finis medii. Simul autem intendit aliquis et finem proximum, et ultimum; sicut confectionem medicinae, et sanitatem." See *Sententia Metaphysicae*, book 5,

Preparing medicine is certainly a means to health, yet it is intended. Of course, Aquinas does not call it a means when he says that it is intended, but rather a proximate end. His mediate and proximate ends, however, are precisely what we call means; preparing medicine, when viewed in relation to the goal of health, is a means; at the same time, it is an end of the agent or an end of other actions, such as moving one's hands.[7] When Thomas says, then, that intention concerns the end and choice concerns the means, he does not exclude the possibility that they both concern the same object; one may both choose to prepare the medicine and intend to prepare the medicine. Both concern the "means" of preparing medicine, but they differ in the formality under which they move toward that means. Intention moves toward the means as a mediate end (and therefore as achieved by way of something yet more proximate), while choice moves toward it precisely as something ordered toward a more ultimate end.[8]

Long correctly notes that we can intend an end such as health without yet choosing or knowing the means, which is indeed a sign that intention concerns the end.[9] It is no sign, however, of the point Long truly needs to make, namely, that intention does not concern the proximate end. When we intend health without yet knowing

lect. 2, no. 771 (in *In duodecim libros Metaphysicorum Aristotelis expositio,* ed. M.R. Cathala and R. M. Spiazzi [Taurini-Romae: Marietti, 1935], 256).

7. Finnis et al. ("Direct and Indirect," 16–19) lay emphasis upon the proximate end for the object of human actions. Brock points out (*Action and Conduct,* 201) that there need not be some "means"—an action—that is directed to the proximate end; sometimes the agent himself is that which is directed to the action as toward an end.

8. See I-II, 12, 4, ad 3. "Motus qui est unus subiecto, potest ratione differre secundum principium et finem, ut ascensio et descensio, sicut dicitur in *iii Physic.* Sic igitur inquantum motus voluntatis fertur in id quod est ad finem, prout ordinatur ad finem, est electio. Motus autem voluntatis qui fertur in finem, secundum quod acquiritur per ea quae sunt ad finem, vocatur intentio. Cuius signum est quod intentio finis esse potest, etiam nondum determinatis his quae sunt ad finem, quorum est electio."

9. Long, *Teleological Grammar,* 1–2; see I-II, 12, 4, ad 3.

the means, then we do not intend the as yet undetermined means. It in no way follows that once we have determined the means, then we still do not intend them. Aquinas's example indicates otherwise. Having determined the means of preparing medicine, we now intend not only health, but we intend also to prepare medicine. We intend this means, of course, not as a means, but as a more proximate end.

2.1.2. Means-Intention

John Finnis is noted for his defense of what might inaccurately be called means-intention, the view that we intend not only the further end or goal but also the means to achieve the goal.[10] More precisely, we intend the mediate end, for intention does bear upon the end and not the means. For convenience, however, we may readily say that we intend the means. We intend it, of course, only insofar as it is an end. On this view, then, Jones intends to kill as well as to make money, but he does not intend to make noise.

Someone might suggest that the means are intended but only in a secondary or analogical sense.[11] Unfortunately, there is no good reason to suppose so. Thomas nowhere indicates that intention of the mediate end is a secondary meaning of the term.[12] Certainly, intention is primarily of the end. It does not follow that taking the medicine cannot be the object of intention—properly speaking— for taking the medicine need not be conceived merely as a means; it might also be conceived as a proximate end. One might, for instance, intend to take the medicine by way of preparing it.

What matters for our purposes is identifying the sense of inten-

10. See Finnis et al., "Direct and Indirect," 16–17; Finnis, "Object and Intention," 10–14; also Boyle, "Praeter Intentionem."

11. Long, "Brief Disquisition," 50–51; Long, Teleological Grammar, 28–29.

12. Long provides no explicit text. He merely repeats that intention is primarily of the end and choice of the means. See, for instance, "A Response to Jensen on the Moral Object," Nova et Vetera 3 (2005): 101–8, at 103; Teleological Grammar, 41, 48, 49, 51, 71.

tion from which the species of actions are derived. Does intention of the means provide species for human actions, or does only intention of the end? Fortunately, Thomas leaves no doubt on the matter; Pilsner shows conclusively that actions take their species from the proximate end intended, which can also be called the means.[13] A few samples will suffice.

> An end is either proximate or remote. The proximate end of an act is the same as its object, and from this the act receives its species. On the other hand, the act is not specified by the remote end, but the order to this end is a circumstance of the act.[14]

> Profit or glory is the remote end of the hypocrite as well as the liar. Therefore, from this end the species is not taken, but from the proximate end, which is to show oneself other than one is.[15]

Some texts, on the other hand, emphasize the importance of the remote end, claiming that the remote end also gives species; indeed, it gives the more defining species. Aquinas says, for instance,

> The species of human actions is considered formally according to the end but materially according to the object of the exterior action. Therefore, the Philosopher says that he who steals so that he can commit adultery is properly speaking more an adulterer than a thief.[16]

13. Pilsner, *Specification*, 219–22.

14. *De malo*, 2, 4, ad 9 (Leonine ed., vol. 23, 41, 335–39). "Duplex est finis, proximus et remotus. Finis proximus actus idem est quod obiectum; et ab hoc recipit speciem; ex fine autem remoto non habet speciem, sed ordo ad talem finem est circumstantia actus." Also see *De malo*, 2, 6, ad 9 (Leonine ed., vol. 23, 49, 347–53); I-II, 1, 3, ad 3; I-II, 60, 1, ad 3; II-II, 11, 1, ad 2; II-II, 66, 4, ad 2.

15. II-II, 111, 3, ad 3. "Lucrum vel gloria est finis remotus simulatoris, sicut et mendacis. Unde ex hoc fine speciem non sortitur, sed ex fine proximo, qui est ostendere se alium quam sit."

16. I-II, 18, 6. "Actus humani species formaliter consideratur secundum finem, materialiter autem secundum obiectum exterioris actus. Unde philosophus dicit, in *v Ethic.*, quod ille qui furatur ut committat adulterium, est, per se

While these texts pose a difficulty of their own, they need not concern us at the moment. They do not deny that the proximate end gives species; they merely state that the remote end provides an additional and more significant species (for further treatment see section 6.4). The man who steals in order to commit adultery still commits theft, even if he is more an adulterer.[17] Even Long, who insists that choice—not intention—concerns the means (and proximate end), acknowledges that the means chosen does give species, although a subordinate species.[18] If both intention and choice give species, then end-intention amounts in practice to means-intention, using different terminology. With regard to that which gives species to human actions, Thomas seems to have preferred the terminology of intention of the proximate end rather than choice of the means.[19]

---

loquendo, magis adulter quam fur." Also see *De malo,* 7, 3 (Leonine ed., vol. 23, 167, 183–190); I-II, 75, 4; II-II, 11, 1 ad 2; II-II, 181, 2; III, 88, 4.

17. See *De malo,* 8, 1, ad 15 (Leonine ed., vol. 23, 196, 488–96).

18. Long, *Teleological Grammar,* 17, 43, 51, 52; Finnis uses *II Sent.,* d. 40, q. 1, a. 2 (Mandonnet, vol. 2, 1013–15) to argue that choice ultimately gives species to human actions ("Object and Intention," 19).

19. Although Long insists repeatedly that intention does not concern the means, his point is not all that relevant for the question of the species of human actions. If the means chosen give species, then it matters little that the means do not give species *from intention;* in either event, from choice or from intention, the means do give species. What is significant about Long's view is not his insistence upon end-intention, but his analysis of the manner in which the end intended might modify or classify the species that comes from the means chosen, a point that we will address further along (section 6.4). Long himself states that the importance of the terminology (intention of the end and choice of the means) is to understand the case in which the object chosen is *per se* ordered to the end intended (*Teleological Grammar,* 29). He grants that perhaps what is chosen as a means might be an end in another respect, "Yet this alters nothing of the proposition that where an object is *per se* ordered to the end the most formal and defining species is from the end" (*Teleological Grammar,* 48). In other words, while the proximate end might give species, nevertheless, what is important is that such species will fall under the species from any further end to which the action is *per se* ordered.

The *per se* effect, then, from which an action takes its species, is determined by the intention of the proximate end or, put differently, from the choice of the means. In the craniotomy case, the doctor intends not only the goal of saving the mother's life but also the means, or proximate end, by which she attains this goal, and her action takes its species from this intended means. Of the three accounts of intention, then, means-intention best reflects the thought of Aquinas, especially insofar as he uses intention for the specification of actions. For convenience, we will often speak of intending the means, although strictly speaking we choose the means and intend the proximate end.

SECTION 2.2. *Self-Defense*

Let us turn our attention to what for Thomists has proven to be the *experimentum crucis* of intention theory, namely, self-defense(see also sections 5.3.5 and 6.4).[20] I wish to suggest that various accounts of intention—in particular, end-intention (section 2.2.2) and a version of means-intention that I will call description-intention (section 2.2.3)—cannot be reconciled with Aquinas's own treatment of self-defense, at least for the standard form of self-defense assumed by most contemporary discussions, namely, firing at one's assailant with a gun.[21] To avoid certain confusions we will press the case to its farthest extreme by considering a situation in which merely injuring the assailant is not likely to stop him, so that the only plausible way to defend oneself is to fire the gun with a near certain-

20. Portions of this section are taken from my article, "The Trouble with Secunda Secundae, 64, 7: Self-Defense," *The Modern Schoolman* 83 (2006): 143–62.

21. G. E. M. Anscombe, "War and Murder," in *Ethics, Religion and Politics* (Minneapolis: University of Minnesota Press, 1981): 51–61, at 54. Thomas A. Cavanaugh, "Aquinas's Account of Double Effect," *The Thomist* 61 (1997): 107–21, notes that Aquinas would not allow cutting off someone's head in order to stop the attack (114–15) nor would he allow shooting someone with a flamethrower as some have asserted (121).

ty that the assailant will die (supposing that one has good enough aim). Later, we will see that the same considerations apply to situations in which one fires the gun thinking that one will wound (but not kill) the assailant (section 2.2.4).[22] Finally, we will consider a way of lessening the desire to conform Aquinas's treatment of self-defense to our own intuitions (section 2.2.5).

2.2.1. Aquinas's Account

Thomas justifies self-defense as follows:

> Nothing prohibits one act from having two effects, one of which is within intention and the other outside intention. Moral acts, however, receive their species from what is intended, not from what is outside intention, since the latter is *per accidens*. From the act of self-defense two effects can follow: the preservation of one's life and the killing of the assailant. Therefore, the act is not illicit from the fact that one intends the preservation of one's own life, for it is natural to everything that it preserve its own existence insofar as it is able. Sometimes, however, an act arising from a good intention becomes illicit if it is not proportioned to the end. Therefore, if someone uses more force than is necessary to defend his own life, his action will become illicit. If he repels the attack moderately, his defense will be licit, for according to the jurists, "It is lawful to repel force with force if one does not exceed the limits of blameless defense." Nor is it necessary for salvation that a man set aside an act of moderate defense in order to avoid killing another, for a man is held more to provide for his own life than for the life of another.[23]

22. It is worth noting that the closest approximation to a gun for Aquinas would be a bow and arrow; furthermore, Aquinas was much more likely to be thinking of something like a sword, or even one's bare hands.

23. II-II, 64, 7. "Nihil prohibet unius actus esse duos effectus, quorum alter solum sit in intentione, alius vero sit praeter intentionem. Morales autem actus recipiunt speciem secundum id quod intenditur, non autem ab eo quod est praeter intentionem, cum sit per accidens, ut ex supradictis patet. Ex actu igitur alicuius seipsum defendentis duplex effectus sequi potest, unus quidem

The Angelic Doctor says that an action of self-defense can be morally acceptable if it meets two conditions, and he takes it as given that it already meets a third condition. First, the defender must have right intention, that is, she must intend to save herself but not to kill. Second, she must not use unnecessary force in defending herself; if she can repel the attack with less force, and so with less likelihood of killing, then she should. Finally, he says that justified self-defense meets a third condition, namely, the defender must have a greater responsibility to perform the action intended than to avoid the unintended consequence.[24] It is more important, says

conservatio propriae vitae; alius autem occisio invadentis. Actus igitur huiusmodi ex hoc quod intenditur conservatio propriae vitae, non habet rationem illiciti, cum hoc sit cuilibet naturale quod se conservet in esse quantum potest. Potest tamen aliquis actus ex bona intentione proveniens illicitus reddi si non sit proportionatus fini. Et ideo si aliquis ad defendendum propriam vitam utatur maiori violentia quam oportet, erit illicitum. Si vero moderate violentiam repellat, erit licita defensio, nam secundum iura, vim vi repellere licet cum moderamine inculpatae tutelae. Nec est necessarium ad salutem ut homo actum moderatae tutelae praetermittat ad evitandum occisionem alterius, quia plus tenetur homo vitae suae providere quam vitae alienae."

24. Most accounts of the principle of double effect, which is said to be derived from this text, elide the second condition into the third, resulting in a single condition, for example, that the good effect must be proportioned to the evil; see, for example, J. T. Mangan, "A Historical Analysis of the Principle of Double Effect," *Theological Studies* 10 (1949): 41–61. That Aquinas has two separate conditions in mind is evident from the text. He says that the action of defense must be proportioned to the end, and when the defense is so proportioned he calls it moderate. He then goes on to say that we need not forego moderate defense in order to avoid killing the assailant, because we have a greater responsibility to save our own life. In other words, he first defines moderate defense as involving a proportion to the end, and then he justified moderate defense as being more important. The greater importance does not determine what counts as proportionate, although that is how the word is used within the context of the principle of double effect. Aquinas uses "proportion" only for the second condition, where he means the proportion of a means to an end; see Brian Johnstone, "The Meaning of Proportionate Reason in Contemporary Moral Theology," *The Thomist* 49 (1985): 223–47. Although the word "proportion" is reasonably applied to the third

Thomas, to defend one's own life than it is to avoid killing one's assailant.

Our concern is with the first condition, the statement of which Aquinas completes only at the end of the article, together with a notable exception. So far he has stated only that it is licit to intend to save one's own life, but he has not mentioned that one cannot intend to kill. He concludes the article, however, as follows:

> Since it is not lawful to kill a man, except with the public authority on account of the common good, as is plain from what has been said, it is unlawful for a man to intend to kill a man in order to defend himself, except for those who have public authority, who while intending to kill a man for self-defense, refer this act to the public good, as is plain for soldiers fighting the enemy, or for a minister of the judge fighting against robbers, although even these sin if they are moved by private desires.[25]

We should note that the public official does defend his own life. He is not defending others, executing a sentenced criminal, or simply apprehending criminals. No doubt a public authority can intend to kill for these reasons as well, but Aquinas is concerned here with self-defense, and he explicitly states that the official is defending his own life. He does so for the sake of the common good, nevertheless he does seek to defend his own life. In other words, the case of the public authority and the private individual are precisely parallel ex-

---

condition as well, it certainly implies a different sort of proportion. It is better, therefore, to keep these two conditions distinct, and to use "proportion" for only one of them; see Thomas Cavanaugh, *Double-Effect Reasoning: Doing Good and Avoiding Evil* (Oxford: Clarendon Press, 2006), 25–32.

25. "Sed quia occidere hominem non licet nisi publica auctoritate propter bonum commune, ut ex supradictis patet; illicitum est quod homo intendat occidere hominem ut seipsum defendat, nisi ei qui habet publicam auctoritatem, qui, intendens hominem occidere ad sui defensionem, refert hoc ad publicum bonum, ut patet in milite pugnante contra hostes, et in ministro iudicis pugnante contra latrones. Quamvis et isti etiam peccent si privata libidine moveantur."

cept with regard to intention. Both are defending themselves, but the private individual cannot intend to kill while the public authority can.

2.2.2. End-Intention

The case of firing a gun with the foresight of the aggressor's death might well seduce someone toward end-intention; it would be simple to claim that the defender intends to save her life without intending to kill, for on this account the means are not intended, and killing her assailant is clearly a means to save her life. Long, for instance, bases his account of self-defense in part upon the supposition that the means fall outside intention.[26] We have already seen that end-intention is inconsistent with Aquinas's more general account of intention (section 2.1.1), but it is also difficult to reconcile with his account of self-defense.[27]

First, from the very beginning Thomas speaks of killing as an effect that can follow the act of self-defense: "From the act of self-defense two effects can follow: the preservation of one's life and the killing of the assailant." It is odd, to say the least, to speak of a means as an effect following upon an action. In the reply to the fourth objection, he continues the terminology of "following": "The act of fornication or of adultery is not ordered of necessity to preserving one's own life, as is the act from which killing sometimes follows."[28]

26. Long, *Teleological Grammar*, 39–63; Long, "Brief Disquisition," 45–71; and Long, "St. Thomas Aquinas through the Analytic Looking Glass," *The Thomist* 65 (2001): 259–300, at 281–87, especially n. 66; also see 290, n. 85.

27. See Boyle, *"Praeter Intentionem,"* 660–61.

28. II-II, 64, 7, ad 4. "Actus fornicationis vel adulterii non ordinatur ad conservationem propriae vitae ex necessitate, sicut actus ex quo quandoque sequitur homicidium." Long interprets the "following" of these passages after the manner of the order of deliberation, that is, we first consider the end, and then deliberate about the means ("Response to Jensen," 105; "Brief Disquisition," 55). As we will see when we look at the resolutive process (section 3.2.4), however, even for deliberation Aquinas refers to the means as causes: we must resolve the end

Second, within the article itself Aquinas twice speaks about intending to kill as if the killing were a means to some further end. Augustine, it seems, opposed all killing by private individuals. When faced with this objection Aquinas responds—so his words imply—by claiming Augustine was speaking of those instances in which a private individual intends to kill as a means, for he "intends to kill a man *so that* he might be freed from death" [emphasis added].[29] Likewise, in the body of the article Thomas says that the public official intends to kill *in order* to defend himself. Twice, then, Aquinas speaks of intending in a manner that implies intention bears upon killing as a means. If he had wished to emphasize that the means are outside intention, as end-intention would have it, then it seems he would have been more careful with his language.

One might try to distinguish the public authority through some special character or formality under which he seeks the death of the aggressor. End-intention might claim that something is an end—and therefore intended—when it is sought precisely under the formality of an end; he must seek it for its own sake, or as a good in itself, or some such thing.[30] The public authority would

---

into its causes. Even if one grants this interpretation, in which the means "follow" the end, it is difficult to imagine what Aquinas was thinking when he called the means "effects." Certainly, Aquinas could have expressed himself much more clearly, had he wanted to say what Long says. Long glosses over another difficulty occasioned by Aquinas's use of the word "sometimes." Killing, Long says, "sometimes follows" self-defense because it is not always needed to attain the end of self-defense ("Brief Disquisition," 61). Unfortunately, in those particular cases in which lethal defense is justified on Long's account, that is, in those cases in which killing is *per se* ordered (by Long's meaning) to defense, then the killing *is necessary* to attain the end. It becomes difficult to follow all the twists and turns that Long must use in order to interpret this text.

29. II-II, 64, 7, ad 1. "Auctoritas Augustini intelligenda est in eo casu quo quis intendit occidere hominem ut seipsum a morte liberet."

30. Long, for instance, says of self-defense that, "killing is not the end for the sake of which the action is performed—it is not intended *qua* end" ("Analytic Looking Glass," 287).

be allowed to seek the death of the assailant precisely as an end (in this special meaning of intending as an end), while the private individual would not.

That, of course, is not what Thomas says. If he wished to emphasize that intention bears upon the end, then he should have said some such thing of the public official, rather than speak in terms that imply the official intends killing as a means or proximate end.

Someone might turn to capital punishment, or some other instance of the public official killing someone, as an instance of killing under the special formality of an end. Since capital punishment is fulfilled only when the criminal has been killed, death belongs to the very notion of capital punishment.[31] Unfortunately, we have already noted (section 2.2.1) that in II-II, 64, 7, Aquinas is not concerned with capital punishment but only with the case of the public official who defends his own life.

2.2.3. Description-Intention

Many commentators on *Secunda secundae*, 64, 7, most notably, John Finnis, Germain Grisez, and Joseph Boyle, explain self-defense by way of a variation of means-intention that I will call description-intention. It claims that a means is intended only under the description or formality under which it serves as a means. As Finnis puts it, "The means are included in the proposal under the description that makes them intelligibly attractive as a means."[32]

31. See Long, "Response to Jensen," 106; Long also uses an example of a public official trying to contain some bandits, so that they do not hurt society at large ("Brief Disquisition," 65; *Teleological Grammar,* 47). Long later says that acts of punishment are defined by the formal element taken from the end, which is the common good; evidently, even punishment is a means to the end of the common good (*Teleological Grammar,* 59). No doubt such officials can intend to kill and perhaps such a killing would have some special sense of being an end, but Aquinas's example is clear: a public official defending himself. Flannery makes a move similar to Long (*Acts Amid Precepts,* 172).

32. John Finnis, *Moral Absolutes: Tradition, Revision, and Truth* (Washington, D.C.: The Catholic University of America Press, 1991), 68. William May seems to

On this account, the defender intends simply to stop the attack of the assailant; she does so by aiming a lethal shot, but she does not intend, even as a means, the death of her assailant. Germain Grisez, for example, says that a woman may shoot a would-be rapist in the head, and that bank guards can shoot a robber in the chest, without intending to kill.[33] Finnis and others, speaking of a woman shooting a robber, claim that her intention, "was no more than a self-defensive act, chosen, without any intent to kill, to stop what she mistakenly believed was an assault."[34] Evidently, then, what Thomas is saying in II-II, 64, 7, is that self-defense is justified only when the defender intends her action under the description of "stopping the attack" but not under the description of "killing the assailant."[35]

Description-intention has discovered one means—stopping the attacker—but has ignored another—killing the assailant. For if stopping the attacker is the means to saving the defender's life, then surely killing the attacker is the means to stop him. How else will firing the gun stop him except that it kill him (given our supposition that he can be stopped in no other way)? Suppose that the defender may stop the assailant by firing at him with a gun, by tripping him with a stick or by throwing a net over him. In this situation she has one end—defending her life—and she even has a single means, namely, stopping the assailant. But she still has three

use this approach for the practical case of shooting the assailant in the head; see "The Management of Ectopic Pregnancies: A Moral Analysis," in *The Fetal Tissue Issue: Medical and Ethical Aspects*, ed. Peter J. Cataldo and Albert S. Moraczewski, O.P. (Braintree, Mass.: The Pope John Center, 1994): 121–47, at 136–37. Jeff McMahan attributes this view to the "followers of Aquinas" and cites Finnis et al., see "Revising the Doctrine of Double Effect," *Journal of Applied Philosophy* 11 (1994): 201–12, at 202–3. He also cites G. E. M. Anscombe, interpreting her quite contrary to her meaning. He rightly concludes that this position allows nearly everything to fall outside intention.

33. Germain Grisez, *The Way of the Lord Jesus 2: Living a Christian Life* (Quincy, Ill.: Franciscan Press, 1993), 473, 484.

34. Finnis et al., "Direct and Indirect," 35.

35. These "double-think" redescriptions are the target of Stanley Windass, "Double Think and Double Effect," *Blackfriars* 44 (1963): 257–66.

possible ways of stopping him; we might call them means to a means. In her deliberations she might well wonder by what means she may stop him, and answer with the three possibilities. Identifying "stopping the attack" as a means does not exhaust all of the means needed for the defense. The situation changes not in the least simply because there is only one option, killing, rather than the three suggested. A necessary means is a means as much as an optional means.[36]

If killing the assailant is not a means to stopping him, then it seems that our intentions are so ill-defined that they may be tailored to any situation or desire. Indeed, Jean Porter points out that, "As long as the agent acts in pursuit of an aim which is admittedly good . . . it will always be possible to describe the act in question in terms of the attainment of the good which is sought, omitting any reference to the bad which is brought about."[37] Jonathan Bennett has suggested that the terror bomber, the bomber who kills innocent civilians in order to demoralize the enemy and so bring a quick end to the war, need not intend the death of innocent civilians. She intends, rather, simply to put the civilians in a state so as to demoralize the enemy.[38] If at the end of the war they happen to

36. May ("Ectopic Pregnancies," 136) implies that killing is a means only when there are other alternatives to stop the attack, and Grisez (*Way2*, 484) suggests that shooting with the foresight of death is a means if it is seen as forestalling future threats. But what if it is seen as forestalling *this* threat? The defender requires the assailant's death not only to stop a future attack, but given our supposition, in order to stop this attack. Aquinas, in contrast to May and Grisez, gives the example of willing to cross the sea and necessarily willing that by which it is attained, namely, a ship (I, 82, 1). Surely, the ship is a means to cross the sea, although it is necessary.

37. Jean Porter, "'Direct' and 'Indirect' in Grisez's Moral Theory," *Theological Studies* 57 (1996): 611–32, at 626. Porter's target is Germain Grisez. Long ("Brief Disquisition," 48) makes a similar point: "All we need do in order to change the nature of the object of one and the same act is to change our descriptions."

38. Bennett, *Act Itself*, 210–11; also see his "Morality and Consequences," in *The Tanner Lectures on Human Values*, vol. 2, ed. Sterling McMurrin (Salt Lake City: University of Utah Press, 1981): 45–116.

get up and walk away healthy, then so much the better. Surely Ben-
net is right to this extent: if the defender need only intend to stop
the assailant but not intend to kill him, even though she aims to
kill, then the terror bomber need only intend to "put into a state
that demoralizes" even though she bombs so as to kill them.
John Finnis draws a similar conclusion concerning killing of
combatants in warfare; he says,

> If, as Aquinas seems to assert and never denies, one can spear an
> assailant's heart in self-defense without intending to kill, [then] it
> is possible to wage war too—lethally and often successfully—with-
> out that intent.[39]

Finnis, of course, means to posit the antecedent, but it seems much
more plausible to deny the consequent. One person's *modus ponens*
is another's *modus tollens*.

It is easy enough to avoid Bennett's conclusions, as long as
we keep *all* of the means in view, for while it is true that the terror bomber aims to put the civilians in a state in which they appear
dead, thereby demoralizing the enemy, she chooses to do so by the
most obvious means, namely, by actually making them dead.[40]
Similarly, the defender may well intend to stop the attacker, but
even on a minimalist notion of means, she surely does so by means

39. John Finnis, *Aquinas: Moral, Legal, and Political Theory* (Oxford: Oxford
University Press, 1998), 287. See also Gerard Bradley, "No Intentional Killing
Whatsoever: The Case of Capital Punishment," in *Natural Law and Moral Inquiry: Ethics, Metaphysics, and Politics in the Work of Germain Grisez*, ed. Robert P.
George (Washington, D.C.: Georgetown University Press, 1998), 155–73, at 157,
who says that soldiers need only intend to render the enemy harmless. "Sound
fantastic?" he asks. Yes, it does.

40. Of course, both the terror bomber and the defender intend to kill in order to achieve their ends (of making the civilians appear dead and of stopping
the assailant), so Bennett does not make his stronger point, that there is no
way to include the death of civilians within intention as a means. For this point
against Bennett see Neil Delaney, "To Double Business Bound: Reflections on
the Doctrine of Double Effect," *American Philosophical Quarterly* 75 (2001): 561–
83, at 577.

of the assailant's death. Bullets would not stop attackers if they did not injure them, and in our current supposition, they will not stop this particular attacker unless they kill him. Killing him, then, is the means intended to stop the attacker. We have here a series of means and ends. The defender intends to kill (means #1) in order to stop the attacker (means #2) in order to save her own life (end). Description-intention, which says that the defender intends to stop the attacker but not to kill him, has merely focused upon the middle means, stopping the attacker, and skipped over the first means of the assailant's death.[41]

2.2.4. Intending to Injure

Perhaps someone will protest that our supposition is unrealistic. An attacker can invariably be stopped by harming him in some manner or other; the defender need not go so far as killing the assailant. Of course, she might end up killing him, if her aim is not precise, or if help cannot come soon enough to mend his wounds, but the killing is itself not necessary to stop his attack. Therefore, description-intention might claim that the defender intends merely to stop the attack, which she does by wounding her assailant. The aggressor's death in no manner serves her goals, and so it is not intended.

This account of the defender's intention does indeed meet the conditions laid out in II-II, 64, 7, and if we had only this article to contend with, then description-intention would have given a satisfactory account of self-defense. Unfortunately, this account cannot be reconciled with other aspects of Aquinas's teaching, for ultimately he does not allow for even the deliberate intention to injure.[42]

---

41. It is difficult to see how Finnis et al. reach the conclusion that in capital punishment the executioner must intend to kill. Paraphrasing Finnis's conditional, we might say, "If, as Finnis explicitly states, soldiers can kill combatants while they sleep without intending to kill, then it is possible to kill in capital punishment without that intent."

42. Finnis recognizes that we may not intend to injure the innocent (for example, *Aquinas*, 276, 278; *Moral Absolutes*, 74–81); see also Thomas D. Sullivan

While question 64 concerns killing, question 65 concerns bodily injury, and in the first article Thomas says that just as only a public authority can take a human life, so too only a public authority
can maim a healthy organ (for the sake of punishment), and that
the private individual can in no way do so (although she may au-
thorize the amputation of her own sickly organ).[43] Certainly, aiming a gun to injure someone falls within the maiming of an organ,
even if it does not involve the complete removal of an organ. And
just as we have seen that "intending to kill" seems unavoidable
when someone aims to kill in order to stop an assailant, similarly,
when someone aims to stop him by injuring him, it is hard to imagine how she can avoid intending to injure.[44]

Furthermore, in II-II, 41, 1, where Aquinas also discusses the
morality of self-defense, he condemns both seeking to kill and
seeking to injure the person seriously. This article is not addressing
the narrow question of homicide, as does question 64, but rather
the question of strife, which would include both killing someone
and injuring him, so Aquinas does not hesitate to include injury
within his censure.

Yet we find the most explicit statement against injuring in question 64. The third objection of article 3 states that private individuals are to be praised for doing the good of killing evildoers. Thomas
responds as follows:

---

and Gary Atkinson, "*Malum Vitandum:* The Role of Intentions in First-Order
Morality," *International Journal of Philosophical Studies* 1 (1993): 99–110, at 108.

43. II-II, 65, 1; see also II-II 65, 2. Christopher Kaczor argues that intentionally mutilating an organ is impermissible; see *Proportionalism and the Natural
Law Tradition* (Washington, D.C.: The Catholic University of America Press,
2002), 112–15. On the other hand, neither the removal of a diseased organ nor
mere physical pain count as evil (160–62), so both of these may be intended. Furthermore, Aquinas says that anyone (even the private individual) may intend to
temporarily restrain someone from doing evil (II-II, 65, 3, ad 3).

44. Nicanor Austriaco, "On Reshaping Skulls and Unintelligible Intentions," *Nova et Vetera* 3 (2005): 81–100, at 94–97, recognizes the difficulty with

Doing something for the benefit of the common good that harms no one is lawful for any private person, but if the benefit involves harm to another person, then it should not be done, except on the basis of the judgment of him to whom it pertains to decide what may be taken from the parts for the safety of the whole.[45]

When we look beyond question 64, article 7, then, we see that the defender cannot intend even to injure her assailant. Once again, therefore, description-intention cannot account for self-defense with a gun, and it, like all other views of intention, fails the *experimentum crucis* of self-defense.

2.2.5. Avoiding Intention

It seems that no account of intention can reconcile our intuitions concerning self-defense with Aquinas's justification for self-defense, but perhaps we can yet salvage our intuitions by way of another account of self-defense, an account that would allow the defender to act as a kind of emergency public official. This less restrictive account of self-defense, suggested in passing by the late G. E. M. Anscombe,[46] is not necessarily given in *Secunda secundae*, 64, 7, but it can be derived readily from principles that St. Thomas himself advances. We begin with the principle that human laws apply only imperfectly to concrete situations; they cannot cover every possible circumstance.[47] Laws concerning speed limits, for instance, cannot

---

shooting to kill, but is willing to describe shooting to injure simply as "shooting to stop him."

45. II-II, 64, 3, ad 3. "Facere aliquid ad utilitatem communem quod nulli nocet, hoc est licitum cuilibet privatae personae. Sed si sit cum nocumento alterius, hoc non debet fieri nisi secundum iudicium eius ad quem pertinet existimare quid sit subtrahendum partibus pro salute totius." Long quotes this passage and fails to realize that it contradicts his account of self-defense (*Teleological Grammar*, 54). Earlier, Long has stated that he can find nothing to exclude killing as a proportionate means to self-defense (see also "Analytic Looking Glass," 282). Six pages later he quotes the very exclusion that he could not find.

46. Anscombe,"War," 54.

47. I-II, 96, 6; II-II, 51, 4; II-II, 120, 1.

possibly enumerate all the circumstances in which it might be legitimate to exceed the limit. Similarly, Thomas allows that in case of necessity one can take what (ordinarily) belongs to another, because in need all things are held in common; a starving man can take a loaf of bread, if there is no other sustenance available.[48] Since no human law can possibly articulate all the circumstances in which such "theft" is legitimate, one must rely upon one's good judgment to discern when the human law must be set aside on account of some higher principle; Aquinas calls this good judgment the virtue of equity (*epikeia*) or *gnome*.[49]

A similar analysis can be made concerning the role of public officials in self-defense. Just as human laws designate which objects belong to which individuals, so human laws designate which individuals are public officials. And just as property laws "break down" under certain circumstances, requiring the discernment of equity rather than a servile submission to the letter of the law, so the laws designating public officials may also "break down." Circumstances may arise in which a public official is needed, but in which no humanly designated official is available; in such situations ordinary citizens may act as public officials. Through the virtue of equity, an individual can recognize the situations in which necessity demands that she act as an official.[50] If she is being attacked, and she cannot expect help from designated public officials, and if the situation is such that "repelling the attack" is an inadequate means of defense, then it seems that she herself serves as the official; she acts in an official capacity, and as such she may intend to kill in order to defend her own life.

In order to avoid unwarranted license with the law, Aquinas insists that exception to the law can be taken only when necessity prevents one from having recourse to the proper authority.

48. II-II, 66, 7; II-II, 110, 3, ad 4.
49. II-II, 120, 1.
50. II-II, 40, 1, ad 1, recognizes that private individuals can sometimes be charged with public authority.

If there arises a case in which following a law is harmful to the common welfare, then it should not be observed. . . . Nevertheless, if following the letter of the law has no imminent danger in need of immediate correction, then not just anyone is competent to determine
what is useful or harmful to the city, but only the rulers, who consequently have the authority to dispense from laws. When the danger
is imminent, however, not allowing time to refer the matter to some
superior, then the necessity itself brings with it a dispensation, since
necessity knows no law.[51]

Self-defense appears to be just such a case of imminent danger.

Secunda secundae, 64, 7, itself does not appear to offer this justification of self-defense, although some have thought it does.[52] Still,
64, 7, is open to this justification. After all, Aquinas does not say
that a public official can intend to kill in self-defense; rather, he says
that someone *with public authority* can intend to kill. Furthermore,
this account is based upon Thomistic principles, and it allows us to
retain our intuitions of self-defense without tailoring our notion of
intention. In these situations of what Aquinas calls *epikeia* or equity, intending to kill the assailant is permissible, for we act with
public authority.

Unfortunately, even if we can set aside the concerns over self-
defense, it remains that a coherent account of the specification of
actions through intention still proves elusive. The troubles that
plague intention have only begun.

51. I-II, 96, 6. "Si emergat casus in quo observatio talis legis sit damnosa communi saluti, non est observanda. . . . Sed tamen hoc est considerandum, quod si
observatio legis secundum verba non habeat subitum periculum, cui oportet sta-
tim occurri, non pertinet ad quemlibet ut interpretetur quid sit utile civitati et
quid inutile, sed hoc solum pertinet ad principes, qui propter huiusmodi casus
habent auctoritatem in legibus dispensandi. Si vero sit subitum periculum, non
patiens tantam moram ut ad superiorem recurri possit, ipsa necessitas dispensa-
tionem habet annexam, quia necessitas non subditur legi."

52. Gregory Reichberg thinks it does; see "Aquinas on Defensive Killing: A
Case of Double Effect?" *The Thomist* 69 (2005): 341–70.

SECTION 2.3. *More Troubles with Intention*

The diverse views of intention are forced in some cases to draw an awkward line between what is intended and what is foreseen. No single account is consistently able to draw a satisfactory line between intention and foresight. Of course, what counts as satisfactory depends in large part upon our intuitions, and one person's intuitions differ from another's, especially for the difficult situations considered, in which our intuitions are most strained. Often, however, the diverse views of intention fail to draw an acceptable line between the species of an action and the consequences of an action even for the most straightforward of cases, cases for which we can rely upon Aquinas's judgment and not merely on our own intuitions. We will suggest that the ailments that chronically plague intention are unavoidable (section 2.3.4). The project of separating the species of an action from its consequences by way of intention is doomed to failure.

2.3.1. Under a Description

Description-intention is apt to conclude that in the craniotomy case the doctor need not intend to kill the baby. Her action serves as a means to end the labor only under the description "reducing the size of the baby's head," for it is the smaller size of the head that allows the baby to pass through the woman's pelvis. The death of the baby is a consequence that in no way contributes to end the labor.

In some people's minds, description-intention has already run afoul on the craniotomy case, drawing the line between action and consequences too loosely, allowing the doctor to get away with murder. But even if one's intuitions concerning the craniotomy case are friendly towards description-intention, they may not be so kind for its troubling conclusions concerning the spelunker case. In this case, designed by Philippa Foot precisely to parallel the craniotomy case, a fat spelunker is stuck in the only exit from a cave, thereby trapping the remainder of his party, who have tried but failed to dislodge him from his predicament. Floodwaters are rising in the cave, and it is only a matter of time before all the spelunkers will drown, if they cannot dislodge their companion. The only means remaining appears to be a stick of dynamite too weak to put a dent in the solid rock but strong enough to blow the fat spelunker to bits. If the spelunkers choose to blow up their companion, then have they intended to kill him? Not according to description-intention, for the death of the spelunker is not what frees the passageway to the surface. As Foot satirizes it: "'We didn't want to kill him . . . only to blow him into small pieces' or even '. . . only to blast him out of the mouth of the cave.'"[53]

To Boyle, however, it is no satire. The spelunkers intend to introduce some change in their companion that will free the passageway to the surface; "his death is not what opens the cave but rather his being removed from the entrance."[54] Therefore, the form the spelunkers seek to introduce in their companion is not the form of death, but the dispersal of his parts. Other changes follow upon the form that they introduce, including their companion's death, but Boyle claims that subsequent changes are intended only if they are "conceptually" connected to the act. Since we can separate, in our minds, the dislodging of the potholer and his death, the spelunkers need not intend to kill.

Similarly, in the craniotomy case, "the bringing about of the death of the fetus is not conceptually related to the performance of the craniotomy" since, "it seems to be *logically* possible that the craniotomy be performed and the fetus not be killed."[55] Consequently, the doctor need not intend to kill the baby.

Description-intention also seems to fail in some rather straightforward cases. When a thief steals a car, the car's belonging to some-

53. Philippa Foot, "The Problem of Abortion and the Doctrine of Double Effect," in *Killing and Letting Die*, ed. Bonnie Steinbock (New York: Fordham University Press, 1994), 266–79, at 268.

54. Boyle, "Embryotomy," 307.   55. Boyle, "Embryotomy," 308.

body else does not serve his purpose; this feature is not formally a means to his goal, so he does not intend it. His action, therefore, will not be specified as "taking what belongs to another," since he did not intend to take the car insofar as it belongs to another. Similarly, an adulterer does not intend to have sexual relations with another man's wife, since the woman's marital status in no way serves his purpose. His action, therefore, should probably be specified as having sexual relations with a blonde, or with a 120 pound woman, or whatever feature serves his purpose of getting pleasure.

2.3.2. End-Intention

End-intention fares no better for these straightforward cases. The adulterer intends pleasure as an end, while the evil means fall outside his intention. The thief intends profit and merely *chooses* to take what belongs to another. As Anscombe remarks, "it is nonsense to pretend that you do not intend to do what is the means you take to your chosen end. Otherwise there is absolutely no substance to the Pauline teaching that we may not do evil that good may come."[56] Of course, if one insists upon end-intention but then grants that the means chosen still give species, albeit as a material element, then the difference between ends-intention and means-intention becomes merely verbal and these difficulties are avoided.

2.3.3. "Too Close"

An objection often raised against description-intention claims that the death of the spelunker is "too close" to the dispersal of his body; the two cannot be separated in the agent's intention. Similarly, the death of the baby is "too close" to the crushing of his skull. Flannery, for instance, wonders whether "One can separate the crushing of the fetus's skull from its death."[57] And G. E. M. Anscombe asserts that "Doing that is doing this, and so closely that you can't

56. Anscombe, "War," 59.
57. Flannery, "What is Included," 504; see also Flannery, "More on Abortion," *Gregorianum* 79 (1998): 163–67, at 166; see also Foot, "Problem of Abor-

pretend only the first gives you a description under which the act is intentional."[58] The difficulty with this objection, however, is determining what counts as "too close."[59] When the soldier blows up the bridge, is the death of the child "too close" to the bridge's destruction? When the doctor performs the hysterectomy, is the death of the baby "too close" to the removal of the womb?

2.3.4. The Bane of Intention

We need not hold our breath waiting for someone to come up with the right formulation of intention that can account for the many cases of specification of human actions. No such account will be found. The whole project of identifying the precise object of intention by which actions are specified seems to be plagued by some curse. It is doomed from its inception. We will search in vain for some object of intention that will serve to specify exterior actions. Why? Because the object of intention, for which we have been searching, is none other than the exterior action itself.

That intentions are specified by exterior actions should be no surprise. Rhonheimer repeatedly insists upon the point.[60] Thomas himself is clear enough on the matter. He says, "The exterior act is the object of the will insofar as it is proposed to the will by reason as a certain good known and ordered through reason."[61] Even in a

tion," 268; Austriaco ("Reshaping Skulls," 99) also thinks that the death of the baby is too "immediate."

58. Anscombe, "Action, Intention and 'Double Effect,'" in *Human Life, Action and Ethics,* ed. Mary Geach and Luke Gormally (Charlottesville, Va.: Imprint Academic, 2005): 207–61, at 223.

59. Bennett has given a careful analysis and critique of possible accounts of "closeness" (*Act Itself,* 204–12); see also Delaney, "Doctrine of Double Effect," 568–71.

60. See Rhonheimer, "Perspective," 464, 468, 469, 470, and many other places.

61. I-II, 20, 1, ad 1. "Actus exterior est obiectum voluntatis, inquantum proponitur voluntati a ratione ut quoddam bonum apprehensum et ordinatum per rationem, et sic est prius quam bonum actus voluntatis." Also see *De malo,* 2, 3 (Leonine ed., vol. 23, 36, ln. 58–59) and *De malo,* 2, 3, ad 8 (Leonine ed., vol. 23,

text in which he clearly delineates the specifying role of intention upon the exterior action, he explicitly states that a person intends "to do such a voluntary act in such material."[62] As Pilsner says, "The best illustrations [of external actions playing the role of object] can be found in passages where Aquinas is considering the relationship between 'interior acts' of the will and 'exterior acts' which are realized through them."[63]

Specifying intention in terms of actions is so natural that when it is fully brought to our attention, we marvel that we ever sought some other object for intention. Of course, if we suppose that the role of intention is to specify the exterior action, then it would be fruitless to specify intention in terms of the very action. How can the action that needs to be specified by intention serve as the very object that specifies intention?

2.3.5. Conclusion

While intention is certainly central to Aquinas's doctrine of the specification of human action, it is no panacea for the woes of action theory. Disputes over the nature of actions often merely shift to disputes over the nature of intention. With regard to interpretations of Aquinas, we have considered primarily two views, end-intention (section 2.1.1) and means-intention (section 2.1.2). The former has little support in the texts of Aquinas and indeed has rarely been entertained in the history of Thomism. The latter appears to be the view of Aquinas. Nevertheless, one of its more common variants, description-intention, when applied to the specification of actions, neither conforms to commonsense judgments of actions nor to Aquinas's own identification of actions (sections 2.2.3 and 2.3.1).

37, ln. 152–53); also see ad 1 (Leonine ed., vol. 23, 37, ln. 100–1). Texts stating that the exterior action is the object or end of the will provide yet one more argument against end-intention, since the exterior act is often a means for some further end.

62. I-II, 72, 1. "Qui intendit talem actum voluntarium exercere in tali materia."

63. Pilsner, *Specification*, 80.

More than anything else, what has led to a variety of loose interpretations of intention is Aquinas's teaching on self-defense, in which intention plays an essential role, for Aquinas thinks that self-defense by a private individual cannot be an act of killing, properly speaking, and as such any killing that occurs must be outside intention (section 2.2.1). Two ideas seem impossible to unite: our common intuitions concerning justified self-defense and a plausible account of intention, consistent with the words of Aquinas, in which the killing of self-defense falls outside intention. The upshot, it seems, has been an attempt to stretch the meaning of intention and the words of Aquinas to fit our intuitions concerning self-defense. Another Thomistic alternative, however, is to recognize the limitations of human laws that designate who is and who is not a public official, so that in emergency situations a person takes on public authority and is justified in intending to kill her assailant (section 2.2.5).

As if these difficulties surrounding intention were not enough, the crowning perplexity comes from the object of intention, which is the exterior action itself (section 2.3.4). Intention, then, is specified by the exterior action, and cannot serve in turn to specify the exterior action. Rather, the exterior action must have some character of its own by which it can specify intention. We have already seen, however, that the exterior action by itself, apart from its origin in the will, cannot provide the moral species of human actions (section 1.4).

With neither physicalism nor Abelardianism to provide us with the moral species of human actions, where are we to turn? Is there some third alternative? Not really. But as is often the case, we need not look beyond our starting positions. Both physicalism and Abelardianism have failed only because each is incomplete. When combined, the truth concerning the species of human actions begins rapidly to unfold. We need only the piece of the puzzle that will fit everything together. For that purpose we now turn to the exterior act conceived.

3 | EXTERIOR ACTIONS

We are trying to discover the species of human actions, the *per se* order arising from within the agent and moving to some object. Intention seemed a plausible place to look for the source of this order, both on account of the very words of Aquinas and because intention is a principle of human actions. Unfortunately, the effort to draw the line between what is intended and what is outside intention is plagued with difficulties. Indeed, rather than intention drawing the line between action and consequence, it seems that the action itself must draw the line between intention and what is outside intention. We must turn our attention, therefore, to the exterior act of will.

We will begin by noting that this exterior action is itself two-fold, namely, the exterior action performed and the exterior action conceived (section 3.1). The remainder of the chapter will focus upon the exterior action conceived, which arises in our deliberations. We must examine how this action, the exterior action conceived, takes on a *per se* order to some object. In particular, we will focus upon what role, if any, the causal structure of the physical act plays (section 3.2), and we will see how the causal structure of the craniotomy bears upon its species (section 3.3). We will then see that what belongs to the species of the exterior action goes beyond intention. Some characteristics of an action give species even though they are not intended (section 3.4). The central feature of the exterior action, it will turn out, is the object upon which it is directed, the subject acted upon (section 3.5).

SECTION 3.1. *The Exterior Act Conceived*

Apparently, we have wound ourselves into a vicious circle.[1] On the one hand, the exterior action—insofar as it is an act of will and not merely physical activity—does not provide its own moral endpoint but must be formed by intention. On the other hand, intention must be specified by its object, which is none other than the exterior action. The exterior action must receive its character from intention, but intention must receive its character from the exterior action.

Two distinctions are needed to unravel this philosophical Gordian knot. We must first distinguish two ways in which something can be said to specify (section 3.1.1). Both the exterior action and intention play roles in the specification of human actions, but they do so in different ways. Second, we must distinguish between the exterior action as it is actually performed and as it is conceived in deliberation (section 3.1.2).

3.1.1. Two Specifications

Something may be said to specify in two senses. We say that the agent's intention specifies his actions, but we also say that the end or object of the action specifies the action. We should not presume, however, that the single word "specify" has but a single meaning. It might mean one thing for intention and something else for the end or object.

An action is essentially a directional reality; it is headed somewhere. Just as a trip to Chicago is headed to Chicago, so the act of killing is headed to death. To "specify" the action is in some man-

---

1. Portions of this section are taken from my article, "A Defense of Physicalism," *The Thomist* 61 (1997): 377–404.

ner to determine or identify the direction that an action takes. Intention determines this direction by giving rise to it, by being its originating or efficient cause. The object, on the other hand, characterizes the direction through being the end toward which the action is directed.

Just as the archer is the cause that directs the arrow, so the soldier's intention is the cause that directs his action. Without intention his action would be directionless; it would simply be a series of events. And without direction, there would be no *per se* action; everything would be accidental, and no species would remain. The physical act of pulling a trigger may have the upshot of death, but it has the *per se* direction towards death only because the agent intends to bring about death. The agent's intention, then, specifies by giving direction to the exterior action.

The object or end of the action plays a different specifying role. While intention *gives* direction to the act, the object *characterizes* the direction so given. A movement or direction, being a relational term, has no inherent character; it must be characterized by its end. My trip to Chicago, for instance, is characterized by its destination. Likewise, the act of killing is characterized by the endpoint of death. An action directed towards death has one character, quite distinct from an action directed toward the endpoint of heat. We know the kind of action, what it is like, through its endpoint.

This endpoint does not attach to an action of itself, but rather comes from the agent's intention. The two specifying roles, therefore, that of the endpoint and that of intention, work in tandem, playing complementary roles.[2] An action can have no character unless it is headed toward some endpoint that gives it character, but it can be headed in some direction only because it is directed by intention. My trip to Chicago is specified by its destination, for this termination gives it a different character than if it terminated in Los Angeles. It would have no destination, however, if my inten-

2. See Brock, *Action and Conduct*, 91.

tion did not direct it towards Chicago. Jones's act of killing is characterized by the endpoint of death to which it is directed, but that Jones is right now performing an action directed towards death depends upon his intention.

While this distinction between two different senses of specifying is insufficient to resolve our perplexity, it does reveal the weaknesses of both physicalism and Abelardianism. Each of the two views fails in one of the two specifying roles. Physicalism seems to say that the exterior action has direction in and of itself, thereby forgetting the specifying role of intention, which gives direction to the action. Abelardianism, on the other hand, fails not with the exterior act but with the interior act of will, by failing to provide intention with its proper object, namely, the exterior action.

3.1.2. From Conception to Performance

A further distinction is needed to resolve our perplexity. Thomas says that the exterior action may be considered in two ways, either as it is conceived or as it is performed.[3] For example, before the soldier actually bombs the bridge, he thinks about it. He plans exactly where he must lay his charges. After planning his attack, he then executes it. In effect, he first plans to destroy the bridge, and then he actually destroys it. His action occurs twice, once in his deliberation and then again in actuality.

Now these two actions, the exterior action as conceived and as performed, have different relations to the agent's intention. The exterior action performed is specified by intention, for intention gives it a *per se* direction. The exterior action conceived, on the other hand, specifies intention after the manner of an object.

Let us follow the specification of the soldier's action. He first conceives of the possibility of destroying the bridge, perhaps even

---

3. *De malo*, 2, 3 (Leonine ed., vol. 23, 36, 70–74); also ad 1, ad 3, ad 8. Also I-II, 20, 1.

planning some details of his attack. Only after so conceiving, can he then intend to bomb the bridge, for we cannot desire or intend anything unless we have first of all conceived of it in some manner or other. His intention, then, is specified by the exterior action that he has conceived. After he intends to bomb the bridge, then he actually executes his plan. The exterior action that he now performs receives its direction from his intention.

We can already see our knot beginning to unravel. Our perplexity took the form of a circle involving two actions, the exterior action specifying intention and intention specifying the exterior action. But now rather than two actions we have three, the exterior act conceived, intention, and the exterior act performed, and our circle has disappeared. Intention is specified, it is given its characterization, by the exterior act conceived. Intention then specifies the exterior action performed, that is, it provides the direction to the endpoint that does specify. What appeared to be a circle of specification, turns out to be a linear series of specifications. The beginning and the end of the series are ostensibly alike, thereby giving the illusion of a circle.

The circle of specification, then, has been replaced with a series that begins with the exterior action conceived. Since the beginning point of specification is in the exterior action rather than in the will, physicalism might find in this new account of specification a confirmation of its view. A triumphant attitude, however, would be hasty, for a perplexity still remains: what specifies the exterior action conceived? Indeed, in one way or another, this question might well characterize the remainder of our pursuit.

Up to this point we have been concerned with the other two elements of the series. In chapter 1 we investigated the exterior action performed, noting that this action—as a human action—must arise from the will and receive its direction from the will. Any impulse or direction that the exterior action performed has from nature, apart from intention, provides only a natural species. In this regard, a surprise awaits us, for this same impulse or direction, at the level of the exterior action conceived, can play an essential role for the moral species of human actions.

In chapter 2 we investigated intention, which gives direction to the exterior action executed. Intention can provide direction, however, only if it already has its own characterization and direction. Therefore, we investigated the nature of intention. Does it concern only the end, or the means also? Does it concern the means only under certain formal descriptions? We can now see that these attempts must remain fruitless, unless we examine the final element of the series, the exterior action conceived.

As we investigate the exterior action conceived, we will discover two important features. First, the exterior action has an order or direction to some natural form, abstracted from its moral character. The craniotomy, for instance, is directed to some endpoint, such as a smaller head or death. Second, identifying this order does not yet provide the moral characterization of the action. For both of these features, the order to some form and the moral characterization of this order, reason will play a central role, so much so that the will and intention will become secondary. This prominence of reason should not obscure what we have already learned: when speaking of the exterior action as actually performed, intention provides the order of the action (section 3.1.2); also, the exterior action, even as conceived, is an act of will, not merely a physical or natural activity arising from some power (section 1.4.2).

We will begin, then, in the next two sections (sections 3.2 and 3.3), investigating the order to some end or form found in the exterior action conceived. The moral character of this order will occupy the remainder of the book. The next section (section 3.2) will investigate three possible ways in which the exterior action conceived has an order to an end, either from nature, from intention, or from reason. Section 3.3 will then apply the conclusions to the case of the craniotomy.

SECTION 3.2. *Proposals*

The exterior action conceived must be specified by its endpoint or object. The act of killing, for instance, is specified by the endpoint of death. This observation, however, accounts for only one of the two senses of specification discussed in the previous section (3.1.1). The act of killing is directed to some endpoint, and so it is characterized by this endpoint; but it must also receive this direction from some agency. The exterior action performed receives its direction from the intention of the agent. Jones's action of pulling the trigger is directed to the endpoint of death because Jones himself has so directed it through his intention. The exterior action conceived, on the other hand, cannot receive its direction from intention, for the agent's intention must itself be characterized through the exterior action conceived. From where, then, does the exterior action conceived receive its direction? As Smith conceives the act of pounding nails, how does he discern whether it has or does not have a *per se* order to making noise? He cannot turn to his intention, for he has not yet intended to act.

We will consider three possible sources for the order or direction of the exterior action conceived. First, physicalism will suggest that exterior actions have a natural order inherent to them (section 3.2.1). Second, Abelardianism will suggest that exterior actions do in fact receive their direction from the agent's intention, even as does the exterior action performed (section 3.2.2). Finally, Abelardianism will turn to what has been called a kind of Kantianism, suggesting that reason designates the order of the action (sections 3.2.3, 3.2.4, 3.2.5, and 3.2.6).

3.2.1. Natural Orders

Physicalism claims that reason apprehends the inherent order of actions. Just as reason perceives a triangle and understands its various attributes, such as its three sides, its interior angles, the sum of these angles, and so on, so reason perceives diverse actions and their properties. Within the act of killing, for instance, it perceives an order to death. Reason is, in this sense, passive, merely apprehending the realities of the world around it.

On this account, an exterior action already has various physical features, including its nature or species, and reason simply becomes aware of these characteristics, the way it becomes aware of the attributes of a triangle. The exterior action performed is specified by intention, while intention is specified by the exterior action conceived, but this very conception is specified by the object of reason, namely, the reality known, which has a nature of its own. Jean Porter, for instance, says that the act itself has its own causal efficacy, derived from the agent's form, by which it is ordered to some aim.[4]

Abelardianism protests that the most essential aspect of an action, its *per se* order to an end, cannot just be "read off" from a physical observation of the action. As Rhonheimer says, "'Objects' of human acts are not mere 'givens,' that is, 'things,' realities, or physical, biological, technical, or juridical structures."[5] The act of pulling a trigger, for instance, is not by its very nature ordered to death, and the act of pounding nails is not by its very nature ordered to making a noise. Just by observing the activity of pounding nails, we cannot determine whether or not it is *per se* ordered to making a noise. Similarly, if we consider the activity of one person handing money to another, we cannot determine just from the physical characteristics of the action whether she is paying a debt or giving a bribe. In none of these cases can we just "read off" the order of the action from its physical features. As Finnis insists, we cannot simply focus upon "the cause-effect relationships identifiable by outside observers," but we must "adopt and consistently maintain the perspective of the acting person."[6] Is it possible, then, that the or-

4. Porter, *Nature as Reason*, 299–300.
5. Rhonheimer, "Perspective," 461.
6. Finnis et al.,"Direct and Indirect," 19; also Finnis, "Object and Intention," 25.

der of the exterior action conceived arises from the will? Perhaps, suggests Abelardianism, it arises from the agent's intention after all.

3.2.2. Prior Intentions

The act of killing, insofar as it is conceived, certainly cannot be specified by the intention to kill, for while someone is still deliberating, he has not yet intended to kill. He must first conceive an act ordered to death and only then intend it; the order to death, then, cannot arise from the very intention to kill. Rhonheimer maintains, however, that the action conceived receives its order from some other intention, from some prior intention that directs the agent's deliberations.[7] Consider, for instance, the exterior action "shooting a gun." By itself, merely through its physical features, it is not necessarily directed to an individual's death. Reason cannot "read off" some natural direction to death. Nevertheless, this physical action can be directed to death by the agent's intention. Even during deliberation, before it is performed, the action can be formed and shaped by some prior intention.

Jones's deliberations about whether or not to shoot a gun do not occur in a vacuum. Rather, they arise within a certain context and within a set of prior goals already determined by Jones. Jones deliberates over whether to shoot a gun only after he has first determined that he wants to kill Smith. After he has decided to kill Smith, he then considers the possible means, such as poisoning, shooting, and so on. As Bratman says,

> I will frequently reason from . . . a prior intention to *further* intentions. I will frequently reason from intended end to intended means or preliminary steps. . . . And I will frequently reason from more general to more specific intentions. . . . further, my prior [intentions] will constrain the other intentions I form.[8]

7. Rhonheimer, "Perspective," 483–93.
8. Bratman, *Intentions*, 17.

When he considers the act of shooting a gun, Jones is already considering it within the context of an intention to kill Smith. He considers it as charged with the direction of his prior intentions. Even the exterior action conceived, then, receives its direction from intention, not from the intention of the action under consideration, but from some prior intention. The act "shooting a gun" does not receive its direction from the intention to shoot a gun, for Jones does not yet intend this action; but it does receive its direction from the intention to kill, which Jones has already settled upon. Once Jones has settled upon the means of shooting a gun, he will then consider the act of "moving his finger," which will be an action invested with his prior intention, and therefore directed to the end of shooting the gun.

On this account, the exterior action conceived, like the exterior action performed, becomes an intention-exterior-act composite. The action conceived is not simply "shooting a gun," but "shooting a gun in order to kill Smith." Similarly, the exterior action of "handing over money" is conceived as "handing over money in order to pay off a debt." The exterior action conceived is not simply a consideration of physical characteristics but includes an order derived from intention. As Rhonheimer says, "an exterior act, the object of a choice, can be described as such an object only by including an intentional element in the description."[9]

Unfortunately, an infinite regress seems to await this account. The act of "handing over money" may be specified by the prior intention to pay off a debt, but this prior intention must itself be specified by some exterior action conceived, namely, by the exterior act of "paying off a debt." From where does this conceived action receive its direction? It cannot be specified by the very intention to pay off a debt. Rather, it must be specified by some yet prior intention, for while the person is deliberating over paying off a debt, she has not yet intended to do so. Nevertheless, she must be deliber-

9. Rhonheimer, "Perspective," 484.

ating within the context of some other intention. Perhaps, for instance, she intends "to do what is just." She does not consider, then, the abstract action "paying off a debt," but the act of "paying off a debt in order to do what is just." Unfortunately, the exterior action "doing what is just" must itself have some other prior intention built into it. We cannot go on forever, but must arrive eventually at some exterior action with no intention built into it. Similarly, if Jones conceives of the act of "shooting a gun" as directed by his prior intention to kill, then this prior intention must itself be specified by the exterior action of killing. From where does this exterior action conceived receive its direction? From some yet prior intention? We cannot have indefinite recourse to prior intentions. Abelardianism, therefore, suggests another possibility.

3.2.3. Active Reason

Why should we suppose that reason passively apprehends the order of exterior actions? Perhaps reason actively constructs the actions about which it deliberates, providing an order that is not found in the physical activity itself. After all, deliberation does not belong to speculative reason but to practical reason. It is not reason trying to figure out how the world already is, but reason trying to figure out how to change the world. The potter who shapes the clay does not passively "read off" the shape of a vase from the clay, for the clay is not yet formed; rather, she constructs a shape from her own mind, which she then introduces into the clay. Similarly, in our deliberations we introduce into physical activity *per se* orders that are not already present. Precisely because it is practical, reason must introduce features into reality rather than merely observe various features.[10]

When Jones considers the act of shooting a gun, for instance,

10. Aquinas says that ethics concerns that order that we introduce into our own actions. See *Sententia libri Ethicorum*, bk. 1, l, 1 (Leonine ed., vol. 47, 4, 14–54).

he does not passively apprehend some order within the physical activity. Rather, he mentally constructs an action that is directed to death. He does not think merely of the act of "shooting a gun" but the act of "shooting a gun in order to kill." The "in order to" need not imply some prior intention, leading to an infinite regress. It implies only a designation of reason.[11] Reason stipulates that this action is directed to death. It recognizes that shooting a gun can be directed to other endpoints, but it is not now concerned with these other endpoints; it is concerned only with the act of shooting that is directed to death. Reason, not intention, orders our actions, for as Aquinas says,

> The will does not order but it tends into something according to the direction of reason, so that the word "intention" names an act of the will but it presupposes the direction of reason ordering something into the end.[12]

3.2.4. Resolution

Physicalism objects that the realism of Aquinas, in which reason discovers the existing world, has been abandoned for the subjectivism of Kant, in which reason paints itself upon the world. Actions no longer have an inherent nature, but they change depending upon the arbitrary stipulation of reason. Reason becomes free to designate any order upon any action, even as the potter is free to shape the clay. The worst nightmares associated with description-intention become true. We merely stipulate some description of our action, however arbitrary, and intend it under that description. According to Kevin Flannery, for instance, "Boyle's approach

---

11. What Rhonheimer does with the intention-for-an-end can be achieved with reason rather than intention; we need recognize only that reason conceives actions as directed to an end.

12. I-II, 12, 1, ad 3. "Voluntas quidem non ordinat, sed tamen in aliquid tendit secundum ordinem rationis. unde hoc nomen intentio nominat actum voluntatis, praesupposita ordinatione rationis ordinantis aliquid in finem." See also I-II, 13, 1.

threatens to descend into arbitrariness," since the only restraint Boyle places upon reason is that descriptions of actions must include what is "conceptually related," a loose term that allows one to ignore many important features of an action.[13]

The active role of reason, however, need not be arbitrary. The potter cannot arbitrarily assign any shape to the clay, nor can she designate the properties her product will have. She cannot, for instance, suppose that a shape with no bottom will have the property of holding water. If what she wishes is pottery that holds water, then she cannot arbitrarily assign a shape with no bottom. Similarly, if what Jones wishes is the death of Smith, then he cannot arbitrarily conceive of an act of shooting a gun that is ordered only to making a noise; he must conceive the act as directed to death. Just as the potter's conceptions are constrained by the physical realities of clay, so practical reason is constrained by the causal realities in the world around us. As Stephen Brock points out, "What fall under this consideration [of practical reason] are not just features *conferred* on a thing by practical reason.'Given' features of it do too."[14]

According to Thomas, deliberation proceeds in the manner of resolution or analysis, that is, it begins with the desired endpoint and seeks to resolve this endpoint into its causes.[15] The soldier, for

13. Flannery, "What is Included," 505.

14. Stephen Brock, "*Veritatis Splendor* ¶ 78, St. Thomas, and (Not Merely) Physical Objects of Moral Acts," *Nova et Vetera*, English ed. 6 (2008): 1–62, at 40. Brock has a detailed treatment of how objective features of things and actions determine the species as given by reason.

15. I-II, 14, 5. Those authors who have done much to emphasize and elucidate the role of deliberation and resolution in our intentions and actions include Michael Bratman, *Intentions*; Christopher Kaczor, *Proportionalism*, 106–18; "Moral Absolutism and Ectopic Pregnancy," *Journal of Medicine and Philosophy* 26 (2001): 61–74, at 65–68; "Distinguishing Intention from Foresight: What is Included in a Means to an End?" *International Philosophical Quarterly* 41 (2001): 77–89, at 82–85; and John Finnis et al., "Direct and Indirect"; Sullivan and Atkinson, "*Malum Vitandum*"; Flannery (*Acts Amid Precepts*, 60–71, 195–98) is one of the few explicitly to recognize and treat the role of analysis within practical reasoning.

instance, begins with the desire to stop the army in its progress. He then searches for possible causes of this goal. Eventually, he settles upon destroying the bridge as the best possible means to achieve his goal. He next inquires into the causes of destroying the bridge. After concluding that it is best to blow up the bridge, he then searches for the causes needed to achieve this new goal. He proceeds, says Thomas, until he comes to some first action that he must perform. Throughout his deliberations, he is constrained by the real causal relations in the world around him. When the second soldier shoots the child, for instance, he cannot imagine that his goal of destroying the bridge is achieved apart from the means of injuring the child, for the injury is one of the causes that brings about his goal. He could conceive of an act of shooting the bridge itself, but such an action would not causally accomplish his goal. He cannot, therefore, include this action in his deliberations about how to destroy the bridge.

Boyle has claimed that only what is conceptually connected to a means need be intended, and has thereby freed himself from concerns over the real causal connections in the world.[16] In fact, the real causal connections are precisely what form our deliberations concerning the means.[17] Bratman identifies two constraints upon our deliberations.[18] First, our deliberations must be consistent with our current intentions. If the soldier intends to stop the army, then his deliberations concerning the child must be consistent with this goal. Second, our deliberations must be consistent with our background beliefs. If the soldier believes that clapping his hands will not stop the army, then he cannot plan to clap in order to stop the army. Amongst our background beliefs, some of the most important are our beliefs about causal structures in the world, about what causes will bring about our goals. Causes are significant be-

16. Boyle, "Embryotomy," 306–8.
17. Such is the main criticism that Flannery ("What is Included") lays against Boyle.
18. Bratman, *Intentions*, 31–37.

cause they must enter into and shape deliberation. We deliberate about how to do something, and we do things by way of causes. As Bratman puts it, "A good coordinating plan is a plan for the world I find myself in."[19]

In the process of analysis, the active role of reason might be viewed as connecting the dots. Reason moves backwards, from the goal sought, back to the initial causal input needed. If Jones wishes to steal from Smith, he then moves back to the realization that he must get Smith out of the way; from there, he moves back to killing Smith as a way of getting rid of him; from there, he moves back to shooting him as a way of killing; from there, he moves back to pointing the gun and pulling the trigger as a means to shoot.

3.2.5. What Real Causes Do Not Do

When we consider the possible descriptions of an action we often move forward from the initial causal input. We see that Jones pulls the trigger, which then fires a gun, which then kills Smith, and so we say his action can be described as pulling a trigger, firing a gun, or killing Smith. But we can also move forward to other effects. Firing the gun also results in making a noise, so we can describe his action as making a noise. Making a noise wakes the neighbors, so his action can be described as waking the neighbors. Of course, as Jones works backwards from the goal, making the noise and waking the neighbors do not play into the causal factors that contribute to the goal (indeed, they work against it). He does not propose to himself, therefore, the act of "firing a gun in order to make a noise"; rather, he proposes the act of "firing a gun in order to kill Smith."

Every action is directed to its proper effect. The act of killing is directed to death; the act of growing is directed to increased size; the act of pulling a trigger is directed to the trigger moving. Actions have no need to receive this direction from anything, for it belongs to their very nature or to the very notion of their descrip-

19. Bratman, *Intentions*, 31.

tion. "Killing" simply is the name of the activity directed towards death, as "growing" describes the action ordered to increased size. Rhonheimer's insistence upon the order to the end has perhaps led him to forget this fact.[20] He almost seems to deny that we can conceive of an act of killing directed simply to death; he would want some further end to which it is directed. He wishes to emphasize that an action such as "pulling the trigger" is not inherently directed toward death. He need not go so far as to deny that pulling the trigger is inherently directed to the trigger moving. That is just what it means to pull the trigger.[21]

Such inherent endpoints are of little use as we move forward, for the very question before us is whether we should describe the action of pulling the trigger as a killing or as something else.[22] We do not wonder whether the act of pulling a trigger is directed to the trigger moving; we wonder whether it is directed to death or to a noise or to some other effects. As Jones moves backward in deliberation, on the other hand, he begins with the description "kill-

20. Rhonheimer, "Perspective," 490–91.

21. Rhonheimer might wish to deny that these action descriptions (without a further end) are human actions. But why? Just because they are considered without a further end, it does not follow that they must be considered as nonvoluntary or unintended. We can conceive the act of "pulling the trigger" as a voluntary and intentional action, while abstracting from the further end toward which it might be directed. If Aquinas grants that "picking up sticks" can be a human action, then why not "pulling the trigger"? For a treatment of this issue see Brock, "Veritatis Splendor," 46–55.

22. Cavanaugh also notes that we might approach causality from two directions (Double-Effect, 29–30). He further notes that if an evil effect is the only cause by which an action brings about some further presumably intended effect, then the evil must also be intended. In using a gun for self-defense, for instance, the evil effect of injury cannot fall outside intention, since the gun is a cause of defense only insofar as it harms the assailant. This approach still uses resolution, for it presumes the end of self-defense; it does not trace this resolution back to the injury, but rather discovers that the resolution *must* go to the injury, since the injury is the only cause of the desired end. Herein lies the truth to the claim that we can sometimes determine someone's intention merely by looking at his physical activity.

ing," since death is the goal he seeks, and what is undetermined, at that time, is whether the killing will be achieved by shooting, stabbing, strangling, or some other means. When he considers the act of shooting Smith, he does not have to worry whether it is directed to the death of Smith, for his deliberations forge a link between the act of shooting, which is itself indeterminate toward many effects, and the effect of death. He conceives the shooting precisely as a way of killing. Reason connects the dots as it moves backward, joining the various effects with a direction or ordering between them, with what might be described as an "in order to" link.

The "in order to" link is not built into the nature of the physical activity, especially as approached forward. The act of firing a gun is directed to the discharge of a bullet from a gun, but this effect can result in various other effects, such as a noise or the death of an individual. As we move forward, the action is not *directed* toward any of these effects; it merely results in them. We cannot move forward on account of some special causal feature of the action to some further effect, beyond the proper effect, as if the action must include particularly salient or "close" effects. We cannot move, for instance, from the crushing of the skull to the death, as if these two effects must necessarily be linked into a single action.[23] We cannot, as William May suggests, move from "cutting off someone's head" to his death.[24] We can move forward to say that the death follows necessarily. The same, however, can be said of the death of the baby in the hysterectomy case. Any effect moving forward, however inevitable, is not necessarily a *per se* effect and the human action is not necessarily directed toward it.

As we move backward in deliberation, however, the action is immediately connected by reason to the desired effect. The connection forged is made by reason, not by the physical nature of the activity. As we look at the action—moving forward—of one per-

23. This approach is criticized by Finnis et al., "Direct and Indirect," 19–20.
24. May, "Ectopic Pregnancies," 141.

son handing over money to another, we do not know to what end
it is directed, because it has no intrinsic direction toward its many
possible effects. The action might be in order to pay off a debt or in
order to give a bribe or for many other things. The action of handing over money, just as such, is not necessarily directed to any of
these. As reason moves backwards in deliberation, however, it immediately directs the action to the most recent goal in the chain.
Perhaps the person has deliberated, beginning with the goal of doing what is just, from which she moves back to the goal of paying
off her debt, from which she moves back to the activity of handing over money. Offering a bribe never enters into the equation as
a possibility. She connects one activity to another as she moves
backward. Handing over the money is for the sake of paying off her
debt. It *is* an act of paying off a debt, or at least that is how she conceives it.

3.2.6. What Real Causes Do

This active role of reason is fairly minimal. It does not allow reason
to redescribe an action in any way it pleases. Reason must follow
the real causal connections in the world;[25] reason merely provides
the *per se* order between these causal connections. As reason directs an action, it cannot skip one of the real causal connections.
The soldier, for instance, cannot redescribe his action of firing the
gun simply as "setting off the explosives," thereby excluding the
link of killing the child, for in his reasoning he begins with the goal
of setting off the explosives, and then recognizes that he must kill
the child in order to do so. He has forged the first link. Next he recognizes that he must fire the gun in order to kill the child. The next
link is forged. He cannot now eliminate the link that connects
"shooting the gun" to "setting off the explosives," namely, "killing
the child." Likewise, the person who defends herself cannot de-

---

25. Or more precisely, what the person believes to be the real causal relations.
Sullivan and Atkinson emphasize this role of causes (*"Malum Vitandum,"* 103).

scribe her action as "firing a gun to stop the attacker," leaving out the step of "injuring the attacker," since firing a gun stops an attacker precisely by injuring him. Such redescriptions are the tools of rationalization, not of deliberation. As Finnis suggests, we must consider "clear-headed practical reasoning," not fanciful redescriptions of actions.[26] And as Rhonheimer insists,

> That which an agent can reasonably propose (and consequently choose) in a given situation is understood by reason, not simply as a function of "proposals" or "intentions" that can be freely oriented by the agent, but [is] subject to the concrete circumstances in which the choice is carried out.[27]

In what way, then, do causes operate to determine the *per se* order of the action? Not by moving forward, in which we recognize a cause and perceive its various effects, some necessary, others not; rather, by moving backwards, in which we begin with the effect and look for the causes. These causes are real, and so constrain our deliberations.

In what way, then, do exterior actions conceived receive their order? Primarily from reason, which conceives actions precisely with some *per se* order. Nevertheless, the other two possibilities— prior intention and nature—also play a role in our deliberations, for reason is constrained by the goals we seek to attain and by the real causes in nature by which we can attain those goals. We begin with some goal and move backwards searching for the causes that can bring about this goal. Reason forges the links between the causes and the goal, thereby giving exterior actions a *per se* order.

---

26. Finnis, "Intention and Side-Effects," in *Liability and Responsibility: Essays in Law and Morals,* ed. R. G. Frey and Christopher W. Morris (New York: Cambridge University Press, 1991): 32–64, at 43–44. The emphasis upon being clear-headed is reiterated in Finnis et al. ("Direct and Indirect," 34).

27. "Perspective," 473. See also 489, in which Rhonheimer argues that reason must understand the link between swallowing a narcotic and relieving pain.

SECTION 3.3. *A Deliberation*

By applying the considerations of the previous section (3.2) to the case of the craniotomy some details can be flushed out. In particular, we will see that our deliberations determine two defining features of actions, namely, the subject that we act upon and the form that we aim to introduce in this subject (section 3.3.2). When fire heats water, it introduces the form of heat into water; similarly, when Jones kills Smith, he introduces death into the subject of a human being. What, then, is the subject acted upon in a craniotomy, and what is the form introduced?

3.3.1. Engaging Powers

We have seen that intention primarily concerns actions rather than end-states (section 2.3.4). All the more does deliberation. We do not deliberate over end-states or results but over actions.[28] The soldier does not deliberate over the army being stopped, but over stopping the army. Jones deliberates over killing, not over death.

Typically, we deliberate over exterior actions. Jones deliberates over whether he should kill, not over whether he should choose or intend to kill. In some unusual circumstances, we might deliberate over acts of will, but these instances need not concern us. The exterior actions over which we deliberate, however, are not mere physical activity; rather, we deliberate over voluntary actions, actions conceived precisely as arising from the will and belonging to the will (section 1.4.2). Our deliberations tend to focus upon the engagement of some external power, such as the power to move about. We do not usually deliberate about our will engaging these powers, but about engaging these powers as from the will. We do not wonder whether we should choose to move our hand; we wonder whether we should move our hand, recognizing that if it is indeed *we* who move the hand, then the action arises from the will.

28. I-II, 14, 3.

As Anscombe says, "The voluntariness is presupposed in [one's] *considering whether* to do [something]. Thus it does not come into [one's] considerations of what to do, but it does come into a later judgment—[one's] own or another's.—of what was done."[29]

The external powers that we engage are generally of two sorts, mental or physical, for example, we might engage in the mental activity of looking at a picture or in the physical activity of throwing a ball. The most important physical activity is the activity of moving about, through which we use various objects as instruments (section 1.4.1).[30] Jones, for instance, moves his finger and thereby moves the trigger and fires the gun and kills Smith. We also move our body in order to engage other powers. We move our head and our eyes, for instance, in order to see some object. Similarly, through various movements concerning our reproductive organs, we engage the power to reproduce.

The craniotomy case is an instance of activity in which we use our power of movement to use things as instruments in order to bring about some desired effect. The doctor moves her hands in order to move various medical instruments in order to crush the head of the baby in order to remove the baby and end labor. Our conceptions of such actions are constrained by the realities of the causal relations of the instruments we use (sections 3.2.5 and 3.2.6). The doctor cannot suppose, for instance, that she can reduce the size of the head of the baby without some movement of her hands, for it is precisely by bringing about a change in her hands that she also brings about a change in her instruments, which then change the baby.

3.3.2. Who Is Acted Upon?

The soldier who shoots the child must conceive his act as achieved by way of acting upon the child, for it is precisely by bringing about

---

29. G. E. M. Anscombe, "Two Kinds of Error in Action," in *Ethics, Religion and Politics* (Minneapolis: University of Minnesota Press, 1981): 3–9, at 8.
30. See I-II, 93, 5.

a change in the child that he detonates the explosives. In his deliberations, he must plan to bring about a change in the child in order to bring about a change in the detonator in order to destroy the bridge. The other soldier, in contrast, must plan to bring about a change in the bridge, recognizing that he thereby brings about a change in the child. He does not need a change in the child as a cause to destroy the bridge, as does the soldier who shoots the child.

The craniotomy and the hysterectomy differ in a similar respect. In both of them, some change is brought about in the child, but in the hysterectomy this change does not causally bring about the desired change of removing the cancer; rather, removing the cancer brings about the change in the child. In contrast, for the causal reality of the craniotomy, the change in the child (and we do not here stipulate whether this change is death or merely reducing the size of the head) causally contributes to the desired goal of bringing the labor to an end.

As Kevin Flannery points out, the doctor in the craniotomy case must act upon the child; the child is one of the objects, or matter, upon which the doctor acts.[31] In contrast, in the hysterectomy case, the doctor need not act upon the child, for bringing about a change in the child is neither the end sought nor a causal means of bringing about the desired change; the child, then, need not serve as the material of any action in the hysterectomy case. Likewise, the soldier who destroys the bridge, foreseeing the death of the child, need not act upon the child.[32]

While the doctor performing the craniotomy must act upon the unborn child, it does not follow that she must kill the child. In

31. Flannery, "What is Included," 511–12.

32. As Finnis et al. ("Direct and Indirect," 28) and Kaczor ("Distinguishing," 82) point out, the material alone is not sufficient to determine the precise nature of intention. While it is not sufficient, it is certainly relevant, for the material is one thing that is intended, as well as the effect. That to which the agent reduces her goal is the bringing about of certain changes in certain materials.

her deliberations she must plan to bring about some change in the child in order to obtain her further goal of ending the labor. But what change must she propose to introduce, death or merely resizing the head? Once again, the desired goal must be resolved into its causes. Not all the changes that come about in the child need serve as the objects to which the doctor's action is directed. The doctor must plan to bring about only those effects that causally contribute to bringing about the desired goal. The death of the child, it seems, does not causally bring about the end of the labor; rather, the reduced size of the head is the causally instrumental change that brings about the desired effect.

The doctor, then, must propose to bring about some change in the child in order to end the labor, but she need not propose to bring about death, which does not causally bring about the desired result. Since intention is specified by the exterior action conceived, it seems to follow that the doctor need intend only to reduce the size of the child's head and not to kill the child.[33]

3.3.3. Crushing Skulls

The affair of the craniotomy, however, is not quite settled. We have not sufficiently resolved the goal into its causes. It may be true that the death of the child does not causally contribute to the desired goal. It may be true that the smaller size of the head is the effect that causally ends the labor. Nevertheless, we must yet consider the manner in which the doctor plans to reduce the size of the head. She does so by introducing other changes in the child, namely, by crushing the skull of the child. Christopher Kaczor and Stephen Brock have argued that this action, crushing the skull, is at the very least an act of harming the child.[34] To crush a skull is to do dam-

33. Many thinkers grant that the death need not be intended. See Kaczor, *Proportionalism*, 111; Sullivan, "Malum Vitandum," 108.

34. Brock, *Action and Conduct*, 204–5, n. 17; Kaczor, "Distinguishing," 86; Kaczor, *Proportionalism*, 11–113; see also Sullivan and Atkinson, "Malum Vitandum," 108; Cavanaugh, *Double-Effect*, 202.

age to a major organ, which is certainly a kind of harm. Indeed, it appears to be an act of lethal harm. The doctor, therefore, in order to reduce the size of the head, plans to crush the skull, which is to plan harm to the child.

Finnis and others claim that Brock has not established the priority of the description "crushing the skull" over "narrowing the cranium."[35] Surely, they have missed the point. Both descriptions are perfectly legitimate; indeed, both are *per se* and proper descriptions of the action. We must not view the action from the outside, moving forward, and wonder which description, given the causal structure of the action, seems the best fit. We must move backwards, from the perspective of the doctor's deliberations, and realize that she cannot stop short at the description "narrowing the cranium," for she must resolve *this action* into its causes as well. She must recognize that she narrows the skull by way of crushing. If we are to adopt the perspective of the acting person, then we must do so to the very end; we must "steadily maintain the perspective of the acting person."[36] We must consider the deliberations of the doctor to the point where she has finally resolved her goal into the most immediate cause of her own initiative. If we wish to include a proximate end, that is, a means, within intention, or rather within deliberation, then we must include all the means, even the crush-

35. Finnis et al., "Direct and Indirect," 26, n. 38.

36. Finnis et al., "Direct and Indirect," 12. Finnis correctly notes that we should not say that "intentionally firing a shotgun at close range directly at robbers just is acting with intent to kill them." ("Intention and Side-Effects," 54–55). Nevertheless, he misses the point that stopping the violent assault is reduced to their death in deliberation. It is not the closeness of the range or the directness of the aim that makes the action to be *per se* killing, or at least an "injuring," but the fact that the acting person has recognized she can stop the assault by injuring the robber, which she does by firing the gun. What sort of clear-headed deliberations Finnis imagines the defender to be making is difficult to grasp. No one defending herself stops at the cause "I must stop the attacker"; she deliberates about some means to stop the attacker. And no clear-headed defender leaps from "stopping the attacker" to "firing a gun at close range." She invariably includes the middle step: "injuring the attacker."

ing of the skull. We must be careful, warns Finnis, not to describe an action "only in terms of the purposes that motivated it, omitting what the acting person chose to do as a means of pursuing those purposes."[37]

The hysterectomy is a different matter. The doctor does not plan to introduce any change into the child. Rather, she plans to introduce a change into the womb, which consequently changes the child. She need not, then, plan to do any harm to the child; she need only plan other actions that consequently bring about harm to the child. Doing something to the child, whether it be harm or otherwise, is not any part of the causes that bring about her desired goal. She need not reason, "I must introduce some change into the child, such as death, which will then causally bring about the end of the cancer."

In contrast, in the craniotomy case the doctor reasons that some change in the child, namely, crushing the skull, causally brings about a reduced size of the head, which in turn causally brings the labor to an end. When she recognizes that the change she plans to introduce is in fact a harm or damage to the child, then her plans include doing harm, even lethal harm, to the unborn child.

3.3.4. Trolleys

Before we proceed, we should note an oddity of deliberation that arises from our ability to conceive negations. Amongst the causes that we use in the world around us are included the lack of a cause or the obstruction of a cause. In fact, such must always be the case when we are trying to prevent something; if we wish to prevent some event from happening, then we must prevent its expected cause from acting. If I plan to stop the water from boiling, then I must turn off the burner or take the pot off the burner. In either case, I prevent the stove from acting, either by eliminating its causality entirely or by eliminating its causality upon this water. I do

---

37. Finnis et al., "Direct and Indirect," 35.

so, of course, through some other change or action. Nevertheless, part of what I try to achieve, in the causes around me, is that a cause not act. In other words, when we act we not only aim to introduce some form in some subject; sometimes we aim to prevent a form from being introduced.

This point can be of great importance in certain instances of causing harm. Consider the well-worn trolley example.[38] A runaway trolley is racing toward a divide in the track. Bound to the track on the right is a single individual; bound to the track on the left are five individuals. The trolley is currently directed to the five individuals on the left, but Paula has control of the switch in the track, so in order to save the five, she turns it down the right track, thereby injuring the one person on the track. Must she plan this injury as a cause needed to achieve her goals?

It would seem not. She is trying to prevent the trolley from killing five people on the left track. Reducing this goal to its causes, Paula recognizes that she must eliminate the expected cause, which is the trolley moving down the left track. In other words, the first cause to which she reduces the goal is the negation of a cause. Ideally, of course, she would prevent the trolley from moving entirely—like turning off the stove—but we suppose that option is unavailable. The most immediate cause available, therefore, is that the trolley not go down the left track, which does not prevent the trolley from moving entirely, but it does prevent the trolley from acting upon these five individuals, just as moving the pot off the stove prevents the stove from heating this water. By moving the trolley away from the left track, however, the trolley necessarily moves somewhere else, and given the suppositions, it must move down the right track, where it kills one individual. In other words, by aiming at the negation of a cause—that the trolley *not* go down the left track—another cause is introduced—that the trolley go down the right track, which causes the death of the person. This new cause, however, is a

38. Originating with Foot ("Problem of Abortion," 270).

consequence of the cause that Paula seeks to introduce; it is not one of the causes to which she reduces her goal. As Philippa Foot puts it, "We have here the *diverting* of a fatal sequence and not the starting of a new one."[39]

We might say that the train does not go down the left track *because* it does go down the right track. We can say just as well, however, that it goes down the right track *because* it does not go down the left. The trolley must go somewhere (given our suppositions), and it can only go to the left or to the right. By going one way, it does not go the other; or by not going one way, it does go the other. In either event, some negation is involved, which cannot strictly be the case in the real causes in the world, but which can be the case in our conceptions. What Paula must plan in her deliberations is the negation of a cause, the trolley not going down the left track, which is achieved by throwing the switch and which has as a consequence that the trolley move somewhere else.

Stephen Brock notes that a similar point can be made of the captain who jettisons his cargo in a storm in order to save his life.[40] The captain aims to achieve a negation, namely, that the cargo cease acting as a cause to sink the ship; he does so by moving it off the ship. That it should, afterwards, fall into the sea is not something he need aim to achieve. The captain reduces his goal of saving the ship to the cause of the cargo *not* being on the ship, which is achieved by throwing it off the ship. What happens to the cargo after it is thrown off the ship is no cause to which the captain need reduce his goal.

Long provides another commonly used example.[41] Several rock climbers are tied together with ropes, but one slips and is hanging dangling from the others. His weight, however, threatens to dislodge the one remaining stay, thereby pulling them all down. If

39. Foot, "Killing and Letting Die," in *Killing and Letting Die,* ed. Bonnie Steinbock (New York: Fordham University Press, 1994): 280–89, at 287.
40. Brock, *Action and Conduct,* 206–8.
41. Long, *Teleological Grammar,* 72–74.

one of the climbers should cut the rope, then she aims to achieve a negation that the weight of the dangling climber should cease to pull down the others. That the climber then falls to his death necessarily follows upon this negation, just as the trolley must necessarily go down the right track when it is diverted from the left. This consequent causality, following upon the negation of a cause, however, need not fit within the causes that the climber plans to use. The climber aims to prevent the entire group from falling to their deaths. She reduces this goal to the elimination of the expected cause, which is the weight of the dangling climber. This cause is eliminated by cutting the rope. The consequent fall and death of the climber is not a cause of the goal. In this instance, by introducing the negation of a cause, that is, by cutting the rope so that the weight does not act to pull down the remaining climbers, one also eliminates another cause, that is, one removes the cause that holds up the dangling climber.

Self-defense is also an instance of trying to prevent something, and so it involves the attempt to eliminate the expected cause. Shooting the assailant, however, eliminates the cause by way of killing him, or at least injuring him. One does not divert the cause, thereby leading it to bring about some other injury, as with the trolley; rather, one attacks the cause precisely by way of an injury. In this instance, the assailant himself is the expected cause, and his causality is eliminated by killing or injuring him.

From these considerations, together with all that has brought us to this point, we should recognize that Jonathan Bennett's distinction between making and allowing, to which he attributes no moral significance, misses the mark.[42] "Making" includes all manner of causing, whether *per se* or *per accidens*. In both the craniotomy and the hysterectomy, the doctor "makes" the baby die, and in the trolley example, Paula "makes" the person on the right track die. We are interested in what an agent does, not what she makes,

42. Bennett, *Act Itself,* 62–142.

for through what she does she orders herself to some good or to some evil. The focus should be upon doing, which is not the same as making. In the trolley example, Paula "makes" the person on the right track die. She does not, however, "do" the act of killing, that is, she does not plan in her deliberations to bring about the death of the person as a way to achieve her goals.

The point of this digression is obvious. Someone might suppose that these cases of preventing something are no different from the craniotomy case: they involve damaging one person as a cause of saving others. We might suppose that Paula must harm one person as a means of saving five others; or that the rock climber must kill one person as a cause of saving others. In these cases, however, the injury results by positing the negation of a cause, that is, by preventing an expected cause from acting. As a result, the cause acts upon something else. In contrast, the doctor in the craniotomy case reduces her goal of ending the labor to the crushing of the skull, which is a kind of injury. For the craniotomy case, then, the doctor must intend to do harm.

3.3.5. Intending a Good Formality

Abelardianism insists, however, that the matter is still not closed. While the doctor must intend to crush the skull, and a crushing of the skull is certainly harm to the child, it does not follow that the doctor must intend this action *insofar as it is harm*. The act of crushing the skull can be considered in two ways: first, insofar as it is a harm to the child; second, simply insofar as it reduces the size of the head. The doctor intends it only in the second way, for only as such does it causally contribute to her goals. What is done, says Finnis, "is settled by what one [chooses], under the description which made it attractive to choice."[43] This approach affects the

---

43. Finnis, "Intention and Side-Effects," 57. Porter's criticism of Grisez, that an action can always be described in terms of some good end seems on the mark ("Direct and Indirect," 626). She herself, however, says that any harmful act that

characterization of both the exterior action performed and the exterior action conceived. The exterior action conceived is ordered by reason rather than intention, but our deliberations are constrained by the goals at which we aim, so that even the exterior action conceived is ordered by reason in relation to an end intended. In her deliberations, the doctor plans to crush the head of the baby, but she does so in order to reduce the size of the head, not in order to harm the child.

In short, Abelardianism avoids concluding that the craniotomy is a killing, or at least a lethal harm, through the implications of some version of description-intention (see sections 2.2.3 and 2.3.1), through what Long calls "logicism."[44] The doctor does intend that which is harm, namely, the crushing of the baby's skull, but she does not intend it under the description of harm. We must see once and for all, therefore, whether logicism can be defended, or whether, as Long says, a moral description of an action "materially presupposes the act itself and the integral nature of the act itself."[45] Does the exterior action, whether performed or conceived, have some substance to it beyond the formality that intention provides? The answer to this question, it turns out, will depend once again upon reason. We have seen that reason provides the order of the exterior action conceived (section 3.2.3); it will become evident that reason plays a yet more fundamental role in the species of human actions.

The potter actively conceives the shape of the vase, but then she is forced to recognize various properties that follow; a vase with a rounded bottom, for instance, will not sit upright. The doctor conceives her action as an act of crushing a skull precisely for the purpose of reducing the size of the head. She is forced to recognize,

---

is justified is defined in terms of a positive natural human inclination, and that any damage or loss from such an action is construed as outside intention (*Nature as Reason*, 286). The resulting flexibility is hardly different from that of Grisez.

44. Long, *Teleological Grammar*, 30.

45. Long, *Teleological Grammar*, 34.

however, that the act of crushing is also an act of harming. Should this harming be included in the moral species of her action? That depends. Not upon intention but upon reason. How does the harm relate to reason as it orders to the good?

Surprisingly, this new role of reason for determining the substance of human actions is best approached through that which, by definition, falls outside the substance of human actions, namely, circumstances. Is it possible, Aquinas asks, that a circumstance could give species to human actions?

SECTION 3.4. *Circumstances*

We began our inquiry into the specification of human actions with a distinction between the substance or species of an action and its circumstances (section 1.1.2). [46] When Jones kills Smith, for instance, the substance of his action is a killing while its circumstances include the time it occurred, where it occurred, and so on. The circumstances provide multiple descriptions of an action but they do not enter into the very heart or species of the action (section 1.2.1). As Jones fires the gun, his action may be described as, "making a noise," but that is not what he is most essentially about; what he is going about doing is killing Smith, and the noise is only circumstantial.

The whole question over the craniotomy concerns the substance of the doctor's action. Certainly, her action can be described as lethal, or even as a killing. But is it most essentially a killing? Is its lethality circumstantial, or does it belong to the substance of the action? As we have seen, there is no easy answer to this question.

Although a circumstance, by definition, is that which falls outside the species of an action, Aquinas asks several times whether a circumstance can give species to human actions. On the face of it,

46. Portions of this section are taken from my article, "Do Circumstances Give Species?" *The Thomist* 70 (2006): 1–26.

the answer must be negative, but Aquinas usually answers in the affirmative. Furthermore, Aquinas's various answers appear to be in conflict. At one point he gives an answer that seems to correspond with description-intention: only those formalities, or circumstances, that are intended gives species to an action, so that for instance, the formality of harm associated with crushing a skull would not give species so long as it is not intended. At other points, Aquinas says that circumstances give species, whatever the intention, just so long as they provide some new moral deformity. We will begin with those texts that emphasize the role of motive, thereby seeming to aid and abet description-intention or logicism (section 3.4.1). Then we will consider how these texts can be reconciled with apparently conflicting texts (sections 3.4.2, 3.4.3, 3.4.4, and 3.4.5).

3.4.1. Circumstances and Motive

When asking whether circumstances give species to sins, Thomas provides the following answer.

> Whenever there is a new motive to sin, there is another species of sin, since the motive for sinning is the end and object. Sometimes in the corruption of different circumstances, the motive may remain the same, for example, the greedy person is propelled by the same motive to take when he should not, where he should not, and more than he should, and similarly with other circumstances, for he does all of these things on account of the inordinate desire to accumulate money. The corruption of these different circumstances does not diversify the species of sins, but they all belong to one and the same species of sin. At other times, on the other hand, the corruption of diverse circumstances arises from distinct motives . . . and so leads to diverse species of sins.[47]

47. I-II, 72, 9. "Ubi occurrit aliud motivum ad peccandum, ibi est alia peccati species, quia motivum ad peccandum est finis et obiectum. Contingit autem quandoque quod in corruptionibus diversarum circumstantiarum est idem motivum, sicut illiberalis ab eodem movetur quod accipiat quando non oportet, et ubi non oportet, et plus quam oportet, et similiter de aliis circumstantiis; hoc

As Abelardianism reads this text, the harm done to the baby in the craniotomy belongs to the species of the action only if the doctor intends it as a motive for her action. It appears, then, that if she intends to crush the skull only under the formality of reducing the size of the head, and not under the formality of harm, then the harm does not specify her action.

In a parallel text of the *Secunda secundae* the Angelic Doctor makes a similar point concerning the act of theft and sacrilege. He seems to have in mind two thieves who steal an object, such as a chalice, from a church. The first wants the gold, but in addition he seeks to do damage to God through harming what is sacred. The second simply wants the gold, and the church happens to be a convenient place from which to take it. Both thieves commit the offense of theft, but what of the sin of sacrilege? Do both commit sacrilege, or only the first? Although the second thief is aware that his action harms God, he does not intend the action insofar as it brings harm; he only wants the profit from the gold. On the face of it, Aquinas states that the thief commits sacrilege only if he intends to do harm.

> When the corruption of diverse circumstances has the same motive, then the species of sin is not diversified, for example, it belongs to the same species of sin to take what is not one's own, either where one ought not or when one ought not. But if there are diverse motives, then there would also be diverse species, for example, if someone takes from where he ought not in order to do harm to a holy place then the species would become sacrilege; but if someone else takes when he ought not simply on account of an excessive desire for possessions, then the species would be simply greed.[48]

---

enim facit propter inordinatum appetitum pecuniae congregandae. Et in talibus diversarum circumstantiarum corruptiones non diversificant species peccatorum, sed pertinent ad unam et eandem peccati speciem. Quandoque vero contingit quod corruptiones diversarum circumstantiarum proveniunt a diversis motivis. . . . Unde in talibus diversarum circumstantiarum corruptiones inducunt diversas peccati species."

48. II-II, 53, 2, ad 3. "quando corruptio diversarum circumstantiarum habet

The holy place from which the thief steals, which may be tak-
en as a circumstance of the action, provides species to the action,
claims Abelardianism, only if the thief intends to steal precisely
from a holy place, insofar as it is holy. If he intends to steal only under the formality of riches, then the holy place remains a circumstance and does not give species to the action. Certainly what the
thief does—take the chalice—is a kind of harm to the holy place,
even as crushing a skull is harm to a child. Nevertheless, the thief
need not intend his action insofar as it is harmful to God. Likewise,
the doctor need not intend her action insofar as it is harmful to the
child. The species of either action is taken from the motive of the
one who does it. The thief who seeks only riches commits theft but
not sacrilege, and similarly, concludes Abelardianism, the doctor
who seeks only to reduce the size of the skull, without intending
the damage, does not commit murder.

Unfortunately, this account is open to the worst sorts of abuses
endemic to description-intention. For instance, the adulterer may
claim that he did not intend sexual relations with this woman *insofar as she was another man's wife*. Even if he could be found guilty
of some other sin, such as excessive desire for pleasure, his action
could not be specified as adultery. The thief who steals the chalice
would avoid not only the sin of sacrilege but also the sin of theft
itself, just so long as he intended to take the item insofar as it was
valuable, rather than under the formality of its belonging to someone else. Many murderers would not in fact commit murder, if they
intend the action only under the formality of its usefulness rather
than under the formality of harming the victim.

Furthermore, this interpretation of Aquinas falls apart under

---

idem motivum, non diversificatur peccati species, sicut eiusdem speciei est peccatum ut aliquis accipiat non sua ubi non debet, et quando non debet. sed si sint
diversa motiva, tunc essent diversae species, puta si unus acciperet unde non de-
beret ut faceret iniuriam loco sacro, quod faceret speciem sacrilegii; alius quando non debet propter solum superfluum appetitum habendi, quod esset simplex
avaritia."

scrutiny. Certain texts of Aquinas seem to contradict the teaching that circumstances give species only when they are intended, and upon further examination the texts adduced in favor of this account bear a more plausible interpretation.

3.4.2. An Early Text

The view that circumstances give species only when intention formally bears upon them is explicitly rejected by Thomas. Indeed, he seems to have the two thieves in mind.

> Some have said that circumstances make for a new species only insofar as they are taken as an end of the will, for moral actions receive their species from the end. This view, however, is insufficiently considered, for sometimes the species of sin changes without the sinner's intention bearing upon that circumstance. For example, a thief just as readily takes a gold vessel that is not sacred as one that is sacred, yet the action changes into a new species of sin, namely, from theft simply speaking into sacrilege. Furthermore, according to this view the only circumstance that could change the species of sin would be "that for the sake of which," which is plainly false. We should say, therefore, that all circumstances can change the species of a sin but they do not always do so.[49]

When do they give species, if not when intended? Thomas goes on to say that they give species to sin when they give rise to some new deformity.[50]

49. In *IV Sent.*, d. 16, q. 3, a. 2C (Mandonnet, vol. 4, 803–4). "Quidam enim dicunt, quod hoc accidit inquantum illae circumstantiae accipiuntur ut fines voluntatis, quia a fine actus moralis accipit speciem. Sed hoc non videtur sufficienter dictum; quia aliquando variatur species peccati sine hoc quod intentio feratur ad circumstantiam illam: sicut fur ita libenter acciperet vas aureum non sacratum sicut sacratum; et tamen in aliam speciem peccatum mutatur, scilicet de furto simplici in sacrilegium. Et praeterea secundum hoc sola illa circumstantia quae dicitur cujus gratia, speciem peccati mutare posset; quod falsum est. Et ideo aliter dicendum, quod omnis circumstantia potest speciem peccati mutare, sed non semper mutat."

50. Grisez is troubled by this practice of Aquinas of including within the

How is the above text to be reconciled with that quoted earlier, which appears to say that circumstances gives species only when intention bears upon them? Two texts could hardly seem more opposed. One plausible possibility, suggested by Cajetan, is that Aquinas changed his mind.[51] After all, the above text comes from Thomas's commentary on the *Sentences*, which dates from 1252 to 1256, while the text quoted initially comes from the *Prima secundae*, dating around 1269 to 1270 (and the text cited concerning the two thieves is from the *Secunda secundae*, dating around 1270 to 1272). Early in his career, then, Aquinas held the view that circumstances give species whenever they give rise to some new deformity, whether or not that circumstance is itself intended as an end. But later he changed his mind, holding that circumstances give species only when they are sought by the agent as an end or motive.

It is not clear, however, that Thomas did change his mind. In many later texts Aquinas reiterates the teaching that circumstances give species to sin whenever they add some new deformity. In the *De malo*, for instance, when he asks whether circumstances give species to sin, he does not mention intention, but rather says,

> Not every circumstance of a more general act constitutes the species of a more specific act; it does so only if it pertains *per se* to the act. Something pertains *per se* to the moral act, however, insofar as it is compared to reason as appropriate or repugnant. Therefore, if an additional circumstance implies no special repugnance to reason, it does not give species to the act. For example, to use some-

---

species of an action that which makes it wrong, even when it is not intended; see Grisez, *The Way of the Lord Jesus 1: Christian Moral Principles* (Chicago: Franciscan Herald Press, 1983), 233. Finnis also fears that this practice of Aquinas is a source of confusion ("Object and Intention," 17, n. 43). For arguments against these concerns see Flannery, "The Field of Moral Action According to Thomas Aquinas," *The Thomist* 69 (2005): 1–30.

51. Thomas de Vio Cajetan, *Commentaria in Summam theologicam s. Thomas Aquinatis* (in *Opera omnia iussu Leonis XIII P. M.*, vol. 7 [Rome: Editori di San Tommaso, 1892], 23).

thing white adds nothing pertaining to reason, so "white" does not constitute the species of the moral act. On the other hand, using another person's possession does add something pertaining to reason, so it constitutes the species of the moral act.[52]

Perhaps, then, Aquinas did not change his mind. But then what are we to make of the texts in which Thomas seems to say that circumstances give species only when intended? Let us re-examine the texts to see whether they can bear another interpretation.

3.4.3. Circumstances Do Not Give Species

A rereading of I-II, 72, 9, reveals that Aquinas is up to something quite different from the first impression he leaves. He is not arguing that circumstances give species only when they are intended as an end. Rather, he argues that circumstances do not give species. He is apparently reversing not only the *Sentences* article but the many other texts where he says that circumstances do give species when they add a new deformity. Even this reversal, however, is only apparent.

In the article, Thomas asks, "Whether sins take on a new species from distinct circumstances." If we do not read the article carefully, then we will assume that he answers, as he does elsewhere, that circumstances sometimes do give species. But if we forget what Aquinas says in other places and approach the text afresh with no presuppositions, then we see that he answers in the negative: circumstances do not give species. All of the objections ar-

---

52. *De malo*, 2, 6 (Leonine ed., vol. 23, 48, 215–27). "Non oportet quod omne quod est circumstantia communioris actus, constituat speciem aliquam in actibus, set illud tantum quod per se pertinet ad actum; iam autem dictum est quod ad actum moralem aliquid per se pertinet, secundum quod comparatur ad rationem ut conueniens et repugnans. Si ergo circumstantia addita nullam specialem repugnantiam ad rationem importet, non dat speciem actui, puta uti re alba, nichil addit ad rationem pertinens: unde album non constituit speciem actus moralis; set uti re aliena addit aliquid ad rationem pertinens: unde constituit speciem actus moralis."

gue that sometimes circumstances do give species. The *sed contra,* on the other hand, argues that circumstances do not give species. Both the objections and the *sed contra,* then, prepare us for a negative answer; Thomas should conclude that circumstances do not give species.

This negative answer, however, remains opaque unless we examine the immediately preceding articles. The general principle that moral actions take their species from the motive is implied, but not explicitly stated, in articles 6 and 7. It is stated for the first time in article 8, which asks whether excess and defect diversify sins. Not surprisingly, he answers that they do, as wanting too much pleasure is distinct from wanting too little pleasure. The true source of the specification, however, lies with the distinct motives that underlie excess and defect. Wanting pleasure too much arises from the love of pleasure, while wanting pleasure too little arises from the hatred of pleasure. In the reply to the first objection Thomas clarifies the point:

> Even if more and less are not the cause of diversity of species, nevertheless they sometimes follow upon the species insofar as they arise from diverse forms, for example, as when it is said that fire is lighter than air. Therefore, the Philosopher says in book 8 of the *Ethics* that those who thought there were not diverse species of friendship, because they are said to be more or less, based their belief upon an insufficient indication. In the same way, to exceed reason or to fall short of it pertains to diverse sins according to species insofar as they follow upon diverse motives.[53]

---

53. I-I 2, 72, 8, ad 1. "Magis et minus, etsi non sint causa diversitatis speciei, consequuntur tamen quandoque species differentes, prout proveniunt ex diversis formis, sicut si dicatur quod ignis est levior aere. Unde philosophus dicit, in viii ethic., quod qui posuerunt non esse diversas species amicitiarum propter hoc quod dicuntur secundum magis et minus, non sufficienti crediderunt signo. Et hoc modo superexcedere rationem, vel deficere ab ea, pertinet ad diversa peccata secundum speciem, inquantum consequuntur diversa motiva."

It turns out, then, that excess and defect do not themselves give species; rather, they follow upon a new species. We might identify fire as the element that is lighter than air, but the lightness itself does not give species; rather, it follows upon the form of fire, which does give species.[54] Similarly, we might identify sins through excess and defect, but these quantities do not in fact give species; they follow upon the form that does give species, namely, the new motive.

Aquinas now proceeds to ask whether circumstances give species to sins. The objections and the *sed contra* prepare us for a negative answer, but instead the answer parallels that given in article 8. Yes, they do, but not really. Actually, diverse motives give species, but sometimes circumstances follow upon these diverse motives and serve to identify the new species. In a parallel text of the *De malo*, Thomas drops any pretense that the circumstances themselves give species, and simply states that the motive serves as a new form of the will, thereby giving species to sin: "These species of gluttony are not diversified on account of diverse circumstances, but because of diverse motives."[55]

Prima secundae, 72, 9, is striking in its singularity. In several places, dated both before the *Summa* article and after it, Aquinas asks whether circumstances give species to actions or to sins. Everywhere else, whether in the *Sentences*, in the *De malo*, or earlier in the *Prima secundae*, Aquinas responds that they do indeed give species, but in question 72, article 9, his answer reverses. There, and there alone, Aquinas states that circumstances do not give species. Aquinas himself, however, seems oblivious to this radical change.

3.4.4. Two Kinds of Circumstances

The reason behind Aquinas's unconcern is rather straightforward; Aquinas's use of the term "circumstance" is ambiguous. Initially,

---

54. See *In libros de generatione et corruptione*, bk. 1, cap. 3, lect. 8, no. 5 (Leonine ed., vol. 3, 292–93).

55. *De malo*, 14, 3, ad 1 (Leonine ed., vol. 23, 265, 115–17). "predicte species non diversificantur propter diversas circumstantias, set propter diversa motiua."

it refers to what is outside the essence or species of an action, but Thomas proceeds to give a list of circumstances, including place, time, effects, and so on.[56] Confusion arises from supposing that these two—the definition and the list—are interchangeable. What are we to do, after all, with a circumstance that gives species? For example, when a thief steals from a holy place and thereby commits sacrilege, what are we to do with the circumstance of place? It is amongst Aquinas's list of eight circumstances, but in this particular instance it falls within the very essence of the action.

The term "circumstance," then, has two meanings. In a loose sense, it refers to anything on the list of circumstances, whether it gives species or not; in a strict sense, it refers to that which falls outside the species of an action.[57] Clearly, in this second meaning of circumstance, there can be no way in which circumstances truly give species to actions. A specifying circumstance is a contradiction. If it specifies, then it is no longer a circumstance, at least in the strict sense. In a text concerning the species of lust, Thomas says as much.

> Since circumstances, insofar as they are circumstances, cannot give species to moral actions, the species of moral actions must be taken from the object, which is the material of the action; therefore, the species of lust must be assigned from the material or object.[58]

Yet elsewhere Thomas says that the species of adultery, which is a kind of lust, arises from some circumstance.

> A circumstance does not always gives species to the moral act, but only when it adds a new deformity pertaining to another species of sin. For example, if beyond this, that someone takes to himself

56. I-II, 7, 3, or *De malo*, 2, 6 (Leonine ed., vol. 23, 47, 175–97).

57. Pilsner gives a detailed account of the strict and loose meanings of circumstance (*Specification*, 193–98).

58. II-II, 154, 1. "Quia circumstantia, inquantum huiusmodi, non dat speciem actui morali, sed eius species sumitur ab obiecto, quod est materia actus; ideo oportuit species luxuriae assignari ex parte materiae vel obiecti."

a woman who is not his wife, it is added that he takes the wife of another man, then there is added the deformity of injustice. Therefore, that circumstance gives a new species, and properly speaking it is no longer a circumstance; rather, it is a specific difference of the moral act.[59]

This apparent conflict, however, is easily resolved, as is done by Aquinas himself, by recognizing that adultery is specified by a circumstance only in the loose sense.

Usually when Aquinas asks whether circumstances give species to human actions, he uses the term "circumstance" in the loose sense, and so he answers in the affirmative. But when he comes to *Prima secundae*, 72, 9, he is concerned to address another phenomenon, namely, circumstances—in the strict sense—that appear to give species. These circumstances do not add some new deformity to the sin, and yet they enter into our definitions of various species. Thomas explains that the circumstances do not really give species; rather, they serve as signs of a new species that arises from distinct motives.[60]

The conflicting articles in the *Sentences* and in the *Summa*, then, reach opposite conclusions about the role of circumstances because they use different senses of the term "circumstance." In the *Sentences*, Aquinas concludes that circumstances—in the loose sense—give species to sins when they add a new deformity. In the *Summa*, Aquinas concludes that circumstances—in the strict

59. *De malo*, 7, 4 (Leonine ed., vol. 23, 170, 45–54). "Circumstantia non semper dat speciem actui morali, set solum tunc quando nouam deformitatem addit ad aliam speciam peccati pertinentem: puta, cum aliquis super hoc quod accedit ad non suam accedit ad eam que est alterius, et sic incidit ibi deformitas iniustitie; unde ista circumstantia dat nouam speciem, et proprie loquendo iam non est circumstantia, set efficitur specifica differentia actus moralis." Also see I-II, 7, 3, ad 3; II-II, 154, 1, ad 1; *IV Sent.*, d. 16, q. 3, a. 2C, ad 1 (Mandonnet, vol. 4, 804).

60. Pilsner recognizes the distinctiveness of this teaching (*Specification*, 199–216). He correctly distinguishes between those circumstances that do give species, and so cease to be circumstances, and the circumstances that merely give the name to the sin, while the motive gives species.

sense—do not give species, but they can sometimes serve to identify a new species when they follow as proper accidents upon some distinct motive.

Furthermore, the view that Thomas considers but rejects in the *Sentences* is not the view adopted in the *Summa*. In the *Sentences* Aquinas rejects the view that a circumstance, in order to give species, must serve as the end of the sinner, so that a thief commits sacrilege only if he wants the chalice precisely insofar as it is sacred. In the *Summa*, Aquinas adopts the view that circumstances give species, or rather they serve as signs of species, when they are the proper accidents of some new motive. The circumstance need not itself be a new motive; rather, it must follow upon some new motive. The two articles express two different relationships between a motive and a circumstance. The circumstance might be the motive, as in the *Sentences*, or the circumstance might follow upon the motive, as in the *Summa*. The apparently conflicting articles are in fact addressing two disparate matters.[61]

61. There remains the troubling text, quoted above, from the *Secunda secundae* (II-II, 53, 2, ad 3), which seems to contradict Aquinas's conclusion concerning theft in a holy place. We should note that Aquinas here speaks about greed rather than the act of theft, which he discusses in the *Sentences* article. Is there some reason to suppose that these two actions, theft and greed, might relate differently to sacrilege? Is there some reason why theft might be further specified without intention, while greed requires intention for its further specification? We can only speculate. Thomas says that justice and injustice concern exterior actions insofar as they relate us to other people; the virtue of generosity and the vice of greed, on the other hand, immediately concern our desires for possessions and the internal relation they bear to reason; see II-II, 118, 2, and especially, II-II, 118, 3, ad 2. Perhaps, then, the further specification of greed into sacrilegious greed requires a new motive because greed is already a vice concerned primarily with our desires and our motives. The unjust act of theft, on the other hand, is further specified through any defect relating to others (including God), whether there is any new motive or not. As Pilsner suggests, "Perhaps Thomas would have reserved 'motives' for factors inordinately moving passions in opposition to right reason" (*Specification*, 215–16). Whether or not this attempt to distinguish theft from greed is successful, we are still left with a difficult text. This text of the *Secunda secundae*, however, is troublesome for any interpretation of

3.4.5. New Deformities

Circumstances can give species even when intention does not bear upon them; it follows that the harm involved with the craniotomy can specify the action, even though the doctor does not intend to crush the skull precisely insofar as it is harm. As she plans her action, resolving her goal of ending the labor into its causes, she recognizes that she must crush the skull and that this act of crushing is in fact an act of harming the baby. It causes the desired result not insofar as it is an act of harm but only insofar as it reduces the size of the skull; nevertheless, it is inseparably an act of harm, even an act of lethal harm. Formalities of intention cannot change the nature of the action.

Unfortunately, this approach raises more questions than it answers. If intention does not delineate between those circumstances that give species and those that do not, then what does? New deformities? Repugnance or fitness to reason? Certainly. Aquinas says as much. But what do these ideas mean in practice? What counts for a new deformity, or what is repugnant or fitting to reason? Is the harm done to the baby in the craniotomy case a deformity of the action? If so, then what of the harm done to the baby in the hysterectomy case? Aquinas lists the effects of an action amongst its circumstances. Although we have seen that the doctor performing the hysterectomy need not act upon the baby (section 3.3.2), nevertheless the death of the baby is an effect and circumstance of her action. If circumstances can give species without being intended, then perhaps this circumstance can as well. Without intention, it seems, we are unable to discriminate between circumstances. All effects, intended or not, potentially give species to an action.

We will see, however, that one of the circumstances, namely, that which is acted upon or the *materia circa quam*, takes prece-

---

Aquinas's doctrine concerning specification through circumstances; it does not correspond well with what Thomas says of sacrilege anywhere else.

dence over the others. It plays such a central role in the specification of human actions that Aquinas calls it the object of the action. Furthermore, other circumstances specify actions only insofar as they make for some new condition in the object or material.[62] Let us examine, then, in what manner the material specifies human actions.

SECTION 3.5. *Materia Circa Quam*

Aquinas clearly states that the subject acted upon, which he often calls the *materia circa quam*, gives species to exterior actions, even going so far as to distinguish this species from the species of the interior act of will, which arises from the end.[63]

> Within a voluntary action there are two acts, namely, the interior act of will and the exterior act, and each of these acts has its own object. The end is the proper object of the interior act of will, while that upon which it acts is the object of the exterior action. Therefore, just as the exterior action takes its species from the object with which it is concerned, so the interior act of will takes its species from the end, as from its proper object.[64]

Only a few articles earlier, when Aquinas is concerned to identify the moral species of actions, he turns to the material.

> The object is not the material out of which something is made, but the material on which an activity bears, which, in some manner, has the aspect of a form, insofar as it gives the species to the activity.[65]

62. See I-II, 18, 10; *De malo*, 2, 6, ad 2 (Leonine ed., vol. 23, 48, ln. 263–94).
63. Portions of this section are taken from Jensen, "Circumstances."
64. I-II, 18, 6. "In actu autem voluntario invenitur duplex actus, scilicet actus interior voluntatis, et actus exterior, et uterque horum actuum habet suum obiectum. Finis autem proprie est obiectum interioris actus voluntarii, id autem circa quod est actio exterior, est obiectum eius. Sicut igitur actus exterior accipit speciem ab obiecto circa quod est; ita actus interior voluntatis accipit speciem a fine, sicut a proprio obiecto."
65. I-II, 18, 2, ad 2. "Obiectum non est materia ex qua, sed materia circa quam; et habet quodammodo rationem formae, inquantum dat speciem."

This identification of the object and the material is not uncommon. As Pilsner notes, "Thomas so frequently [alternates] object and matter [which] indicates that he often took their synonymity for granted in certain contexts."[66] After his careful examination of Aquinas's usage, Pilsner concludes that the *materia circa quam* is "that reality to which an action is specially related,"[67] which he has previously identified as a primary usage of "object."[68] It seems incontrovertible, then, that the material serves in some manner as the object of human actions. Nevertheless, this straightforward reading of Aquinas is sometimes vigorously denied.

3.5.1. Actions and Things

Martin Rhonheimer has recently taken up the standard of Theo Belmans in rejecting "things" as objects of human actions.[69] Both correctly point out that just *as such* things are insufficient to give species. "What belongs to another" does not by itself make an action to be theft; after all, one might be "returning what belongs to another," which is far from theft. Both also rightly fear a kind of physicalism in which the mere physical activity, precisely as physical activity, gives moral species. Unfortunately, both have gone too far in their concerns. In their denial that "things" can be the objects of human actions, they conclude that the exterior action itself, and that alone, is the object of human actions. For the interior act of will, we have seen, they are correct (section 2.3.4).

Pilsner shows conclusively that for Aquinas the term "object" has many and diverse meanings, including the thing that is acted

---

66. Pilsner, *Specification*, 143.
67. Pilsner, *Specification*, 147.
68. Pilsner, *Specification*, 70–91.
69. See Belmans, *Le sens objectif de l'agir humain: pour relire la moral conjugale de Saint Thomas* (Vatican City: Libreria Editrice Vaticana, 1980); Rhonheimer, "Perspective," 464–75. For a detailed refutation of Rhonheimer's position see Brock, *"Veritatis Splendor,"* and Lawrence Dewan, "St. Thomas, Rhonheimer, and the object of the human act," *Nova et Vetera*, English ed. 6 (2008): 63–112.

upon by the exterior action.[70] As even Rhonheimer acknowledges, the thing can "be significant and at times decisive for the morality of an act."[71] When Rhonheimer denies that the exterior action can have any "thing" as an object, then where does he turn instead? What does he say is the object of the exterior action? The exterior action itself, he concludes, must be its own object.[72] He is not afraid to express this circularity, although he seems to think that bringing in reason relieves the circle of its viciousness: "The objects that morally specify such actions are . . . the respective actions inasmuch as they are the intelligible contents of concrete ways of acting, 'goods understood and ordered by reason.'"[73] As we will see (section 3.5.3), Rhonheimer is correct to stress the importance of reason, but if reason is to understand actions as good and to order them, then it must understand them as directed to some end, and this end is an object that specifies it; reason must also understand them as directed upon some material, which is another object. Rhonheimer himself emphasizes that exterior actions have a direction to an end built into them.[74] He is simply unwilling to acknowledge that this end itself might give species to the exterior action. He even recognizes that the material is a kind of end to which the exterior action is directed—he even calls it the form of the action[75]—but once again he is unwilling to grant that this material

---

70. Pilsner, *Specification*, 78–80.

71. Rhonheimer, "Perspective," 478.

72. Long also falls into the trap of making the terminus of the exterior action be the action itself, although defined morally. He says, for instance, that, "this act of murder has its own *per se* terminus: the unjust killing of an innocent or of one awaiting sentence by a higher authority" (*Teleological Grammar*, 20–21). Jean Porter, as well, makes a similar mistake: "Hence, the object, properly so-called, should not be identified with some person or thing on which the agent acts; rather, 'the object' refers to the act itself under a description along the lines indicated" (*Nature as Reason*, 299).

73. Rhonheimer, "Perspective," 480.

74. Rhonheimer, "Perspective," 483–93.

75. Rhonheimer, "Perspective," 493.

is an object that can give species to the act. He even says that the good and evil of an action derives from its matter, but in the next breath protests that this matter is not the object of the action.[76] At one point he even admits that the *materia circa quam* can be the moral object in relation to the order of reason, but then he goes on to insist—contrary to the explicit statement of Aquinas—that it is not the object of the exterior action.[77]

What is going on here? Why grant to the material everything that we would suppose the object to be, but then insist that the object of the action can only be the action itself? Evidently, from fear of physicalism: "If one were to further seek an 'object' of the exterior act itself as such, he would inevitably fall into physicalism."[78] Or again, "Whoever looks for an 'object of the exterior act' *as an external, observable behavior,* will end by reducing the human act to its non-moral elements, in a crude physicalism that ignores the regulating and morally ordering role of reason."[79] Apparently he thinks that if "things" are objects, then the will must have as an object something non-moral, for only actions are moral and not things. As Brock points out, however, even things can be morally good, when viewed as the object of an action:

> [Pleasures] fall under the intention of temperance, *as* objects of this act of "curbing." Temperance intends to curb them, for the good of reason. In this respect, the temperate agent even sees something good about them, though no doubt he would be less likely to say simply that they are good ... [, but he will] regard them as good to curb.[80]

76. Rhonheimer, "Perspective," 477.

77. Rhonheimer, "Perspective," 476. In *Natural Law,* Rhonheimer seems to grant that the *materia circa quam* is the moral object (422), but then asserts rather that the moral object must be an action (424), saying that the object of theft is theft.

78. Rhonheimer, "Perspective," 476.

79. "Perspective," 481, emphasis Rhonheimer's. See also *Natural Law,* 424.

80. Brock, "*Veritatis Splendor,*" 28.

When Rhonheimer cautions against finding an object for "the exterior act itself as such" he seems to mean the exterior act "as an external, observable behavior." In other words, Rhonheimer is referring to the exterior act simply as physical activity, arising from some external power, and not to the external act insofar as it arises from the will. Finding morality in this action is indeed a kind of physicalism. Unfortunately, Rhonheimer's point lacks clarity, for surely even the physical action must have some object that gives it species; it just does not have a moral object, nor a moral species. For clarity sake, Rhonheimer should insist that we not look for a *moral* object of the exterior act.

Even this point, however, can be readily misunderstood. Recall that the exterior action is twofold: the act just as it arises from the external power and the act as it also arises from the will. Rhonheimer wishes to emphasize that there can be no moral object for the external act just as such, that is, insofar as it is an act of the external power and not of the will. Has his fear of physicalism led him to forget what he himself has so much emphasized, namely, that the exterior act itself—as human—must be considered as an act of will?[81] Does he suppose that looking for an object of *this* action, this act of will, drags one to physicalism?[82] I think not. He always insists that the exterior action *as such* cannot have an object. Unfortunately, he seems to elide the two exterior actions, thereby concluding that *no* exterior action (not just the exterior action *as such*) can have an object beyond itself. Rhonheimer's fear of physicalism has led him to fear a certain terminology. Unfortunately, it is a terminology regularly used by Aquinas.

81. See, for instance, Rhonheimer, *Natural Law,* 418–19.
82. In *Natural Law,* Rhonheimer rightly identifies the object as the object of the act of will (as opposed to being the object of mere physical activity), but he seems to mean the interior act of will, for which the object is, as Rhonheimer says, the exterior action. He acknowledges (418) that the exterior act is also an act of will, but he does not seem concerned to identify the object of this act of will.

When freed from this fear of calling "things" objects, we can begin to bring clarity to the question of the moral species of the exterior action. Both Belmans and Rhonheimer say much that is true about how the exterior act must be characterized through reason. In the end, however, their accounts are vague and dissatisfying. They must be so. Reason does indeed specify human actions, but it does so only by providing some object. Actions are always relational realities, directed toward some object. We can conceive of an action in no other way. If we free ourselves from this fear of "things" specifying human actions, if we instead follow the terminology of Aquinas that Pilsner identifies, then we will be able to take the truth Rhonheimer grasps and more clearly apply it to the exterior act as willed, thereby determining the moral species of the exterior act. Let us see, then, in what way the material gives species to actions.

3.5.2. Under a Formality

When fire heats wax, it may be difficult to imagine how wax can specify the act of fire. Surely there is not some new species of action for each distinct subject, as if heating wax were one kind of action, heating water another kind, and heating wood yet a third species of action. All of these actions seem to be, in kind, simply heating, and the diverse subjects serve as different circumstances.

We should not suppose that the wax specifies the act of heating simply insofar as it is wax; rather, the material specifies under some particular formality, even as the act of seeing is specified by its object under the formality of being colored.[83] A rock is not seen insofar as it is a rock, nor insofar as it is hot or cold, but insofar as it is colored.[84] The rock specifies seeing, then, precisely insofar as it is

83. Pilsner gives a detailed account of the formal aspect of the material or object (*Specification*, 92–133).

84. I, 59, 4. "Cum potentiae non distinguantur secundum distinctionem materialem obiectorum, sed solum secundum rationem formalem obiecti." See also I, 80, 1, ad 2; I-II, 54, 2, ad 1; *Q. de caritate* 4 (in *Quaestiones disputatae*, vol. 2: *Quaestio disputata de caritate* [Taurini-Romae: Marietti, 1942], 763); and *Q. de anima* 13,

able to be seen. Similarly, wax specifies the act of heating precisely insofar as it is able to be heated.[85] The wax does not specify the act of heating insofar as it is soft or round or fragrant; rather, it specifies the act of heating insofar as it is able to undergo the change of becoming hot. And just as diverse objects, such as a rock, a tree, and a dog, all specify the act of seeing insofar as each is colored, so diverse materials such as wax, water, and wood all specify the act of heating insofar as each is able to become hot.

We may say, more generally, that the material of any action must be able to undergo the appropriate change. If a billiard ball is to be moved then it must be movable; if a wire is to conduct electricity, it must be electrocutable. The material specifies an action precisely under this formality—its ability to undergo the change.[86]

This idea appears in Aquinas's commentary on the *De anima*. He is concerned with what we might roughly call the act of digestion, of which the material is food. The change that the food undergoes is a transformation into the organism; when I digest an apple I transform the apple into my very being. Food serves as the object of the action because it, unlike poison or a rock, is able to undergo this transformation; the apple is able to be changed into my being.[87] The material, then, in its potential to take on the form introduced by the agent, gives species to human actions.

3.5.3. Material and Reason

In a certain sense, then, the material specifies potentially, since the formal aspect under which the material specifies depends upon the

---

ad 2 (Leonine ed., vol. 24, 120, 373–85). In this text, and in others that follow, Aquinas uses the more general term "object" rather than material, which is a particular kind of object. What he says, however, clearly does apply to the more specific "material"; indeed, his examples often indicate he has the material in mind.

85. See I, 25, 3.

86. See Brock, *Action and Conduct*, 89.

87. *Sentencia libri De anima*, bk. II, cap. 9 (Leonine ed., vol. 45, 104–5, ln. 122–83).

form in the agent.[88] The same material of wax, for instance, might be the object both of the act of heating and of the act of seeing, but it will specify these actions under different formalities. Which formal aspect we look to, whether the ability to be seen or the ability to be heated, depends upon the form in the agent. Or, as Thomas says, we must look to the principle of an action to determine what aspects of an object give species.

> When it is compared to one active principle an act will be specified according to some formality of an object, but when it is compared to another active principle it will not be specified by that same formality. For to know color and to know sound are different species of acts if they are referred to the senses, because these are sensible in themselves. But if they are referred to the intellect, they will not differ in species because the intellect comprehends both of them under one common formality, namely, being or truth. Similarly, to know white and to know black differ in species if they are referred to sight but not if they are referred to taste. One may conclude that the act of any potency is specified according to that which *per se* pertains to that potency, not by that which pertains to it *per accidens*.[89]

Thomas proceeds to identify the principle of human actions as reason, so the material specifies insofar as it refers *per se* to reason.[90]

---

88. Nevertheless, Aquinas is willing to say that the material of an action is in a certain sense its form. See I-II, 18, 2, ad 2. See also II-II, 154, 1, ad 1.

89. *De malo*, 2, 4 (Leonine ed., vol. 23, 39–40, 184–99). "Secundum aliquam rationem obiecti specificabitur actus comparatus ad unum actiuum principium, secundum quam rationem non specificabitur camparatus ad aliud. Cognoscere enim colorem et cognoscere sonum sunt diuersi actus secundum speciem si ad sensum referantur, quia hec secundum se sensibilia sunt, non autem si referantur ad intellectum, quia ab intellectu comprehenduntur sub una communi ratione obiecti, scilicet entis aut veri. Et similiter sentire album et nigrum differt specie si referatur ad uisum, non si referatur ad gustum. Ex quo potest accipi quod actus cuiuslibet potentie specificatur secundum id quod per se pertinet ad illam potentiam, non autem secundum id quod pertinet ad eam solum per accidens." Also see I-II, 18, 5 and I, 77, 3.

90. Rhonheimer emphasizes the role of reason in the object of human ac-

If we consider objects of human actions that differ in something pertaining *per se* to reason, then the acts will differ in species insofar as they are acts of reason, but they might not differ in species insofar as they are acts of some other power. For example, to know one's wife and to know one who is not one's wife are two actions whose objects differ in something pertaining to reason, for to know one's own and to know what is not one's own are determined by the measure of reason. This same difference, however, is related *per accidens* in comparison either to the power of generation or to the sexual desire. Therefore, to know one's own and to know what is not one's own differ in species insofar as they are acts of reason but not insofar as they are acts of the generative power or of the sexual desire. An act is human, however, insofar as it is an act of reason. Clearly, then, the two differ in species insofar as they are human actions.[91]

What refers *per se* to the act of sensing, whether the color of a rose, its odor, or some other aspect, depends upon the power of sensation under consideration. Similarly, what aspects of a woman refer *per se* to the sexual act depends upon the power being considered, reason or the power of generation, for the single act of sexual intercourse arises from multiple active principles, and each of these principles may aim to introduce its own form into the material. If

tions; see "Perspective," 467–75; "The Cognitive Structure of the Natural Law and the Truth of Subjectivity," *The Thomist* 67 (2003): 1–44, at 28, n. 64.

91. *De malo*, 2, 4 (Leonine ed., vol. 23, 40, 200–18). "Si ergo obiecta humanorum actuum considerentur que habeant differentias secundum aliquid per se ad rationem pertinentes, erunt actus specie differentes secundum quod sunt actus rationis, licet non sint species differentes secundum quod sunt actus alicuius potentie: sicut cognoscere mulierem suam et cognoscere mulierem non suam sunt actus habentes obiecta differentia secundum aliquid ad rationem pertinens: nam suum et non suum determinantur secundum regulam rationis; que tamen differentie per accidens se habent si comparentur ad uim generativam vel etiam ad uim concupiscibilem. Et ideo cognoscere suam et cognoscere non suam specie differunt secundum quod sunt actus rationis, non autem secundum quod sunt actus generativae aut concupiscibilis. In tantum sunt actus humani in quantum sunt actus rationis: sic ergo patet quod differunt specie in quantum sunt actus humani."

the woman is one's wife, then the material is able to take on the form introduced by reason, even as wax can take on heat, but if the woman is not one's wife, then the material is unable to take on the form introduced by reason. These same aspects of the woman, however, are irrelevant to the power of generation, for any woman is capable of taking on the form introduced by the power of generation. Everything hinges, then, on the form that reason seeks to introduce into the *materia circa quam*. Those aspects by which the material is able or unable to bear this form will give species to human actions. All other aspects of the material will be circumstantial.

Evidently, then, the material specifies without reference to the end of the will, but rather in relation to reason. As Rhonheimer says, "the moral configuration of an exterior act . . . does not depend . . . on the will of the subject. Rather, it depends on reason."[92] And as Aquinas himself says, "The good or evil that an exterior action has in itself, on account of required material and required circumstances, is not derived from the will but more from reason."[93]

3.5.4. The Action Performed Is Intended

In a couple places, however, Aquinas seems to minimize the specifying role of the material, reducing it in some manner to the will. He says, for instance,

> Objects, insofar as they are compared to exterior acts, have the notion of *materia circa quam;* but insofar as they are compared to the interior act of the will they have the formality of ends, and it is from this formality that they give the species to the act. And even as they are *materia circa quam* they have the formality of terms, from which motion is specified, as is said in V *Physics* and X *Ethics*. But even the

92. Rhonheimer, "Perspective," 481.
93. I-II, 20, 1. "Bonitas autem vel malitia quam habet actus exterior secundum se, propter debitam materiam et debitas circumstantias, non derivatur a voluntate, sed magis a ratione."

terms of motion give species to the motion insofar as they have the formality of an end.[94]

Certainly, the action that an individual actually performs, as opposed to the exterior action conceived, is some particular kind of action because the will moves to bring about this particular change in this particular material.[95] The fornicator commits an act of fornication because he wills to do so. There is no pure act of fornication existing merely by material and reason; there are only individual acts of fornication that exist because certain men choose to perform acts of sexual intercourse with certain women. The point, then, must be conceded: "the *materia circa quam* is the end and form of the act,"[96] and only as such does it specify human actions.

The agent must, as Thomas says, "intend to do such and such a voluntary action in such and such material."[97] Only in this manner is his action directed to this material, and if it were directed to some other material, then it would be another action. It does not follow that the formality under which the material specifies depends upon intention. The material specifies because it is intended, but those aspects of it that serve to specify depend not upon intention but upon their relation to reason. The action of adultery is not specified by the woman insofar as she is able to give pleasure, which might well be the formality that the adulterer intends while acting; rather it is specified by the woman insofar as she is able to bear the form that reason aims to introduce.

94. I-II, 72, 3, ad 2. "Obiecta, secundum quod comparantur ad actus exteriores, habent rationem materiae circa quam; sed secundum quod comparantur ad actum interiorem voluntatis, habent rationem finium, et ex hoc habent quod dent speciem actui. Quamvis etiam secundum quod sunt materia circa quam, habeant rationem terminorum, a quibus motus specificantur, ut dicitur in V *Phys.* et in X *Ethics.* Sed tamen etiam termini motus dant speciem motibus, inquantum habent rationem finis."

95. Brock (*Action and Conduct*, 90) argues that what is intended is both the patient or matter acted upon and the form introduced by an agent.

96. Rhonheimer, "Perspective," 493.

97. I-II, 72, 1. "Qui intendit talem actum voluntarium exercere in tali materia."

For the exterior action performed, the material specifies because it is intended by the will. Nevertheless, given that it is intended, the material specifies the action insofar as it relates to reason. Intention does not specify human actions; rather, the species of human actions is taken from that which is intended. As such, intention provides the stuff for specification, which stuff consists in some action upon some subject.

The exterior action conceived (as opposed to the exterior action performed) bears upon one material rather than another not on account of intention, which has not yet been specified, but on account of the conception of reason, which conceives of an action as directed upon some material and not upon others. While considering the hysterectomy, for instance, the doctor considers an action as directed upon the womb and not upon the baby. The soldier who blows up the bridge, conceives of an action directed upon the bridge and not upon the child walking on the bridge. The soldier who shoots the child conceives of his action as bearing upon the child.

In either event, then, for the exterior action performed or for the exterior action conceived, the formality of intention does not specify an action. At most, intention picks out a certain activity and directs it upon a certain material. What aspects of the material then morally specify the action depends not upon intention but more upon reason. In short, logicism is false. The exterior action does have a character independent of the formality of intention.

The thief, for instance, intends to use the chalice for his purposes, presumably making money. Even if he does not intend to take the chalice insofar as it is holy, even if he does not intend to take it insofar as it belongs to someone else, his action still might be specified by these circumstances. It depends. Do these features of the object taken affect its relation to reason? Do they affect whether the chalice is able to bear the form introduced by reason?

3.5.5. A Review

Before we attempt to answer these questions let us review what we have so far seen concerning the specification of human actions. The exterior actions that people perform receive their direction from intention (section 1.2). An action is directed to this or that end, upon this or that material, depending upon what the agent intends. In this manner, intention may be said to specify human actions, for it provides the direction an action takes (section 3.1.1). This intention, however, does not characterize the direction once given.

Intention itself must be specified by its own object, which is none other than the exterior action conceived (section 3.1.2). The exterior action conceived, on the other hand, cannot be specified through intention, for it precedes the intention for the particular action (3.2.2). Rather, the exterior action conceived receives its direction from reason, not from a purely passive reason, merely perceiving some inherent direction to an action, but from practical reason actively conceiving actions as directed to this or that end and upon this or that material (section 3.2.3). Jones does not find in his action of pulling a trigger some inherent order to the death of Smith. Rather, he conceives precisely that action which is directed to the death of Smith.

Nevertheless, reason is not entirely active in its conceptions. Reason cannot concoct any action with any attributes for any and all deliberations. Jones cannot conceive his action as directed merely to making a noise, for such an action would not fit into his deliberations, in which he seeks to achieve the death of Smith. Reason is passive in at least two ways. First, reason must resolve the end sought into the real causes that the person can muster through his actions (sections 3.2.4, 3.2.5 and 3.2.6). As the soldier deliberates about how to destroy the bridge, he cannot speculate about huffing and puffing and blowing the bridge down. The causes that the agent finds in the world around her serve as the tools or the material out of which she constructs her action. If a defender is to stop her assailant, then she must use the causes available to her. If she uses a gun, then she must recognize that it achieves her goal by way of injuring the assailant. As Porter says, "an agent can only intend what he can reasonably expect to bring about through his specific causal powers."[98]

Second, reason is passive in its perception of the attributes that an action has. Just as reason does not actively construct the properties of a tree or a cat but passively observes them, so reason passively perceives the attributes of an action (sections 3.4 and 3.5). Whether the action is directed upon this or that end, upon this or that material, depends upon reason; but given it has this end and this material, certain attributes follow. In her deliberations, the potter is not passively determined by the clay to form a vase rather than a bowl, but given that she is now considering a vase, she must passively recognize certain properties of that vase. Similarly, the soldier does not passively observe this or that means to destroy the bridge, but given that he is actively considering this means, for example, shooting the child to set off the detonator, he must passively recognize certain attributes of the action.

We have recently turned our attention to this second passivity of reason. An action conceived has certain properties or circumstances and sometimes the circumstances give species (section 3.4). Whether they give species depends upon their relation to the material acted upon. A circumstance gives species when it in some manner affects how the material relates to the active principle of reason (section 3.5.3). If the circumstance changes the material so that it is unable to bear the form of reason, then it refers *per se* to reason; it is said to give rise to a new deformity and it specifies the action. The holy place, for instance, affects the object taken by the thief such that it can no longer bear some form introduced by reason, so that the action becomes sacrilege.

Applied to the craniotomy case we see that this specifying role

98. Porter, *Nature as Reason*, 298.

of circumstances places great emphasis upon the material acted upon, which is the child. As we have seen, the doctor seeks to introduce the form of a reduced size of head, which she accomplishes by introducing the form of a crushed skull (section 3.3.3). The question now is whether the unintended death affects the material such that it is no longer able to bear the form introduced. Does the condition of the material—that death follows necessarily from the form introduced—change its relation to reason? Can we say that the child is unable to undertake the form of a crushed skull—seen as a human good useful for ending labor—because death follows from this crushing? In short, does the circumstance "lethal" refer *per se* to reason?

However we answer these questions, we can see that this analysis does not even begin to apply to the hysterectomy case, in which the doctor does not act upon the child. We need not worry whether the child is in potential to some good, for the doctor is not seeking to direct the child to any good. She is acting upon the womb and directs her action to the good of saving the woman's life. She is not acting upon the child, and she is not seeking to direct the child to any useful good, such as saving a life.

The species of actions will prove to be a simple two-piece puzzle. On the one hand, there is an order that an agent gives to his actions; on the other hand, there is an order of reason, an order that the action should have. When these two orders agree, then the action is good; when they conflict, then the action is evil. The act of murder, for instance, is directed by the agent to the death of his victim; by reason, it is directed to the good of the one acted upon. Since these two orders conflict, the moral species of the action is evil. This relation is simple to recognize. The difficulty is in discovering the contours of the two separate pieces. What exactly is the order that the agent gives to the action? Does the doctor order her action to the death of the child? Then again, what is the order that reason aims to introduce, the order that the action should take on? Must our actions upon others always be directed to their good?

Up to this point we have been analyzing the first order, the order that an action has on account of the agent. The agent directs his actions through intention. Intention itself, however, is shaped through deliberation, which is in turn constrained by the situations and causes in the world. We are not yet through with this first order, for it will take a prominent role in chapter 5. Nevertheless, we have already begun to see intimations of the second order. An action of introducing some form into some material has moral characteristics that go beyond this form and this material. The act of theft aims at possession of some object; its moral character, however, depends upon the ownership of the object, for this ownership relates to the order of reason, the order that the action should have. To this second order, then, we must now turn. In some form or other it will occupy the remainder of our inquiry.

4 | LOVE OF OTHERS

We have seen that the material or subject acted upon is central to the moral species of human actions. Why does it play this central role? We can get a good idea by considering those cases when another human being is the subject acted upon. The act of murder, for instance, has another human being as its subject or material. The victim does not appear to be a fitting subject for this act of killing. Why? Because we should not bring about his evil but rather his good. In short, we should seek his good; we should love him, in some broad sense of the word love. We should love other human beings by seeking their good, so that when we act upon them we should not harm them but benefit them, or at least leave them undamaged. The divide between the craniotomy and hysterectomy might be worked out in these terms. In the craniotomy case, the doctor aims to bring about some change in the baby—a harmful change—in order to achieve her goals. As such, she does not seek the good of the child but his evil. In the hysterectomy case the doctor does not act upon the baby, so that she does not seek to change him for her purposes. She does not aim to bring about his evil in order to achieve her goals.

Two prominent questions face this line of thought. First, if love is at issue, then how does the doctor in the hysterectomy case love the baby? Perhaps she does not seek his evil, but she certainly does not seek his good. It seems, then, that the hysterectomy case is no different from the craniotomy case. In neither does the doctor love the baby. Second, are we not sometimes justified in harming some individuals in order to benefit many more? Should we not love the good of a greater number rather than forsake the good of the many simply to avoid damaging one person? Typically, the second question swallows the first, for some argue, in consequentialist fashion, that it does not really matter how one harms an individual, either in one's very action or merely as a consequence of one's action. In either event, the harm is done. What matters is whether the harm is worth it, that is, whether the harm brings about some greater good. If the child crossing the bridge dies so that many others might live, then it should not matter whether she dies because the soldier has acted upon her, intending to bring about the damage within her, or because the soldier acted upon the bridge, with the child dying as a consequence. The total overall benefit is all that really matters.

This chapter, therefore, will try to resolve the tension between two intuitions: first, that we should love others, so that we should not aim to harm them; second, that we should love the greater good, so that sometimes one person must suffer so that many more will benefit. Abelardianism will defend the first intuition, while Proportionalism will advocate the second. We will begin with Aquinas's distinction between two kinds of love: a love of friendship and a useful love (section 4.1). We will aim to see that human beings are not to be used but to be loved for their own sake. We will then investigate the idea that a lesser good must sometimes be sacrificed for a greater good (section 4.2), suggesting by way of Proportionalism that the life of a baby might sometimes be sacrificed in order to save the life of the mother. This suggestion will draw our attention to the common good and the manner in which the individual relates to the common good (section 4.3). Finally, we will investigate how punishment, especially capital punishment, corresponds with the requirement to love others with a love of friendship (section 4.4).

SECTION 4.1. *Merely a Means*

The material of an action gives species insofar as it is able or unable to bear the form introduced by reason. Abelardianism argues that human beings are not fit material for certain activities, particularly activities of harming. When we harm others we seek to use them as a means to achieve some further end; we do not love them as subjects of their own good. Many things, such as cars and computers, are perfectly fit material for the activity of using; human beings, however, are not. They are to be loved for their own sakes, not for the sake of some other good. Human beings, then, are unable to realize the good of "using."[1]

4.1.1. Two Kinds of Love

The argument has a Kantian flavor, but it is rooted in St. Thomas, who distinguishes between two distinct kinds of love, love of concupiscence and love of friendship.[2] In any act of love we will some good to some person. The love we have for the good is called love of concupiscence, and the love we have for the person is called love of friendship. If Louis wants Clare to be healthy, for example, then he loves health with the love of concupiscence and he loves Clare with the love of friendship. The term "friendship," however, might refer to a self-interested love, for example, if Louis wants health for himself, then he loves health with concupiscence and he loves himself by love of friendship. The difference between the two loves is not a difference of self-interest and concern for others; it is a difference between the good sought and the subject for whom it is sought. Every single act of love, whether it be self-interested or directed to another, consists of these two elements, a love of concupiscence and a love of friendship.

1. See Porter, *Nature as Reason*, 306; Thomas A. Cavanaugh, "Double Effect and the End-Not-Means Principle: A Response to Bennett," *Journal of Applied Philosophy* 16 (1999): 181–85; Sullivan, "*Malum Vitandum*."
2. I-II, 26, 4.

We can have both sorts of love for other human beings, for instance, Louis can love Clare with a love of friendship, but he can also love her with a love of concupiscence. If he sees her as merely useful for his own good, then he loves her as a useful good for himself. Perhaps she is the doctor who can bring him health. Then he would be the subject for whom he wishes the good, and health would be the good that he loves with concupiscence. But he would also love Clare with concupiscence, for she is a kind of good, a useful good, that he seeks for himself. The love of concupiscence, then, can apply to people as well as to things.

Love of concupiscence for another person seems to correspond to Kant's notion of treating someone as a means. Likewise, treating someone as an end might refer to love of friendship. Aquinas would object to the terminology, for only God is to be treated as an ultimate end. Nevertheless, he contrasts the love we have for others as a subject of the good and the love of others as useful or pleasurable.

> To love someone on his own account may be understood in two ways. In one way, when something is loved as the ultimate end, and in this way only God should be loved on His own account. In another way, when we love those to whom we will the good, as happens in virtuous friendship. We do not love them as the good that we will for ourselves, as happens in friendships of pleasure or utility, in which we love the friend as our good, not because we desire some utility or pleasure *for* the friend, but because we desire our utility and pleasure *from* the friend. In the same way, we love other useful and pleasurable things for ourselves, for example, food and clothing. But when we love others on account of virtue, we will the good for them rather than willing them for ourselves [emphasis added].[3]

3. *Q. de caritatae*, 2, 8, ad 16 (Marietti, 775). "Diligere aliquem propter se potest intelligi dupliciter. Uno modo, ita quod aliquid diligatur sicut ultimus finis; et sic solus Deus est propter se diligendus. Alio modo, ut diligamus ipsum cui volumus bonum, ut contingit in amicitia honesta; non autem sicut bonum quod volumus nobis, ut contingit in amicitia delectabili vel utili, in qua amicum diligimus ut bonum nostrum: non quia utilitatem vel delectationem appetamus

We can say, then, that we should not treat others merely as a means, that is, we must always love others with a love of friendship, as a subject of the good. This requirement for love of friendship arises from our natural inclinations, for with our wills we are naturally inclined to love others with a love of friendship. To eliminate this love, to have only a love of concupiscence for others, is contrary to our natural inclinations, which derive from our union with others in human nature.

> That which is one with something in genus or species is one through nature, and therefore all things love that which is one with them according to species with a natural love, insofar as they love their species.[4]

When we kill another human being it seems we do not love him with a love of friendship, for we seek his evil rather than his good. We love him only as a means, as useful for attaining some other good. Killing an innocent human being, then, is evil insofar as it is opposed to our natural love for others, for it treats someone as a means. If the doctor truly kills the child in the craniotomy case, then the action is morally evil.

In general, Abelardianism claims that the natural inclination to love others with a love of friendship is thwarted by intending others' evil. When we will someone's evil, then we cannot possibly be treating him as the subject of the good; his value to us must be solely instrumental.

---

amico, sed quia ex amico appetimus utilitatem et delectationem nobis; sicut et diligimus alia delectabilia nobis et utilia, ut cibum aut vestimentum. Sed cum diligimus aliquem propter virtutem, volumus ei bonum, non ipsum nobis."

4. I-II, 60, 4. "Id quod est unum cum aliquo, genere vel specie, est unum per naturam. Et ideo dilectione naturali quaelibet res diligit id quod est secum unum secundum speciem, inquantum diligit speciem suam." See also II-II, 114, 1, ad 2.

4.1.2. Equality

Aquinas often approaches this prohibition—against treating others as a means—from the perspective of the equality of justice. Treating someone merely as a means, that is, loving him only as useful and not as the subject of the good, is opposed to the notion of equality that underlies Aquinas's account of justice. Thomas says the justice that is between two equal individuals establishes a relationship of equality. As such, it is founded upon reciprocity, realized most clearly in the exchange of goods through buying and selling. One individual must return equally what he receives from another; he must not overcharge or pay too little.[5]

A failure in equality is ultimately a kind of subjection of one person by another, in Kant's terminology, using a person as a means. If I kill another individual, then I am treating her as a mere instrument, as something that I can move about and direct to my own purposes. Similarly, if I defraud an individual, overcharging her for some item, then I treat her actions as something that may be directed to my ends or purposes, quite apart from her own direction.

The equality of reciprocity, then, might also be called equality of subjection or subordination. An individual is not subject to another, as some instrument to be directed to an end. Thomas occasionally expresses the equality of justice in these terms. For example, when discussing whether there is strict justice between a father and his son, or between a master and his slave, situations in which Aquinas thinks that strict equality does not hold, Aquinas says,

> By "another" we may refer to what is simply another, as that which is in every way distinct, as appears in two men of whom neither is subject to the other, but both are subject to the ruler of the state. Between two such as these, as the Philosopher says in book five of the Ethics, we find justice simply speaking.[6]

5. II-II, 77, 1.
6. II-II, 57, 4. "Alterum autem potest dici dupliciter. Uno modo, quod sim-

Elsewhere, when Aquinas is concerned with the relationship between all human beings, he denies an equality of talents or attributes, but he affirms the equality of subjection, which he calls equality in liberty.[7] Human beings, he says, exist for their own sakes, not to be directed, as a means, to some end.

> Nature made all human beings equal in liberty, but not in natural perfections, for according to the Philosopher in book one of the *Metaphysics,* those are free who exist for their own sakes. According to nature one human being is not ordered to another as to an end.[8]

The application to the craniotomy case is obvious. If the doctor indeed harms the baby, then the action is evil and cannot be made good through any intention to benefit the mother. The unborn child is treated as an instrument, loved only with concupiscence and not as a subject of the good. An attribute of the material acted upon, namely, his humanity, relates *per se* to the order of reason, making the action to be inherently evil.

---

pliciter est alterum, sicut quod est omnino distinctum, sicut apparet in duobus hominibus quorum unus non est sub altero, sed ambo sunt sub uno principe civitatis. Et inter tales, secundum philosophum, in v ethic., est simpliciter iustum."

7. Amartya Sen seems to misunderstand equality of liberty to mean an equal measure of freedom, on parallel with an equal distribution of wealth; see *Inequality Re-examined* (Cambridge, Mass.: Harvard University Press, 1992), 21–24. But equality of liberty is not trying to make people equally free; rather, it seeks a freedom from subjection to others. As such, it is fundamentally a negative concept. Equality means what is not more or less; equality of liberty means not being subject to another. There is no degree here. A person is or is not subjected as a means. Oppression is not wrong because it leads to quantitatively less freedom in some individuals, but because it is an imbalance, which by its nature is making someone subject. Sen views liberty as a freedom to realize one's opportunities; Thomas views liberty as freedom from subjection as a means.

8. *II Sent.,* d. 44, q. 1, a 3, ad 1 (Mandonnet, vol. 2, 1122). "Natura omnes homines aequales in libertate fecit, non autem in perfectionibus naturalibus: liberum enim, secundum philosophum in 1 *Metaphysic.,* cap. iii, est quod sui causa est. Unus enim homo ex natura sua non ordinatur ad alterum sicut ad finem." See also I, 97, 4.

4.1.3. Proportionalism and Useful Love

Proportionalism might provide a response to this line of reasoning by noting that useful love can be benign. No one objects when a patient loves a doctor as useful, for through her he is healed. Such useful loves are commonplace, and human intercourse would cease without them. In truth, there is nothing objectionable about loving others as useful. We do it all the time to those we love most. When we need help we go to our friends, loving in them what is useful. These useful loves are acceptable because they are not alone, that is, we love others not only as useful but also as subjects of the good. We seek not only help from our friends; we also seek their good. Proportionalism, then, claims that the act of killing is consistent with a love of friendship for the victim, for it is possible to love someone both with concupiscence and with friendship, as a patient loves a doctor in both ways.

The difference between Proportionalism and Abelardianism can be expressed in terms of the two soldiers. Proportionalism draws a parallel between the two soldiers, while Abelardianism draws a contrast. According to Proportionalism, the love of the two soldiers is the same. Neither actually seeks the good of the child, but both retain a love of friendship for the child. At the same time, they both have a greater love of friendship for those they wish to save, for by destroying the bridge they save many people. Both, then, choose to love the greater good.

Abelardianism, on the other hand, wishes to distinguish between the two soldiers. The second soldier, the one who intends to kill the child, must set aside his love in the concrete. Why? Because he chooses to love the child as merely useful, with a love of concupiscence. As he resolves his goal into its causes, he comes to see the death of the child as useful for producing some greater good. The first soldier, on the other hand, need not view the death of the child as instrumental to produce his goal. It may be true that the first soldier does not love the child—actually right here and now—for he does not currently will her good, but the phrase "not to will the good" is ambiguous. It might refer to "not willing the good," a failure to actually will what is good. On the other hand, it might refer to a positive act of "willing what is not good." The first soldier fails to will the good of the child, for he foresees her death. In contrast, the second soldier positively wills what is not good for his victim. He pursues his victim's evil as a sort of good, a useful good.

Once again, the subject acted upon becomes important. The first soldier does not act upon the child, for the goal he pursues is not reduced to any change that he brings about in the child. The second soldier, on the other hand, does act upon the child, for as he deliberates concerning his goal, he reduces it to some useful change in the child, namely, death, which he then chooses to bring about. The first soldier simply lacks a present love for the child; the second soldier positively loves what is not good for her. The first soldier need not love the child as useful; he merely fails to love her, in the concrete, with friendship. The second soldier not only fails to love the child with friendship; he positively loves her as useful in producing some other good.

4.1.4. Using Others

Abelardianism distinguishes between the soldier's useful love and the useful love of the patient, for there is a difference between using someone and merely loving someone as useful. While the patient loves the doctor as useful, he does not use her, unless he refuses to pay her, manipulates her, or some such thing. On the other hand, when the soldier kills the child, he not only loves her as useful; he actually uses her as a means to save the others. When we love others as useful we seek some benefit to be gained from them. When we use others we go a step further; we direct or move them to the benefit. When we love someone as useful we allow the person herself to direct herself to the utility, as the doctor chooses to be use-

ful for the patient. In contrast, when we use someone, the usefulness arises from our own activity.[9]

When we use some thing we bring about a change in it, or in its
activity, in order to produce some desired result. When we merely desire it as useful, on the other hand, we need not change it. I
might desire a car as useful, but I do not yet use it until I change
it in some manner, by buying it or driving it or some such thing.
At first, I merely desire it under the formality of some usefulness.
I bring this usefulness to the here and now by using it, by in some
manner engaging my powers upon it, through the activity of will
that Aquinas calls *usus* or use.[10] When we use other human beings,
we bring about some change in them for the sake of some desired
result, as the soldier kills the child in order to save others. When we
merely desire them as useful, on the other hand, we do not bring
about a useful change in them.

According to Thomas, human nature is distinctive in that it
moves itself to an end.

> Something tends into an endpoint in its action or motion in two
> ways: in one way, when one moves oneself to the endpoint, as hu-
> man beings do; in another way, when one is moved to the end by
> another, as an arrow tends to a determined endpoint because it is
> moved by the archer, who directs its action into the end.[11]

9. Thus, Aquinas says that "use" follows upon choice and moves some power of execution (I-II, 16, 4). In a secondary sense, however, we can use things or
people even in our minds: "Insofar as the will in some manner moves and uses
reason, the use of something directed to the end can be understood within the
act of reason referring the thing to the end." (I-II, 16, 4. "Sed quia voluntas etiam
quodammodo rationem movet, et utitur ea, potest intelligi usus eius quod est ad
finem, secundum quod est in consideratione rationis referentis ipsum in finem.
Et hoc modo usus praecedit electionem.")

10. For a thorough treatment of *usus*, see Brock (*Action and Conduct*, 176–
86).

11. I-II, 1, 2. "Aliquid sua actione vel motu tendit ad finem dupliciter, uno
modo, sicut seipsum ad finem movens, ut homo; alio modo, sicut ab alio motum

The soldier moves the child to an endpoint, as an arrow to its target, while the patient allows the doctor to move herself, making her own choice to heal. Consequently, the patient can both will the doctor's good and love her as useful. Indeed, she herself perceives the utility as her own good, for she voluntarily moves herself to it.[12] By requesting to be healed, rather than moving the doctor to heal, the patient places the love of friendship before the love of concupiscence. He loves her good, expressed in her choice to heal, before he loves her utility.

The difference between the two can be perceived readily when approached from the perspective of deliberation. The soldier is aiming at some good, such as protecting the people from the marauding army. In his deliberations, he sees the child as something to be changed for the sake of this good. As such, the child is most formally a means in the Kantian sense, for a means is by its notion directed to some end; we take it up in our actions and change it for the sake of some result. On the other hand, the patient is also aiming at some good, such as health, but in his deliberations he does not see the doctor as something to be changed for this good, for he does not bring about the change in her. The doctor is not a means, for although she is useful, she is not subordinated to the end. Thomas expresses the difference well when he distinguishes between love of friendship and love of concupiscence.

> That is good simply which has goodness, while that is good in some respect which is the good of another. Consequently, that love is love

---

ad finem, sicut sagitta tendit ad determinatum finem ex hoc quod movetur a sagittante, qui suam actionem dirigit in finem."

12. Alan Donagan makes much of the difference between natural causality and human, which breaks the chain of the course of nature. Some such analysis seems to underlie the distinction between using someone and desiring something useful about them. See *The Theory of Morality* (Chicago: University of Chicago Press, 1977), 37–52.

simply speaking in which something is loved so that the good is for it, but that love is a love in some respect in which something is loved so that it is good for another.[13]

To use someone is to love him as existing for another; to love with friendship is to love someone as the one for whom the good exists. To use someone is to direct him toward some good, as a tool or instrument to be used. His good, then, is subordinate; his good is a means in the strict sense. It is not merely something I find useful; it is something I take up in my actions and direct to an end.

Jonathan Bennett, no doubt, would be unconvinced. Speaking of the tactical bomber, who, like the first soldier, bombs a military site (such as a bridge) foreseeing the deaths of civilians, Bennett says we must

> not only clear the tactical bomber of using the civilians as a means, but must imply that he is treating them as ends. Tell that to the civilians! What the tactical bomber does to the civilians, indeed, is in a way worse than treating them as means. He is treating them as nothing; they play no part in his plan.[14]

Like the tactical bomber, the first soldier certainly does not seek the good for the child. Perhaps he does not use her as a means, for he does not, in his deliberations, consider her as something to be changed for the sake of the good; he changes the bridge and consequently she is changed for the worse. The two soldiers, then, differ with regard to the love of concupiscence, for the first soldier does not love the child as a means while the second soldier does; they do not differ, however, with regard to the love of friendship,

---

13. I-II, 26, 4. "Ita bonum, quod convertitur cum ente, simpliciter quidem est quod ipsum habet bonitatem; quod autem est bonum alterius, est bonum secundum quid. Et per consequens amor quo amatur aliquid ut ei sit bonum, est amor simpliciter, amor autem quo amatur aliquid ut sit bonum alterius, est amor secundum quid."

14. Bennett, *Act Itself*, 218.

for neither seeks the good for the child. Indeed, both act such that the child can no longer be the subject of the good. Surely the first soldier cannot be compared to the patient. The patient allows the doctor to direct herself to the end; the soldier gives no such choice to the child. In short, the soldier simply does not love the child, in blowing her up, even if he acts primarily upon the bridge rather than upon her.

Proportionalism, unconvinced as well, insists that we should not be focusing upon love of the child. The child is only a single person. We should not love the child and preserve her life when many more lives are at stake. In short, Proportionalism would claim that we should not focus upon the individual good but upon the greater good.

SECTION 4.2. *The Greater Good*

Proportionalism agrees that human beings are to be loved for their own sakes, but the love must be properly proportioned, so that we love greater goods more and lesser goods less. The soldier who shoots the child crossing the bridge, for instance, does love the child with friendship but he loves those he intends to save even more, for their good far outweighs the good of the child. The soldier cannot do good for all involved, claims Proportionalism, so he chooses to do the greater good. When he shoots the child, he does so out of a love of friendship for those he saves from the invading army. He must choose either to kill the child, and thereby benefit many others, or allow the army to pass, thereby benefitting (at best) only the child. His love of friendship for all involved demands that he kill the child.

4.2.1. Disproportionate Love

Abelardianism fails to recognize, claims Proportionalism, the importance of greater and lesser goods. Finnis, for instance, denies that any basic good is greater or lesser than any other; moral judgments cannot be reached by comparing one good to another.[15] In contrast, St. Thomas himself does not hesitate to say that some goods are greater than others and that the lesser are subordinated to the greater.

> The human good is threefold, as is said in book I of the *Ethics*. One consists in exterior things, for example, money; another consists in goods of the body; and the third consists in the goods of the soul, among which the goods of the contemplative life are better than the goods of the active life, as the Philosopher proves in book X of the *Ethics*, and as our Lord says in Luke 10:42, "Mary has chosen the best part." The exterior goods are ordered to the goods of the body, and the goods of the body are ordered to the goods of the soul, and finally the goods of the active life are ordered to the goods of the contemplative life.[16]

This comparison of goods is not merely abstract or metaphysical but has practical implications in our moral judgments. Aquinas explains the sin of fearlessness, for instance, as arising from an inadequate love of life. It is not that the person fails to love life entirely, a state of mind that Aquinas considers impossible, but that he does not love life enough.

15. See John Finnis, *Moral Absolutes*, 53; Finnis, *Natural Law and Natural Rights*, 2nd ed. (Oxford: Clarendon Press, 1980), 92–95; see also Grisez, *Way1*, 150–56.

16. II-II, 152, 2. "Est autem triplex hominis bonum, ut dicitur in I *Ethic*.: unum quidem quod consistit in exterioribus rebus puta divitiis; aliud autem quod consistit in bonis corporis; tertium autem quod consistit in bonis animae, inter quae etiam bona contemplativae vitae sunt potiora bonis vitae activae, ut Philosophus probat in X *Ethic*., et Dominus dicit, *Luc*. 10: 42, 'Maria optimam partem elegit.' Quorum bonorum exteriora quidem ordinantur ad ea quae sunt corporis; ea vero quae sunt corporis, ad ea quae sunt animae; et ulterius ea quae sunt vitae activae, ad ea quod sunt vitae contemplativae." Also see *Summa contra Gentiles* III, 25, no. 9, and no. 10 (Leonine ed., vol. 14, 66–67); *Q. de anima*, 13, ad. 7 (Leonine ed., vol. 24, 121, ln. 407–18); I, 77, 5; II-II, 73, 3. In "Metaphysics and the Good Life: Some Reflections on the Further Point of Morality," *American Catholic Philosophical Quarterly* 65 (1991): 215–34, at 2, Kevin Staley claims that I-II, 94,

Naturally impressed in everyone is a love for his own life and for those things that are ordered to it. Furthermore, it is naturally impressed that these things should be loved in their proper manner, not as if the end were found in them, but insofar as they should be used for the sake of the ultimate end. Therefore, failing from the proper manner of loving these things is contrary to the natural inclination and consequently it is a sin. No one can fail entirely from such a love, because what is natural cannot be entirely lost. . . . Sometimes, therefore, a person fears death and other temporal evils less than he should because he loves [the opposite goods] less than he should.[17]

Furthermore, the moral disorder of the will, upon which Abelardianism places so much emphasis, involves an improper degree of love, loving lesser goods as if they were greater.

The will is disordered when it loves more that which is a lesser good. But someone chooses to endure the loss of a good he loves less in order that he might save a good he loves more, as when a man wills, with full knowledge, to undergo an amputation of some part in order to save his life, which he loves more. Similarly, when someone with a disordered will loves a temporal good, such as wealth or plea-

---

2, is the most difficult text with which Finnis and Grisez must contend (for finding their incommensurability thesis in Aquinas). I think the above texts are more troubling for Finnis and Grisez because they are more practical. Staley does not explain why Finnis's "metaphysical" claim that the basic goods are incommensurable does appear to have practical import, namely, that one good cannot be attacked for the sake of another.

17. II-II, 126,1. "Inditum autem est unicuique naturaliter ut propriam vitam amet, et ea quae ad ipsam ordinantur, tamen debito modo, ut scilicet amentur huiusmodi non quasi finis constituatur in eis, sed secundum quod eis utendum est propter ultimum finem. Unde quod aliquis deficiat a debito modo amoris ipsorum, est contra naturalem inclinationem, et per consequens est peccatum. Nunquam tamen a tali amore totaliter aliquis decidit, quia id quod est naturae totaliter perdi non potest. . . . Unde contingere potest quod aliquis minus quam debeat timeat, mortem et alia temporalia mala, propter hoc quod minus debito amet ea."

sure, more than the order of reason, or the divine law, or love of God, or something of this sort, then he is willing to suffer some loss of spiritual goods so that he might save some temporal good.[18]

4.2.2. The Good of the Whole

Proportionalism suggests that a properly proportioned love might demand that the soldier kill the child. After all, by killing the child he saves many more individuals. Should he not love these others more than he loves this single child? Proportionalism points out that some goods surpass the good of the individual and should be loved more than the individual. In particular, Thomas teaches that we should always love the common good more than the good of the individual, for an individual is a part within the greater whole of society. Just as a part of the body exists for the sake of the whole body, so an individual is for the sake of society. The lesser good of the part can be sacrificed for the sake of the whole, as when we re-move a gangrened limb. Similarly, an individual can be sacrificed for the good of the whole society, since the good of society is the greater good, to be loved with a proportionately greater love. Aqui-nas uses this reasoning to argue for capital punishment.

> Since every part is naturally for the sake of the whole, if the health of the whole human body requires the removal of one limb—for example, if the limb is putrid or corruptive of another part of the body—then its amputation is praiseworthy and laudable. But every individual person is compared to the whole community as a part to

18. I-II, 78,1. "Est autem voluntas inordinata, quando minus bonum magis amat. Consequens autem est ut aliquis eligat pati detrimentum in bono minus amato, ad hoc quod potiatur bono magis amato, sicut cum homo vult pati ab-scissionem membri etiam scienter, ut conservet vitam, quam magis amat. Et per hunc modum, quando aliqua inordinata voluntas aliquod bonum temporale plus amat, puta divitias vel voluptatem, quam ordinem rationis vel legis divinae, vel caritatem dei, vel aliquid huiusmodi; sequitur quod velit dispendium pati in ali-quo spiritualium bonorum, ut potiatur aliquo temporali bono." See also II-II, 53, 5, *sed contra*.

a whole. Therefore, if some man is dangerous and corruptive of the community on account of some sin, it is praiseworthy and laudable to kill him in order to preserve the common good. As is said in I Corinthians: "A little yeast corrupts the whole lump."[19]

This love of the common good, like the love of friendship for an individual, is founded upon a natural inclination. Indeed, we are naturally inclined to love the whole more than the part, so that in need we will sacrifice the part.

The good of the lover is greater where it is more complete. A part, however, is incomplete in itself and has its completion in its whole; therefore, even by a natural love, the part tends more to conserve its whole than itself. Thus, an animal naturally sacrifices its limb to defend its head, on which the good of the whole depends. Also an individual man exposes himself to death for the preservation of the community of which he is a part.[20]

It follows that if we were to love an individual more than the common good, then our love would be disordered.

19. II-II, 64, 2. "Omnis pars naturaliter est propter totum. Et propter hoc videmus quod si saluti totius corporis humani expediat praecisio alicuius membri, puta cum est putridum vel corruptivum aliorum membrorum, laudabiliter et salubriter abscinditur. Quaelibet autem persona singularis comparatur ad totam communitatem sicut pars ad totum. Et ideo si aliquis homo sit periculosus communitati et corruptivus ipsius propter aliquod peccatum, laudabiliter et salubriter occiditer, ut bonum commune conservetur; 'modicum enim fermentum totam massam corrumpit,' ut dicitur I ad Cor."

20. III Sent., d. 29, q. 1, a. 3 (Mandonnet, vol. 3, 929). "Bonum autem ipsius amantis magis invenitur ubi pefectius est. Et ideo, quia pars quaelibet imperfecta est in seipsa, perfectionem autem habet in suo toto, ideo etiam naturali amore pars plus tendit ad conservationem sui totius quam sui ipsius. Unde etiam naturaliter animal opponit brachium ad defensionem capitis ex quo pendet salus totius. Et inde est etiam quod particulares homines seipsos morti exponunt pro conservatione communitatis cuius ipsi sunt pars." See also I, 60, 5; II-II, 26, 3. Thomas Osborne shows that the love for the common good above oneself is natural to human beings, in Love of God and Love of Self in Thirteenth Century Ethics (Notre Dame, Ind.: University of Notre Dame Press, 2005), 69–112.

Abelardianism, insists Proportionalism, fails to recognize the importance of greater and lesser goods. Finnis, for instance, claims that Aquinas's order of goods is merely metaphysical and "plays no part in his practical (ethical) elaborations of the significance and consequences of the primary precepts of natural law."[21] St. Thomas, however, is unequivocal; not only are some goods greater than others; this distinction in goods has moral implications.[22] Punishment, for example, is justified in terms of the greater good.

> Punishment is opposed to the good of some particular person. But sometimes a particular good is removed while introducing a higher good that is better than the particular good, and then the removal of the particular good is not opposed to the essence of the highest good. For example, the form of water is removed through the introduction of the form of fire. Similarly, in punishment the good of a particular nature is removed through the introduction of a better good, for in punishing, God institutes the order of justice in things.[23]

Proportionalism uses this primacy of the common good to justify harm done to the individual. The soldier may intend to kill the child with a properly proportioned love, for he seeks the greater good. Similarly, the doctor can intend to kill the unborn baby, for by so doing she saves at least one life (the mother), thereby loving a greater good than she would by simply allowing both the mother

---

21. Finnis, *Natural Law*, 94.

22. Flannery distinguishes between counting, in which one unit can be compared to another, and ordering, which is something we do with our minds prior to any comparison (*Acts Amid Precepts*, 84–108). Aquinas, it seems, does compare one good to another with practical import.

23. *De malo*, 3, 1, ad 3 (Leonine ed., vol. 23, 67, 190–99). "Pena opponitur cuidam particulari bono. Non est autem contra rationem summi boni auferre aliquod particulare bonum, cum particulare bonum auferatur per appositionem alterius boni quod interdum est melius: sicut forma aquae aufertur per appositionem forme ignis, et similiter bonum nature particularis aufertur per penam per appositonem melioris boni, per hoc scilicet quod Deus ordinem iustitie in rebus statuit."

and child to die. Her situation is no different than that of the first soldier, who also must choose between his love for the child and his love for those he could save by destroying the bridge. If he destroys the bridge, then he does not seek the good of the child, but if he saves the child by refraining from destroying the bridge, then he does not seek the good of those the army is attacking. His love for the greater good demands that he destroy the bridge. In general, Janssens argues that

> In conflict situations it is our moral obligation to choose the alternative which indicates our preference for the lesser premoral disvalue or for the higher premoral value: "one will try to save one life rather than lose both."[24]

In opposition to Abelardianism, then, Proportionalism claims that we cannot simply identify the act of killing a human being as evil. Not all actions of killing a human being are murder. We cannot look at the nature of harming and the nature of a human being and judge that human beings are unfit material for harming. According to Proportionalism, it is sometimes good to harm them, when the harm is founded upon a love for the greater good. We can identify an action as murder, then, only when we have passed judgment upon the proportion of loves involved. Murder is killing with an ill-proportioned love, while justified killing involves a proper proportion of love.

SECTION 4.3. *The Common Good*

As we have seen, love is of two sorts, either love of concupiscence or love of friendship (section 4.1.1). Human beings are properly the object of love of friendship, to be loved as a subject of the good and

24. Louis Janssens, "Norms and Priorities in a Love Ethics," *Louvain Studies* 6 (1977): 207–38, at 214; see also John G. Milhaven, "Moral Absolutes and Thomas Aquinas," in *Absolutes in Moral Theology?*, ed. Charles E. Curran (Washington: Corpus Books, 1968): 154–85, at 183.

not to be used to achieve some further good. At the same time, it seems that we must love the greater good, so that sometimes, suggests Proportionalism, we must set aside the love of a single individual in preference for the love of a greater number (section 4.2). These two loves, the love of the individual and the love of the greater good, appear to conflict. If we love the greater good, then we must sometimes use individuals; on the other hand, if we are to avoid using the individual, then we must set aside the love of the greater good, or so it seems. This conflict between the good of the individual (or the rights of the individual) and the good of the many is a mainstay of contemporary thought. The medieval mind, however, saw no such conflict.

Aquinas certainly seems to say that the good of the individual takes second place to the common good. One might well conclude, with Proportionalism, that the good of the individual may be sacrificed for the greater good of the whole. The soldier, for instance, may kill the child in order to benefit many more. Aquinas, however, takes an opposite approach. When he explains why the innocent may never be killed, he turns to the common good.

> A person may be considered in two ways, either in himself or through comparison to others. Considered in himself, it is never licit to kill a person, because in anyone, even in a sinner, we should love his nature, made by God, which is destroyed through killing. But killing a sinner becomes licit through comparison to the common good, which is corrupted through sin. The life of the just, however, both preserves and promotes the common good, because the just are the primary part of the multitude. Therefore, in no way is it licit to kill the innocent.[25]

25. II-II, 64, 6. "Aliquis homo dupliciter considerari potest: uno modo, secundum se; alio modo, per comparationem ad aliud. Secundum se quidem considerando hominem, nullum occidere licet: quia in quolibet, etiam peccatore, debemus amare naturam, quam Deus fecit, quae per occisionem corrumpitur. Sed sicut supra dictum est, occisio peccatoris fit licita per comparationem ad bonum commune, quod per peccatum corrumpitur. Vita autem iustorum est

Contrary to contemporary intuitions, then, the common good is not opposed to the good of the individual but provides the very basis by which the individual is protected.[26] How can this be so?

4.3.1. The Chief Parts

Central to Aquinas's claim is an implied distinction between the chief parts of the multitude, that is, those who are just, and other presumably lesser parts, which include evildoers. In a text of the *Summa contra Gentiles* discussing the common good of the whole universe, Aquinas makes a similar distinction. Human beings are the chief parts, while nonrational creatures are lesser instrumental parts. For an army, the same distinction applies to soldiers, who are the chief parts of an army, and ancillary members, such as armorers and grooms.

> Whenever some things are ordered to an end, those among them that are unable to obtain the end through themselves must be ordered to those that do accomplish the end, which are ordered into the end for their own sakes. For example, the end of an army is victory, which the soldiers accomplish through their own act by fighting. Within the army, only the soldiers are sought for their own sakes; everyone else is given other duties, such as caring for the horses or preparing the weapons, and are sought for the sake of the soldiers. Since the ultimate end of the universe, namely, God, is attained in Himself only by intellectual natures, insofar as they know Him and love Him, it follows that intellectual natures alone are sought in the universe for their own sakes, while all others are sought for the sake of them.[27]

conservativa et promotiva boni communis: quia ipsi sunt principalior pars multitudinis. Et ideo nullo modo licet occidere innocentem."

26. Grisez follows the contemporary assumption that the common good is sometimes opposed to the individual good; see "Toward a Consistent Natural Law Ethics of Killing," *American Journal of Jurisprudence* 15 (1970): 64–96, at 68. Long, on the other hand, notes that, "Higher or common goods testify to the unique dignity of the human person" (*Teleological Grammar,* 37).

27. *Summa contra Gentiles* III, 112, no. 3 (Leonine ed., vol. 14, 356). "Quan-

All members of a whole, it seems, are directed to the end of the whole. Soldiers exist for the sake of the whole army, doctors for the hospital, and individual human persons exist for the common good of the community. An individual is a part that exists for the sake of the whole. This principle seems to justify sacrificing the individual for the community, as Aquinas justifies killing evildoers, comparing the killing to an amputation, in which the part is sacrificed for the whole person. When it comes to the innocent, however, Thomas uses another principle, namely, the chief parts of the whole are sought for their own sake. Placed side-by-side, the two principles appear contradictory: parts exists for the sake of the whole; the chief part exists for their own sake.

The apparent contradiction is dispelled when we recall that Aquinas distinguishes two senses in which something might be said to exist or to be loved for its own sake (section 4.1.1). On the one hand, being for one's own sake might mean that someone is the ultimate end and does not exist for the sake of any further end. This meaning applies only to God. On the other hand, being for one's own sake might mean that someone is a subject of the good, to be loved with friendship and not merely with concupiscence. Given these two meanings, a part can both be loved for its own sake and loved for the sake of the whole. It is loved for the sake of the whole as something that is directed to the end of the whole; it is loved for its own sake as a subject of the good.

Within the army we find soldiers, armorers, and grooms. All

---

documque sunt aliqua ordinata ad finem aliquem, si qua inter illa ad finem pertingere non possunt per seipsa, oportet ea ordinari ad illa quae finem consequuntur, quae propter se ordinantur in finem: sicut finis exercitus est victoria, quam milites consequuntur per proprium actum pugnando, qui soli propter se in exercitu quaeruntur; omnes autem alii, ad alia officia deputati, puta ad custodiendum equos, ad parandum arma, propter milites in exercitu quaeruntur. Constat autem ex praemissis finem ultimum universi Deum esse, quem sola intellectualis natura consequitur in seipso, eum scilicet cognoscendo et amando, ut ex dictis patet. Sola igitur intellectualis natura est propter se quaesita in universo, alia autem omnia propter ipsam."

exist for the good of the whole army, in that all are directed to the whole as toward an end. Only the soldiers, however, exist for their own sake, in that they are the subjects of the good. The whole army is directed to the good of fighting for victory. Only the soldiers are the subject of the good of fighting well. Those who prepare the armor or care for the horses are not the subject of the good but in some manner produce this good. If the whole army is to fight well, then the soldiers must actually possess this good; therefore, they are sought for their own sake. In contrast, one who prepares the armor is sought not as one who shares in the good of fighting well but as one who is used to produce the good. The chief parts, then, exist for the sake of the whole by the first meaning, for they themselves are not the ultimate end but are directed to the end of the whole. By the second meaning, on the other hand, they are sought for their own sake, for they are the subject of the good of the whole. The lesser parts exist for the sake of another in both ways. They are directed to the further end of the whole, as are the soldiers, and they are merely useful within the whole, unlike the soldiers who are the subject of the good.

The resulting two kinds of parts involve two different ways in which a part can be directed to the whole, for the whole itself serves as a kind of final cause in relation to the parts. Final causality often leads us to think of the means-end relationship, the relationship of one thing producing another, even as health is the final cause of the surgery that produces it. The soldiers, however, exist for the sake of the whole, but they are not means; they do not produce the army. Rather, they constitute it. The whole is the final cause of the parts, then, insofar as the whole must be made of parts.

Any part, of course, in some manner constitutes the whole, so that even horse grooms constitute an element of the army. For these lesser parts, however, the final causality of the whole is not the finality of constitution. Given that we want a unit to fight well in order to obtain victory, we need parts that do this fighting, and these parts constitute the whole. It turns out, however, that this fighting unit has certain needs, such as the preparation of armor and the tending of horses, which can be attained through other parts. These secondary parts, then, do not constitute the whole in the fullest sense. They do not make up what the whole essentially is but are additions to the essence of the whole. Their final cause, then, is not a matter of constituting the whole but of meeting some need of the whole. They end up in some manner constituting the whole, but that is not the immediate "why" for their existence. These secondary parts, then, do not exist for their own sakes but are subordinated to the chief parts as a means to an end.

4.3.2. The Order of the Whole

Proportionalism views the common good as a mere quantitative accumulation of individual goods, after the manner of a consequentialist summation of goods. Thomas explicitly rejects this notion:

> The common good of the state and the singular good of one person do not differ only as more and less but according to a formal difference, for the common good differs from the singular good just as the whole differs from the part.[28]

Proportionalism seems to think that the whole is constituted simply by adding individuals. You get an army by adding together several individual soldiers. You get a human community by adding together several individual human beings.[29] According to Aqui-

28. II-II, 58, 7, ad 2. "Bonum commune civitatis et bonum singulare unius personae non differunt solum secundum multum et paucum, sed secundum formalem differentiam: alia enim est ratio boni communis et boni singularis, sicut et alia est ratio totius et partis." Also see *Sententia politicorum*, bk. 1, cap. 1 (Leonine ed., vol. 48, A72–A73, 27–163).

29. In "The Common Good," *Review of Metaphysics* 59 (2005): 133–64, Mark Murphy also seems to maintain this view of the common good, although he does not claim that it is Aquinas's. He seems to think that there is some plausible reason why an agent should want to pursue this aggregate good. I don't see it. One might pursue it insofar as his own good is part of it, but then the common good

nas, however, a community is constituted and has its unity through an ordering of its parts. A group of 1000 soldiers does not make an army. The soldiers must be ordered and related to one another such that they act together. Similarly, we do not have a human community merely by gathering together several individuals. These individuals must relate to one another in the appropriate manner, constituting a unified whole through their order.

We can understand an element of the relations that constitutes a human community by considering the three kinds of union that relate to the love of friendship.

> Union relates to love in three ways. One kind of union is the cause of love, which for the love one has of oneself is substantial union and for the love one has for another is the union of similarity. Another kind of union essentially is the love, namely, the union of the joining of affection, which is similar to substantial union insofar as the lover, in the love of friendship, relates to the beloved as to himself, while in the love of concupiscence he relates as to something belonging to himself. A third kind of union is the effect of love, which is a real union that the lover seeks with the thing loved. This union must be fitting to the love, as the Philosopher relates, Aristophanes said that lovers desire that they both might become one, but because that would result in one or both of them being corrupted, they seek a union that is fitting and appropriate, namely, that they might live with one another, converse with one another, and do other things of this sort together.[30]

---

appears instrumental, a view rejected by Murphy. One might pursue it insofar as the overall good is somehow also the good of the individual, but then the common good appears to be what Murphy calls "distinctive," which he also rejects. The trouble, it seems to me, is that he conceives an aggregate good as a shared good—which is distinctive—without realizing it.

30. I-II, 28, 1, ad 2. "Unio tripliciter se habet ad amorem. Quaedam enim unio est causa amoris. Et haec quidem est unio substantialis, quantum ad amorem quo quis amat seipsum, quantum vero ad amorem quo quis amat alia, est unio similitudinis, ut dictum est. Quaedam vero unio est essentialiter ipse amor. Et haec est unio secundum coaptationem affectus. Quae quidem assimilatur unioni

A relation of similarity serves as the foundation upon which is built a relation of affection, which is in turn completed with an actual union of sharing the good through activities. The lovers seek, then, not only that the other has the good, but that the two are united in possessing the good, that they share the good with one another. A human community is formed not merely by bringing together two or more individuals. Rather, the individuals must be united by attaining the good together as a unit. Human beings do this most properly when they attain the good together by sharing it with one another.

Thomas provides us with a much richer understanding of the love of friendship. It is not just that we will some good for the friend; in addition, we will to share the good with the friend. The good is indeed a shared or common good. The common good is not had by adding up individual goods; it is had through sharing the good, so that the good is no longer just mine and yours; it is ours. When I love you, I wish not merely that you have your good but that you have *our* good, that we have the good together.[31]

A sharper contrast, then, can be drawn between the love of friendship and using others. When we use others, we seek to change them for the sake of some further goal. We subordinate them, treating them precisely as lesser parts, as parts that do not share in the good but rather are productive of it. When we love others, we seek to share the good with them. We want them to have our good, rather than to produce our good. Using others is exactly the opposite of sharing the good with them. If I want others to have my

substantiali, inquantum amans se habet ad amatum, in amore quidem amicitiae, ut ad seipsum; in amore autem concupiscentiae, ut ad aliquid sui. Quaedam vero unio est effectus amoris. Et haec est unio realis, quam amans quaerit de re amata. Et haec quidem unio est secundum convenientiam amoris, ut enim Philosophus refert, ii *Politic.*, Aristophanes dixit quod amantes desiderarent ex ambobus fieri unum, sed quia ex hoc accideret aut ambos aut alterum corrumpi, quaerunt unionem quae convenit et decet; ut scilicet simul conversentur, et simul colloquantur, et in aliis huiusmodi coniungantur."

31. See II-II, 27, 2.

good, then I do not want them as instruments to produce my good. The human community consists not merely in an aggregate of individuals; it consists in individuals properly ordered and united with one another. One essential order is that they be united in sharing the good.[32] This union is directly opposed when we use others. By using others we cut them off from sharing our good. We subordinate them to the good, so that they are no longer parts that partake in the good. The chief parts of the multitude, then, should never be violated. They should never be treated as means, subject to the good, for then they are viewed not as chief parts. Precisely because the chief parts share in the good, they are protected from being used. To harm and use a chief part for the sake of the whole is a kind of oxymoron. If we harm a chief part, then our action cannot possibly be for the good of the whole. The good of the whole is precisely sharing the good between those chief parts. To harm, then, is not to share the good but to attack it.

Proportionalism can imagine that the common good justifies harming innocent human beings, then, only by a misperception, by supposing that the good is found not in sharing but in accumulating. To the contrary, the common good protects the innocent, for the common good is nothing other than sharing the good with these innocents.[33] The soldier, then, cannot claim that his act of

32. Finnis's interpretation of Aquinas on the common good, by which the common good of society is not the virtue of its members but only an external peace, need not concern us here. We are concerned not only with the common good of some political community, but ultimately with the common good of the human species; see "Public Good: the Specifically Political Common Good in Aquinas," in *Natural Law and Moral Inquiry: Ethics, Metaphysics, and Politics in the Work of Germain Grisez,* ed. Robert P. George (Washington, D.C.: Georgetown University Press, 1998), 174–209. For criticism see Michael Pakaluk, "Is the Common Good of Political Society Limited and Instrumental?" *Review of Metaphysics* 55 (2001): 57–94; Lawrence Dewan, "St. Thomas, John Finnis, and the Political Good," *The Thomist* 64 (2000): 337–74; Long, "Analytic Looking Glass," 291–99.

33. Flannery states that no good system of law has a provision for depriving the innocent of life (*Acts Amid Precepts,* 224). In his account, unfortunately, the

killing the child is for the sake of a greater good. It attacks the one greater good that matters, the shared good between innocent human beings. It treats the child as a tool, thereby shattering the unity that constitutes the human community. The child is no longer treated as a part that shares in the good; she is treated as an instrument, cut off from the good, existing to produce the good.

4.3.3. The Principle of Limited Responsibility

A host of objections will be raised. What of the innocent people that the soldier seeks to protect by killing the child? Does not the soldier seek to share the good with them? And by refraining from killing the child, thereby letting the army through to massacre the people, does he not prevent the good from being shared? And what of the first soldier, who destroys the bridge but foresees the death of the child? Perhaps he does not use the child, for he does not act upon the child but upon the bridge. Can he, nevertheless, be said to share the good with the child? Does he not, rather, take the good from the child?

We are limited human beings with limited responsibilities. We cannot achieve the common good by ourselves, nor can we share the good with everyone. Even with those who are closest to us we share the good only to some degree. Sometimes circumstances limit us even further. When we are sick, for instance, we might be less able to share the good. Our order to the common good, therefore, is necessarily limited. Generally speaking, we are responsible to comparatively few individuals and our responsibility to them is not entire. We are responsible to share the good with our family, our friends, our colleagues, and those who present themselves to us with need. To most people we are responsible only with a readiness to help when needed.

---

law is supposed to be the *basis* for determining what we can and cannot intend to do. It is not really the law that does the work for Flannery, but some unstated notion of human nature, which then determines which systems of law are good and which not.

Strictly speaking we are unable to benefit everyone by some particular act, but no one can be excluded from those we might be bound
to help in particular. Therefore, charity requires that even if someone does not help another through his actions, he nevertheless must
be prepared in his heart to benefit anyone if an appropriate time
presents itself.[34]

If the first soldier fails to share the good with the child crossing the bridge, then, it should be little surprise. We often fail to
share the good with many people, and we can maintain an order
to the common good without directing ourselves to the good of
each and every individual. We direct ourselves to this or that part
of the community, but not to each and every part. The soldier, then,
is not bound to share the good with the child crossing the bridge;
he need not protect her from every danger that comes her way.
Sometimes, as in this case, he is not even bound to protect her from
dangers that he himself might introduce. He is, after all, limited.
In this instance, in order to protect her he must permit the danger that threatens a multitude of people. He is justified, therefore,
in preventing the danger, thereby sharing the good, insofar as he
is able, with the many people who are threatened. He can choose
not to share the good with the child; he can choose not to protect
her from the danger that he himself has initiated.[35] As Thomas says
concerning self-defense,

34. II-II, 31, 2 ad 1. "Simpliciter loquendo, non possumus omnibus benefacere
in speciali, nullus tamen est de quo non possit occurrere casus in quo oporteat ei
benefacere etiam in speciali. Et ideo caritas requirit ut homo, etsi non actu alicui benefaciat, habeat tamen hoc in sui animi praeparatione, ut benefaciat cuicumque si tempus adesset."

35. Can he choose, rather, to spare the child at the expense of the many?
Perhaps. Many factors might come into play: will the child die anyway (at the
hands of the enemy army)? How strategically important is the destruction of the
bridge? How many people will suffer if the soldier does not destroy the bridge?
Realistically, the soldier might often be obliged to destroy the bridge.

It is not necessary for salvation that a man set aside an act of moderate defense in order to avoid killing another, for a man is held more to provide for his own life than for the life of another.[36]

Similarly, the soldier need not set aside his act of protecting many in order to avoid killing the child.

What of the second soldier? Should he not, likewise, benefit the many to the detriment of the child? First, let us consider whether he need benefit the many? Although the many are many, they are still only a part of the common good, a part of the multitude. Once again, we direct ourselves to this or that part of the community, but not to each and every part. The soldier is not bound to benefit the many. He need not protect them from every danger that comes their way, even when, as in this case, he is physically able to do so. He is a limited human being. As such, he is not bound to share the good with everyone.

But should he share the good in this instance? Should he protect the many from the danger, since he is able? The child, as well, is only part of the common good, so perhaps he should harm the child in order to benefit a greater part.

As we have noted, sometimes our circumstances further limit our ability to share the good. When sick, we might not share the good as much as when healthy. The soldier is in just such a situation; his circumstances limit his ability to share the good with the many, for in order to help the many he must use the child. He must attack and subordinate a chief part of the common good in order to help others. That, says Aquinas, we must never do.

Why not? Because it is one thing, an inevitable thing, not to benefit some parts of the common good. It is another, an incoherent thing, to treat a chief part as if it were subordinate and useful for the common good rather than a subject to share the common

36. II-II, 64, 7. "Nec est necessarium ad salutem ut homo actum moderatae tutelae praetermittat ad evitandum occisionem alterius, quia plus tenetur homo vitae suae providere quam vitae alienae."

good. In the latter, we redefine the common good, excluding this person from it; in the former, we recognize our limitations. The common good is found in activity, in acts of sharing, not in good results. The common good is undermined in activity, in disordered acts of subordinating, not in bad results. By using a chief part of the common good, we actually separate ourselves from this good. We subordinate this good to some other.

4.3.4. Two Kinds of Harm

Our good, as parts, is found in the whole, which means that we are good insofar as we are ordered to the whole. More profoundly, it means that the good of the whole is that at which we aim; it is that for which we are. We might speak of harming this good of the whole in two ways, either constitutive harm or harm of offense. On the one hand, we might do some damage to it; on the other hand, we might turn from it, rejecting it as our good, perhaps subjecting it to some other good. We would then be treating it not as inherently good but as something subservient. We readily sense this difference in our treatment of other human beings. If damage comes to a person by some accident of nature, then his good is harmed constitutively, but if the damage comes deliberately, then he is treated as a tool, as something to be subjected. He is not only damaged; he is also offended against. He is treated as if he were not good. Aquinas makes a similar distinction for God (in the reverse order).

> By sinning one cannot effectively harm God, but for one's own part, one can act against God in two ways. First, one can disdain Him in His commands. Second, one can inflict harm on what belongs to Him, either oneself or another.[37]

---

37. I-II, 47, 1, ad 1. "Peccator enim peccando Deo nihil nocere effective potest; tamen ex parte sua dupliciter contra Deum agit. Primo quidem inquantum eum in suis mandatis contemnit. Secundo, inquantum nocumentum aliquod infert alicui, vel sibi vel alter."

The disdain for God more clearly parallels the harm of offense in the following passage.

> Nothing can be either added to or taken away from God by a human act. Still, a man, with respect to what is his own, adds or subtracts from God when he serves or does not serve the order instituted by God.[38]

We can, by a kind of analogical parallel, perceive a twofold harm against other human beings.

The harm of offense is the greater, for if the good is still loved as good, then it retains its place as end, that place by which it is good. Even if the good is damaged in some way, it is still treated as good. It is an incomplete good, but at least it is good. But if the good is rejected, if people turn from it and offend against it, then it loses its place as end and is treated as if not good. Our human yearning to be loved, to be recognized as one who is a good, reveals the importance of being treated as a good, as an end or subject to be loved. The beneficence of a welfare state inevitably pales before the charity of a Mother Teresa, even if the two produce the same good. Conversely, if a storm or an earthquake produces damage, it is not so harmful as one person subjecting another.

If we turn from the common good, then we must turn toward some other apparent good. We must reject the common good as our good, and place something else above it. The soldier who kills the child, then, turns from the common good, choosing to subject a chief part of the common good as a tool or instrument. He thereby does greater harm to the good than any damage that might result from his inactivity. Furthermore, he rejects the good and turns from it to some other. The first soldier, who destroys the bridge and thereby kills the child, does damage to the common good, for the child dies, but he does not turn from the good; he still treats it as

38. I-II, 21, 4. "Per actum hominis Deo secundum se nihil potest accrescere vel deperire, sed tamen homo, quantum in se est, aliquid subtrahit Deo vel ei exhibet, cum servat vel non servat ordinem quem Deus instituit."

good. It is still his end. Constitutive harm results from his act, but he does no harm of offense.

If we focus only upon the damage that results from our action, and ignore the manner in which we treat the end, then we will never understand how it could be wrong to do some evil no matter the catastrophic consequences. It is precisely our attitude toward the end, our order or direction to it, that truly sets the good as good. The good is found more in reverence than in results. Conversely, our rejection of the end, our turning from it to some other, is the one true evil. We recognize this point more readily when we conceive the good as a person—as God—but it holds for the common good of the community as well.

Proportionalism imagines that we can act for the common good when we kill one person in order to save many others. In reality, by killing we do not act for the common good of any human community; we merely act for an aggregate of individuals. By subordinating one individual to others, we separate him and his good from the community, thereby rupturing the unity found in sharing the good.[39] At most we create a new community, a community of our own, but we break up the community of shared goods that included the individual we kill. Although killing one person can produce a greater aggregate of individual goods, it inevitably does so by excluding a person from the shared good. Ultimately, by killing an innocent person we must be seeking some other good besides the common good.

The two soldiers, then, differ in their relation to the child. Neither actually shares the good with the child. The first soldier, however, does only that: he fails to share the good. The second soldier, in contrast, does more: he uses the child; he subordinates the child as an instrument to some further purpose. This difference between the two makes all the difference.[40] The first does not will the good

39. As Sullivan and Atkinson argue, then, the individual cannot be subordinated to any aggregate (*"Malum Vitandum,"* 100).

40. See Cavanaugh, "End-Not-Means."

of the child; the second wills what is not good for the child. The first fails in the good; the second does evil.

4.3.5. A Defining Circumstance

Proportionalism claims that sometimes a human being is proper and fitting material for the act of killing, namely, when the killing is done for some proportionate greater good. The point must be granted, to a degree. Aquinas holds that it is sometimes permissible directly to kill a human being. This permission, however, is narrowly circumscribed. He allows for harm in the case of punishment, or in quasi-punishing activities such as justified war, but in no other context. "It is not permissible to harm someone except after the manner of punishment on account of justice."[41] The innocent, he says, may never be killed.

The circumstance of being innocent, then, seems to operate in the same manner for the act of killing as does the circumstance of being holy for the act of theft; it serves as a condition of the material, making that material unable to bear the form introduced by reason, namely, an order to the common good through use. While a human being may sometimes be killed, an innocent human being may not. Why? Because the innocent are the chief parts of the common good. As such, we are to love them for their own sake, that is, we are to love them as the subject of the good. This good is not a singular isolated good, but a shared good, a good that is had in the very giving of it. To use a chief part of the common good, then, is to subordinate it and treat it as a means or a lesser part. That which makes innocent human life inviolable, then, is its relation to the community, a relation expressed by the description "innocent."

The evil of killing an innocent human being can be tentatively explained in terms of two orders. First, in his deliberations the agent orders his action by aiming to introduce some form in some

41. II-II, 65, 2. "Nocumentum autem inferre alicui non licet nisi per modum poenae propter iustitiam."

material. He plans to introduce the form of death in this particular individual human being. Intention impresses this order upon the exterior action performed. Deliberation forms this order in the exterior action conceived by way of resolving the agent's goal into its causes. Second, reason aims to introduce some order to the human good. "Reason" must be taken, in this context, to refer to something over and beyond the particular agent's deliberations. The order of reason refers to the order to the true human good; it is the order the action should have rather than the order the action does have. In this case, reason aims to order the action to the common good. The action *should be* ordered to the common good; it *is* ordered to introduce death into an innocent human being.

These two orders, however, conflict with one another. The act of introducing death into this innocent human being cannot be ordered to the common good. Why? Because the material of the action, an innocent human being, cannot bear the form of being used for the common good; he can bear the form only of sharing in the common good. His innocence proclaims him to be a chief part of the common good, and a chief part exists for his own sake, as a part that constitutes the common good rather than as a part that merely produces the common good. The form introduced, the death of the individual, is not his good; as such, it cannot be willed for the individual as a subject sharing in the good but must be willed for the sake of something further. In short, this killing is a kind of using or subordinating. An innocent human being, however, is unfit material for the act of using, since he is a primary part of the multitude. As the argument proceeds, we will see (section 6.3) that this account of the evil of using others is incomplete. At present, however, it will suffice.

Our treatment of the love of others, however, still has unfinished business. We have seen why it is wrong to kill the innocent, the chief parts of the common good, but we have yet to see why it can sometimes be acceptable to kill the guilty, as in capital punishment. If human beings are to be loved for their own sakes, as subjects of the good, then how can we kill anyone, even the guilty? We must turn our attention, then, to the justification of punishment.

SECTION 4.4. *Punishment*

Punishment, especially capital punishment, seems to run contrary to the dictum of Abelardianism that we should not use others. Thomas argues that because the individual exists for the whole, he may be used for the benefit of the whole. Just as a cancerous organ may be removed for the sake of the whole person, so an evildoer may be killed for the sake of the whole community. We seek what is evil for one person on account of the greater good of the community.

Germain Grisez has responded to this difficulty by claiming that we now know better. While Aquinas, in his time, justified capital punishment, we now know that capital punishment, like other killings, is inherently wrong.[42] Unfortunately, we are here concerned with Aquinas's account of good and evil actions, not with some modern view. We cannot modify Aquinas's account of the good and evil of actions at the level of punishment and expect the rest to remain unchanged. Any account of Aquinas's view must explain how capital punishment is justified.

4.4.1. Retribution

Punishment is a kind of setting right, a restoration of the proper order. In particular, it restores a part or member to his proper role as part, for by his offense he has elevated himself above the common good, he has set his will above the will of the whole. Now he must be put back in his proper place. Although the following text speaks of divine justice and the command of God, it ends by indicating an application to human affairs. Furthermore, Aquinas has earlier

---

42. Grisez, "Ethics of Killing," 66–69. See also Christian Brugger, "Aquinas and Capital Punishment: The Plausibility of the Traditional Argument," *Notre Dame Journal of Law, Ethics & Public Policy* 18 (2004): 357–72.

made clear that sin disrupts the order that a person has to the community of which he is a member.[43]

> The act of sin makes a man deserving of punishment insofar as he has transgressed the order of divine justice. He does not return to this order except through a recompense of punishment, which restores the equality of justice. He who has indulged his own will more than he ought, acting contrary to the command of God, should suffer, according to divine justice, willingly or unwillingly, something contrary to that which he desires. And this is observed even in human injuries, where the equality of justice is restored through a recompense of punishment.[44]

In the act of murder, for instance, the murderer places himself above his victim. Properly, the two are equal, that is, one is not to be subjected to the other. But the act of murder is precisely an act of subjecting the victim, using his life as an instrument to achieve some other good. Not only does the murderer subject his victim; he subjects the entire community, for each member, including the victim, is himself part of the common good. The murderer, then, has deemed himself able to do with the common good what he pleases, treating it as an instrument for some other good. The proper order, in which the murderer is subject to the common good, must be restored through punishment. Since the murderer has elevated himself above the community, he must now be put down beneath the community.

> Whatever rises against an order is put down by that order and by the principle of the order. Since sin is a disordered act, whoever sins

43. See I-II, 87, 1.

44. I-II, 87, 6. "Actus enim peccati facit hominem reum poenae, inquantum transgreditur ordinem divinae iustitiae; ad quem non redit nisi per quandam recompensationem poenae, quae ad aequalitatem iustitiae reducit; ut scilicet qui plus voluntati suae indulsit quam debuit, contra mandatum Dei agens, secundum ordinem divinae iustitiae aliquid contra illud quod vellet, spontaneus vel invitus patiatur. Quod etiam in iniuriis hominibus factis observatur, ut per recompensationem poenae reintegretur aequalitas iustitiae."

opposes some order, and the sinner will be put down by that order; this putting down we call punishment.[45]

St. Thomas distinguishes two aspects of the disorder of sin. On the one hand, it turns away from the true good, primarily God; on the other hand, it turns toward some false good, which the sinner elevates above the true and common good.[46] By killing his victim, for example, the murderer turns from the good of his victim and from the common good of which his victim composes a part. Furthermore, he turns to some good as higher and more important, for instance, money or revenge or some such thing.

Corresponding to this twofold disorder are two elements of punishment. Since he has turned from the common good, the sinner must lose a share in the common good. The common good, or at least some aspects of it, must be taken from him. It is unfitting that he should partake of the good against which he has turned.

> It seems that natural equality deprives everyone of the good against which he acts, since he has made himself unworthy of this good. Thus, according to civil justice those who sin against the political community should be entirely deprived of the society of the political community, either through death or through unending exile.[47]

This removal of the good should endure until the sinner submits himself again to the common good, that is, until he once again seeks to be a part that contributes to the common good.

45. I-II, 87, 1. "Quidquid contra ordinem aliquem insurgit, consequens est ut ab eo ordine et principe ordinis deprimatur. Cum autem peccatum si actus inordinatus, manifestum est quod quidcumque peccat, contra aliquem ordinem agit. Et ideo ab ipso ordine consequens est quod deprimatur. Quae quidem depressio poena est."

46. See, for example, De malo, 3, 1 (Leonine ed., vol. 23, 66–67, 141–45).

47. Summa contra Gentiles III, 144, no. 4 (Leonine ed., vol. 14, 429–30). "Naturalis aequitas hoc habere videtur, quod unusquisque privetur bono contra quod agit: ex hoc enim reddit se tali bono indignum. Et inde est quod, secundum civilem iustitiam, qui contra rempublicam peccat, societate reipublicae privatur omnino, vel per mortem vel per exilium perpetuum."

Corresponding to what Thomas calls the conversion of sin, that is, the sinner's seeking to take some good for his own private satisfaction, punishment aims to take away this good and restore it to the community. Punishment, therefore, aims at thwarting or frustrating the preference and desire of the sinner. In this manner, the good that has been seized as private can be taken from the satisfaction of the sinner and become a common good. Indeed, the very dissatisfaction of the sinner is itself a kind of common good, because it takes this private good and submits it to the community, which submission is the very condition of the common good.

The sinner, then, must undergo two evils corresponding to the two aspects of his sin. For turning from the true good, he must lose the true good, at least in part and at least for a time. For taking satisfaction in some private good as if it were greater than the true good, he must undergo dissatisfaction as a sort of restitution of the good to the community.

Aquinas summarizes these two aspects of punishment for mortal sins. Presumably, the duality of punishment can be lifted from the supernatural context and applied *mutatis mutandis* to natural punishment.

> Two things are found in mortal sins, namely, a turning away from the unchanging good and an inordinate turning toward a changeable good. Insofar as it turns away from an unchanging good, a mortal sin makes the sinner worthy of eternal punishment, so that those who sin against the eternal good are punished eternally. Insofar as it turns toward a changeable good, precisely as inordinate, a mortal sin makes the sinner worthy of some punishment, because the disorder of sin cannot be reduced to the order of justice except through punishment; it is just that those who have indulged their will more than they ought should suffer something against their will, for in this is equality.[48]

---

48. III, 86, 4. "In peccato mortali sunt duo, scilicet aversio ab incommutabili bono, et conversio ad commutabile bonum inordinata. Ex parte igitur aversionis

4.4.2. The Order of Justice

What is being set right through all of this is the sinner's relation to the common good. If a thief steals a car, then presumably we must return it to its rightful owner, when possible. This setting right, however, is not punishment. Beyond returning the car to its owner we must set right the relationship of the thief to the community. He has set himself above the community, as if he were not a part. Now he must be returned to his proper role by being subjected to the community.

Ideally, the sinner will voluntarily submit himself to the common good by a conversion of heart in which he now seeks not his own private good but rather to share his good with others. This medicinal effect, however, is not the first submission at which punishment aims.[49] Otherwise, hell could not be punishment. Rather, punishment seeks to introduce submission by externally directing the criminal to the common good. If the criminal has indeed converted, then the first notion of punishment, it seems, ceases to be. The offender is no longer rejecting the common good, so he need not be cut off. There remains, however, the imbalance by which he has set his private good above the community. This private satisfaction, so to speak, must be returned to the community, but this setting right is not most properly punishment, for properly speaking punishment is against the will of the person punished.[50]

Describing punishment in terms of a balancing or equality is

---

ab incommutabili bono, consequitur peccatum mortale reatus poenae aeternae, ut qui contra aeternum bonum peccavit, in aeternum puniatur. Ex parte etiam conversionis ad bonum commutabile, inquantum est inordinata, consequitur peccatum mortale reatus alicuius poenae, quia inordinatio culpae non reducitur ad ordinem iustitiae nisi per poenam; iustum est enim ut qui voluntati suae plus indulsit quam debuit, contra voluntatem suam aliquid patiatur, sic enim erit aequalitas."

49. See Steven Long, "Evangelium Vitae, St. Thomas Aquinas, and the Death Penalty," *The Thomist* 63 (1999): 511–52, at 521.

50. In I-II, 87, 6, Aquinas prefers to call this punishment "satisfaction."

accurate, but it might focus our attention too much upon constitutive harm, whereas punishment properly speaking concerns the harm of offense. It is not simply that a murderer has taken a life, and so his life must be taken, or that he has taken too much liberty upon himself, so that his liberty must now be taken from him.[51] Rather, it is that the murderer has turned against life and turned against the common good; he has rejected the good, and now he must be rejected.

Aquinas says that in punishing one intends the common good and not the evil of the individual.[52] He means that one seeks to introduce the proper order into this individual. If the proper order between the innocent is that they share the good, then the proper order for an evildoer is that he be subordinated to the good. One does not seek his evil as evil, but one does seek his subordination, and his subordination requires that he be cut off and that he undergo dissatisfaction. This cutting off and dissatisfaction are not intended insofar as they are evil for the individual but insofar as they are ordered to the common good.

4.4.3. Loss of Dignity

It remains, however, that in punishing we do direct ourselves to the evil of the individual, even if we do not direct ourselves to it precisely insofar as it is evil. The public authority does intend death, but not death insofar as it is the individual's evil. Christian Brugger wonders how this intention, which amounts to using the evildoer, can be reconciled with the idea that we must love others with a love of friendship.[53]

We have already seen (section 4.3.1) that Thomas identifies

51. In "Ethics of Killing," 70, Grisez misunderstands punishment as merely balancing constitutional harm. See also Grisez, Way2, 891; Finnis, Natural Law, 263.

52. De malo, 1, 3, ad 10 (Leonine ed., vol. 23, 17, 360–68). Also see II Sent., d. 37, q. 3, a. 1, ad 2 (Mandonnet, vol. 2, 956–57).

53. Brugger, "Capital Punishment."

those who are just as the chief parts of the common good, and by implication the guilty are secondary parts; therefore, they do not exist for their own sakes. Those guilty of some serious offense become, like nonrational creatures, instrumental for the good. They are no longer members who share the good.

> By sinning a man recedes from the order of reason and therefore falls from human dignity by which a man is naturally free and exists for his own sake, and he in some manner descends into the servitude of the beasts, who are ordered as useful for others.[54]

The innocent may not be harmed because their personal good is itself a shared good. Their very innocence implies a submission to the community by which their good is not merely their own but is part of the whole. In contrast, the very guilt of the sinner implies a damage to the common good, a tearing of their own good from the community and a clinging to their good as private. They have made their personal good into an affront to the common good rather than a chief part of the common good.

How is it that the order to the common good now demands someone's personal evil? Only on account of some prior disorder of the part. A healthy hand is directed to the whole precisely through its own individual perfection. A gangrened hand, however, is itself harmful to the whole; it has an order or relation contrary to its true purpose and perfection. While introducing the proper order, then, this contrary order must be removed, which therefore requires harm to the part. Likewise, through his sin the sinner is ordered against the community and toward his own private good.

---

54. II-II, 64, 2, ad 3. "Homo peccando ab ordine rationis recedit, et ideo decidit a dignitate humana, prout scilicet homo est naturaliter liber et propter seipsum existens, et incidit quodammodo in servitutem bestiarum, ut scilicet de ipso ordinetur secundum quod est utile aliis." Grisez supposes that human dignity depends upon human nature, and as such it can never be lost ("Ethics of Killing," 69). In fact, we have seen that human dignity depends upon the common good, to which the individual's nature is directed (section 4.3).

When fire comes, water must go. When the order to the common good comes, the private satisfaction of the evildoer must go. What is sought throughout is the good, the proper relation of the part to the whole; on account of a defect in the part, however, some harm results to this part.

Evildoers, then, are subject to the common good as are non-rational creatures. Nevertheless, evildoers are not entirely like non-rational creatures. Thomas says that they descend "in some manner" to the level of the beasts. They are not in all ways mere instruments. After all, they may not be used by just anyone, for only those in charge of the common good, those with public authority, may harm evildoers. Furthermore, even public authorities may not use them in any way they please. Their subordination to the common good is on account of a disorder, a defect in their relation to the community. Their instrumental use, then, demands a re-ordering. Indeed, the "use" of offenders is restricted to punishment in some sense.

4.4.4. The End of Love

Brugger suggests that punishment, or at least capital punishment, abandons the love of others. Does it? In a way yes, and in a way no. Aquinas addresses Brugger's concern when he asks whether we should love sinners with charity.[55] He answers that we should love them according to their nature, insofar as they are at least capable of sharing in the true good. But insofar as their sin is incurable— in effect, insofar as they practically speaking lose the capability of sharing in the good—then they should be cut off, for their sin must be set right. Those who are in hell and therefore are in all ways incapable of sharing in the good, should not at all be loved by charity.[56] Because Aquinas acknowledges that even the grievous sinner

55. II-II, 25, 6, especially ad 2.
56. II-II, 25, 11, corpus, and ad 2. The demons and those in hell may be loved as ordered to the good, with concupiscence, but not as the subject of the good, with friendship.

still holds out a possibility of repentance, and consequently has a nature capable of sharing in the good, he maintains that even capital punishment has a medicinal element, insofar as it prevents the evildoer from sinning again and might even frighten him into repentance.

In short, Aquinas wants to maintain that human punishment is always to some degree medicinal, that is, it is a good for the person being punished.[57] Nevertheless, it is essentially a setting right. Human punishment, then, is both a subordination of the individual to the whole, and as such it is a kind of using the person, and also a seeking of the individual's good, and as such it includes the love of friendship. How can it be both?

Only through a distinction in the person. Aquinas distinguishes between the individual insofar as he has a nature capable of sharing in the good and the individual insofar as he is guilty of an offense. In the first manner, he is to be loved; in the second, he is not.[58] We might, correspondingly, distinguish between two ways an individual can be ordered to the common good: either actually or in potentiality, that is, through at least a nature that is capable of an actual order. While the innocent are ordered to the common good in both ways, the guilty are ordered only in the second way (and that, only while they retain the possibility of turning back to the good). We need not love the sinner given his actual order, and so he may be subjected to the common good. Nevertheless, we can still love the sinner in his potentiality for the good. To love the person according to his nature is to seek that he should turn from his sin and regain an actual order to the good, or at the very least that he should not sin again. This return to the good is best accomplished by taking from him that false good to which he has turned in his sin. In short, it is best accomplished through punishment.

57. Although earlier he allows that it might be medicinal merely by benefitting others; see I-II, 87, 3, ad 2.
58. II-II, 25, 6, especially ad 2.

The single act of punishment, then, is both the subjection of the individual according to his actual order and the love of the individual according to his nature.

Brugger supposes that human dignity depends upon human nature considered in itself, and as such he concludes that it cannot be lost, for no one ceases to be human through his sin.[59] We have seen in the last section (4.3) that complete human dignity depends upon an individual's relation to others, namely, his relation to the common good. We can now see that this relation is twofold, either actual or potential. Perhaps Brugger is correct that the potential order to the common good cannot be lost, at least in this life, because it is connected to human nature. The actual order to the common good, on the other hand, depends upon a person's actions. Through sin, then, human dignity is lost, and yet in some manner retained.[60] Only when the individual loses all possibility of returning to the good does he lose his dignity entirely.[61]

4.4.5. Innocence and Guilt

Wax specifies the act of seeing insofar as it is able to be seen; it specifies the act of heating insofar as it is able to be heated. Likewise, things specify human actions insofar as they are able or unable to

59. Brugger,"Capital Punishment," 365–69. See also Grisez, "Ethics of Killing," 69.

60. Lawrence Dewan, "Thomas Aquinas, Gerard Bradley, and the Death Penalty: Some Observations," *Gregorianum* 82 (2001): 149–65, at 152–61, also makes this distinction between the dignity that comes from nature, which is not lost, and the dignity from our actions.

61. Brugger argues that if human beings lost their dignity through mortal sin then they would be subject to any kind of punishment for even lesser mortal sins and even when they are not a danger to the community ("Capital Punishment," 368–69). His argument is ineffectual, since sinners still retain some element of dignity. Aquinas discusses the loss of dignity within the context of capital punishment, but Brugger ignores the fact that even lesser punishments imply a loss of dignity. Furthermore, Brugger does not make the distinction between punishment for aversion, which is the removal of the good, and punishment for conversion, which is taking away private satisfaction. The former punishment

bear the order to the end introduced by reason, the order that an action should have. In this chapter we have been occupied with the following question: are human beings fit material for the activity of harming? For punishment, yes they can be; otherwise, they cannot. Human beings most properly are fit material for receiving the good, not for harm—which takes the good from them—for they are to be loved for their own sakes, with a love of friendship and not with a love of concupiscence. Proportionalism suggested, however, that an individual might be fit material to be harmed when that harm is necessary to bring about some proportionate greater good; in other words, sometimes individuals are fit material to be used, to bring about a change in them not for their own good, since the change is opposed to their good, but for some further purpose.

An investigation into the common good, however, has revealed that innocent human beings are the chief parts of the common good. The common good is realized precisely by sharing the good with them. Harming the innocent attacks the union between individuals by which the human community is constituted. The common good is not an accumulation of individual goods but a shared good. To harm an individual is precisely to attack this sharing, thereby rupturing the unity of the community, redefining the community by excluding the individual harmed.

This account, which excludes harming, faces two problematic exceptions. First, an individual may be harmed when that harm is a consequence of some other action. When the soldier destroys the bridge foreseeing that the child will die, then his action is not necessarily opposed to the common good. Second, an individual may be harmed in punishment.

The two ways that the child may be harmed, either by destroying the bridge and thereby harming the child or by harming the child so that the bridge might be destroyed, are similar in many re-

---

for mortal sin is infinite; the latter is finite. Finally, Brugger exhibits an inadequate appreciation of the evil of even the smallest mortal sin.

spects. In neither does the soldier share the good with the child; in both, the soldier seeks the good of others instead. Nevertheless, the two differ with regard to the act of using the child. The first soldier does not seek to bring about a change in the child that is causally instrumental for achieving his goals; rather, he seeks to bring about a change in the bridge, which consequently harms the child. The second soldier plans precisely to harm the child as a means of achieving his goals.

We need not at all times share the good with everyone, so that the soldiers do not necessarily harm the good through their failure to share the good with the child. We must not, however, subject a chief part of the good for some further purpose. When we subject the good, we treat it no longer as the good, but as a tool or instrument subordinated to the good. We harm by offense, by rejecting the good in preference for something else. Sometimes damage results as a consequence of our action, as with the first soldier, and yet there is no harm of offense; only constitutive harm results. Damage is done, but the individual is not subordinated, and the common good is not rejected.

What of the second difficulty, punishment? It is permissible under the supposition of some offense, of some rejection of the good that must be set right. The person who rejects the good has cut himself off from the common good, so that he is no longer a chief part but a secondary or subordinate part. An individual does not have his dignity simply from himself, but from his relation to the good, through being ordered to the common good as a part that achieves the end of the whole. Everyone has this order, at least in potential, by his very nature, so that everyone should be directed to the common good insofar as he is able. When someone actually rejects the common good, however, then he must be directed to the common good through subordination. He has rejected his place as part, putting himself above the common good, so that now he must be subjected, subordinated to the whole.

In summary, when we bring about harm in another individual,

three cases must be distinguished. First, we might not act upon the individual but upon something else, with the consequence that the individual is harmed, as when the soldier destroys the bridge and the child dies. Then the question of how we order the individual to the common good—by sharing the good with her or by subordinating her—does not arise, for we do not order her at all; we do not plan to bring about some change in her for the sake of some goal. Second, we might act upon the individual and that individual is innocent. Then the individual may be ordered to the common good through sharing in it. Third, we might act upon the individual and that individual is guilty. Then the individual may be subordinated to the common good, a subordination which may be achieved only through the proper authority of the community.

As reason deliberates it seeks to bring about certain changes in certain subjects. Sometimes those changes are a kind of harm or damage, and sometimes the subjects are human beings. Then reason must recognize certain attributes to the action, as the potter recognizes features of the vase she shapes. Moral attributes depend upon whether the subject, the person acted upon, is able to bear the order to the end that the action should have. Just as color provides the potentiality of an object in relation to the power of sight, so innocence and guilt provide the potentiality of an individual to the common good.

5 | DIFFICULTIES

This chapter addresses a few remaining difficulties before we proceed to consider the order of reason in more detail. First, some challenging texts must be examined in the light of Proportionalism (sections 5.1 and 5.2). Second, what we have learned of the specification of human actions must be applied to some difficult cases, such as self-defense, craniotomy, and hysterectomy (section 5.3).

SECTION 5.1. *Dispensations*

The first set of challenging texts concerns divine dispensations from the Decalogue. God commanded Abraham, for instance, to kill Isaac, an innocent youth. He also commanded the Israelites to despoil the Egyptians, and He commanded Hosea to take to himself a fornicating wife. On a Proportionalist reading, these texts state that actions such as killing, theft, and fornication are universally wrong only because they include, in their very action descriptions, the notion of their evil.

5.1.1. Who Is Innocent?

Proportionalism might argue that the prohibition against killing the innocent is not what we would usually consider an absolute universal norm. To be sure, it has no exceptions, but only in a rather trivial sense, in the manner in which "one should never kill wrongfully" is a universal prohibition. The prohibition is universal, but it is not very helpful. It does not identify those killings that we may not perform and those that we may. Let us suppose that the term "innocent" is merely a placeholder for the moral concept "one whom it is wrong to kill." Then clearly it would always be wrong to kill the innocent, but before we could identify who is or who is not innocent we would first have to pass moral judgment upon the act of killing. In other words, the innocence of the person would not help us to determine which actions are just and which unjust; rather, our judgment of which actions are just would help us determine who is and who is not innocent.

This incorporation of moral judgment into action descriptions distinguishes Proportionalism from both physicalism and Abelardianism. The latter two views maintain that we discover various features of actions, for example, the innocence of the victim, and we thereby pass moral judgment upon the action of killing her. The discovery of the innocence or guilt precedes and determines the moral judgment of the action. Proportionalism, on the other hand, might well claim that the moral judgment upon an act of killing is used to determine whether or not the victim is innocent. Relevant features of an action do not determine our moral judgments but follow upon them. As Jean Porter says,

> the object of the act is not given perspicuously in the description of the act, in a supposedly neutral and straightforward way. Any description focusing on certain aspects of the act as definitive of the object will be the outcome of an evaluative process, not its starting point.[1]

The circumstance "another's" in the act of theft, for instance, is not some real attribute of the item taken, like its color or shape; rather, it is a designation that comes from reason. According to Proportionalism, most specifying circumstances are like "anoth-

---

1. Porter, *Nature as Reason*, 276–77. Unlike Proportionalists, she does not think that this evaluation need always be a moral evaluation.

er's"; they do not belong to the action by itself but only by the designation of reason.[2] The moral species of actions always include
some judgment of reason.[3] For instance, "The word 'murder' precisely *means* illicit homicide. . . . 'Murder' implies immorality. 'Killing' does not."[4] Some physical acts of killing, having no balancing
good to justify the evil of the person's death, are morally evil and
therefore are called murder. Other physical acts of killing, having
a proper proportion to some justifying good, even as self-defense
is proportioned to saving one's life, are morally good and therefore
go by some other name than murder.

Someone might protest that actions such as theft or murder
can be characterized simply through the features of the action itself, independently of any measured term or judgment of reason.
Theft, for instance, is taking what belongs to another, while murder
is killing an innocent human being. To determine whether an action belongs to the moral species of murder we need only passively
consider the one who is killed. If he is innocent and a human being, features that include no judgment of reason, then the action is
murder.

Proportionalism, however, claims that even these actions might
contain some latent moral judgment of reason. Terms, such as

2. Porter again: "in the majority of cases, [Aquinas] does *not* equate the object of an action with a form of behavior that is natural in the sense of being com-
prehensible in nonconventional terms." See "The Moral Act in *Veritatis Splendor*
and in Aquinas's *Summa Theologiae: A Comparative Analysis*," in *Veritatis Splendor: American Responses,* ed. Michael E. Allsopp and John J. O'Keefe (Kansas
City, Mo.: Sheed and Ward, 1995), 278–95, at 285–86.

3. See Louis Janssens, "Norms," 207–16; Peter Knauer, "The Hermeneutic
Function of the Principle of Double Effect," in *Readings in Moral Theology No. 1,*
ed. Charles E. Curran and Richard A. McCormick (New York: Paulist Press,
1979): 1–39, at 14–15. Porter holds a similar view, although she claims that the
judgment built into the species need not be a moral judgment (*Nature as Reason,*
276–77).

4. James Gaffney, "The Pope on Proportionalism," in *Veritatis Splendor:
American Responses,* ed. Michael E. Allsopp and John J. O'Keefe (Kansas City,
Mo.: Sheed and Ward, 1995), 60–71, at 63.

"what belongs to another," are measured terms, including a moral judgment. In a text that we have already seen (section 3.5.3), Thomas apparently says that "one's own" and "not one's own" receive some determination by the measure of reason, and only as such do they refer *per se* to reason.

> To know one's wife and to know one who is not one's wife are two actions whose objects differ in something pertaining to reason, for to know one's own and to know what is not one's own are determined by the measure of reason. This same difference, however, is related *per accidens* in comparison either to the power of generation or to the sexual desire.[5]

When Aquinas asks whether it is permissible to steal in case of need, he answers that it is; ultimately, however, he concludes that such acts are not theft, for the object taken becomes one's own on account of the necessity.

> In the case of extreme necessity using what is taken from another in secret does not properly speaking have the formality of theft, because that which one takes to sustain one's own life becomes one's own property on account of the necessity.[6]

Clearly, then, whether an object belongs to another or to oneself is not some physical feature of the object; it is a feature determined in part by the conditions under which one finds oneself. It is, according to Proportionalism, a measured term, already including a judgment of reason. John Milhaven, for instance, writes,

5. *De malo*, 2, 4 (Leonine ed., vol. 23, 40, 205–12). "Sicut cognoscere mulierem suam et cognoscere mulierem non suam sunt actus habentes obiecta differentia secundum aliquid ad rationem pertinens: nam suum et non suum determinantur secundum regulam rationis; que tamen differentie per accidens se habent si comparentur ad uim generativam, vel etiam ad uim concupiscibilem."
6. II-II, 66, 7, ad 2. "Uti re aliena occulte accepta in casu necessitatis extremae non habet rationem furti, proprie loquendo. Quia per talem necessitatem efficitur suum illud quod quis accipit ad sustentandam propriam vitam."

The question is whether Thomas means by 'stealing' something already defined in moral terms. At least in this context he seems to do so: his point seems to be that stealing should not be done because it is, by definition, unjust.[7]

Even an action such as murder is determined not merely through antecedent features of the act; it involves some judgment of reason. Proportionalism might agree that the innocent should never be killed, for they are directed to share in the good, but it might claim that the term "innocent" is not a simple property like being blue or green. Literally the word means "one that is not harming." Determining whether a given individual is harmful or not might depend upon a comparison and judgment of reason. The unborn child in the craniotomy case, for instance, is far from harmless, for his continued life poses a threat to the mother. Only after reason has passed judgment upon a situation, therefore, can we truly describe someone as innocent or not.[8] Those we may kill are the *nocentes*, those that are harmful, so that their death is due or required. We must never kill the innocent, but who counts as innocent depends upon the circumstances.

While discussing whether God can dispense from the commandments of the Decalogue, Aquinas explains that Abraham can intend to kill Isaac because the murder proscribed by the commandment is "undue killing," a close parallel to the Proportionalists' "wrongful killing." The prohibition against killing, then, seems to incorporate a moral judgment on whether that killing is due or not.

7. Milhaven, "Moral Absolutes," 170. Rhonheimer ("Perspective," 506) also thinks that the taking must be described as unjust. See also Louis Janssens, "St. Thomas Aquinas and the Question of Proportionality," *Louvain Studies* 9 (1982): 26–46, at 39.

8. Janet Smith considers this explanation of "innocent" and rejects it; see "Moral Terminology and Proportionalism," in *Recovering Nature: Essays in Natural Philosophy, Ethics, and Metaphysics in Honor of Ralph McInerny*, ed. Thomas Hibbs and John O'Callaghan (Notre Dame, Ind.: University of Notre Dame Press, 1999), 127–46, at 141.

Killing a man is prohibited by the decalogue insofar as it is unfitting or undue, for the commandment against killing contains the very formality of justice. Human law cannot allow the undue killing of a man, but killing evildoers or the enemies of the political community is not unfitting; therefore, such killing is not contrary to the precept of the decalogue, nor is this killing called murder, which is prohibited by the precept.[9]

The Proportionalists might argue, then, that murder may be described in two ways, but in either event it incorporates a moral judgment. It may be described as "undue killing," which clearly includes the judgment that it is wrong; it may also be described as killing the innocent, but only because the very word "innocent" includes a moral judgment. Those who may be killed are the *nocentes,* whose harm to the community justifies killing them. The innocent are simply those that have been judged benign; whatever danger they might pose to the community is insignificant, not justifying their death.

5.1.2. Killing the Innocent

As the previous chapter has indicated, however, the good or evil of killing, which depends upon who does the killing, a public authority or a private individual, and upon who is killed, an innocent person or an evildoer, can be identified and described objectively. When Thomas argues that killing the innocent is in no way permissible, the clear contrast is not to the *nocentes,* those that are harmful, but to those that he describes as sinners *(peccatores)* or evildoers *(malefactores),* those who have committed some grievous fault. Similarly, Aquinas justifies killing in warfare through the *guilt* of

---

9. I-II, 100, 8, ad 3. "Occisio hominis prohibetur in decalogo secundum quod habet rationem indebiti; sic enim praeceptum continet ipsam rationem iustitiae. Lex autem humana hoc concedere non potest, quod licite homo indebite occidatur. Sed malefactores occidi, vel hostes reipublicae, hoc non est indebitum. Unde hoc non contrariatur praecepto decalogi; nec talis occisio est homicidium, quod praecepto decalogi prohibetur."

the people or nation being attacked.[10] He does not justify killing someone merely because she is in some way harmful, as the unborn baby is harmful to the mother in the craniotomy case. He justifies killing only the guilty, whom he also calls sinners and evildoers. Furthermore, he explicitly states that all intentional harm done to another individual must be a form of punishment: "Any harm inflicted upon anyone is permissible only after the manner of punishment for the sake of justice."[11] Even this punishment can be carried out only by public officials.[12] In no manner, then, can the craniotomy case fit under Aquinas's justification of killing. The doctor is not a public official and the baby is not guilty of any offense, however dangerous he might be to the mother.

What Abelardianism has claimed concerning killing and using others, then, applies unqualifiedly to private individuals. No individual may ever intend to kill another. By so doing, he uses the person, subordinating him to some personal goal. Individuals are equal to one another, sharing in the same good, so that one may not be subordinated to another. Abelardianism's claim also applies universally to the innocent. Not even public officials can intend to harm the innocent. Thomas allows only the killing of the guilty, which must be carried out by some public official. This killing, however, is indeed intended.

In certain places, Aquinas says that the act of killing becomes good when the person is a danger to the community.[13] Is he not, in these texts, extending the class of those that may be killed, now including all *nocentes* and not merely the guilty? It would seem not. He seems to have in mind something like war—which he justifies based upon the guilt of those attacked—or even a dangerous crim-

10. II-II, 40, 1.
11. II-II, 65, 2. "Nocumentum autem inferre alicui non licet nisi per modum poenae propter iustitiam."
12. II-II, 64, 3.
13. I, 19, 6, ad 1. "Sed si addatur circa aliquem hominem, quod sit homicida, vel vivens in periculum multitudinis, sic bonum est eum occidi, et malum est eum vivere."

inal, for at one point he says that capital punishment is justified only for those criminals who are a danger, saying that those who sin without seriously harming others should be allowed to live in order to repent.[14] In other words, being harmful is something concurrent with guilt. It is not an independent factor that can justify killing even apart from guilt. The danger is part of the sin, not some involuntary attribute, such as the baby's head being too large.

Aquinas, then, thought that the good or evil of killing could be identified through features of the action that do not incorporate a moral judgment upon the action itself. The innocence of the victim—meaning his freedom from any grave offense, rather than "one who should not be killed"—prohibits killing. Guilt, on the other hand, can sometimes justify killing by public authority. Judging innocence and guilt may involve a moral judgment upon the *victim* of a killing, but they do not, of themselves, include a judgment upon the *act* of killing. Rather, the moral judgment upon the act of killing follows these features.

5.1.3. Undue Killing

Why, then, did Aquinas justify the killing of Isaac, saying that the commandment prohibits only "undue killing"? Was he not, in this passage, granting that sometimes it is acceptable to kill those who are free from guilt? By no means. The excerpt quoted above indicates that killing is due for evildoers or enemies of the political community. Reading further into the article reveals that even the killing of Isaac is justified as a kind of punishment.

> It was due to Isaac to be killed by the mandate of God, who is Lord of life and death. For God inflicts the punishment of death on all men, the just and the unjust, for the sin of the first parents. If a man executes this judgment through divine authority, then he does not commit murder, even as God does not commit murder.[15]

14. II-II, 64, 2, ad 2.
15. I-II, 100, 8, ad 3. "Debitum erat eum occidi per mandatum Dei, qui est

The killing of Isaac is due, then, because it is a punishment that God has the authority to inflict. Isaac might be innocent of any personal offense, but nevertheless he deserves punishment on account of original sin. God inflicts death upon both the just and the unjust, but even upon the just it is a punishment, not for their personal offense but for original sin.[16] Even God intends death only insofar as it is a punishment.[17] No mere utility will ever justify killing the innocent.

Why, then, does Aquinas describe the murder proscribed by the commandment as "undue killing"? Why not describe it as killing the innocent?

For one thing, "undue killing" cannot be so easily described. It includes not only killing the innocent but also most instances of killing the guilty, which is justified only when carried out by public authorities in the appropriate circumstances. At one point, Thomas says the commandment prohibits unauthorized killings, which perhaps best encompasses all the cases of wrongful killing.[18] There is another good reason, however, for describing murder as "undue kill-

---

Dominus vitae et mortis. Ipse enim est qui poenam mortis infligit omnibus hominibus, iustis et iniustis, pro peccato primi parentis; cuius sententiae si homo sit executor auctoritate divina, non erit homicida, sicut nec Deus."

16. Milhaven makes brief mention ("Moral Absolutes," 171) of this fact: "[Aquinas] adds, as part of the argument, that any divine command to kill merely imposes the penalty due all men because of original sin." Evidently, it is just an aside on Aquinas's part, yet it undermines Milhaven's primary thesis, that God has full liberty to do whatever He wishes with life. John Dedek entirely ignores this statement of Aquinas, as well as Aquinas's statement that the harlot becomes Hosea's wife; see "Intrinsically Evil Acts: The Emergence of a Doctrine," *Recherches de theologie ancienne et medievale* 50 (1983): 191–226.

17. II-II, 164, 1, ad 5. "Unde Augustinus dicit, in *Libro Retractat.*, quod Deus non est auctor mortis, nisi inquantum est poena." Also see I, 49, 2; I-II, 19, 10, ad 2; II-II, 19, 1, ad 3.

18. In a *Reportatio: In decem praeceptis, praeceptum v* (in *Opera omnia*, vol. 7, pt. 2 [Parmae: Typis Petri Fiaccadori, 1865], 108). Long uses this passage in his chapter on self-defense (*Teleological Grammar*, 60–61), evidently unaware that no more explicit exclusion of his position on self-defense could be hoped for.

ing." We find in Aquinas, as in our daily language, diverse ways of describing good and evil acts. Sometimes he refers to the fitting or unfitting material; sometimes he incorporates a moral judgment.[19]

The point may be clarified through an analogy to the game of soccer. If a player deliberately kicks the ball into his own goal, we might say that he is aiming at the wrong goal. We might also say that he is aiming inappropriately. The same defective action, then, has three descriptions: the player is kicking at his own goal; he is kicking at the wrong goal; and he is kicking inappropriately. All three descriptions in some manner convey the unfittingness of the action. The last description corresponds to the Proportionalist's formal descriptions, including within it a judgment of its badness. The second also includes a formal element, but it has been transferred from the action itself to the material of the action. The "wrong goal" is precisely the goal that one should not act upon. The first description, however, does not include a formal element, but nevertheless it implies the unfittingness of the action. The description "kicking at one's own goal" does not include a judgment that the action is bad, yet it takes little knowledge of the game to see that it is bad. Its defect arises in precisely the manner we have seen for human actions, namely, it bears upon unfitting material, material that is not in potency to bear the form. Kicking at a goal is an action directed toward scoring, but one's own goal is not in potential to give scores to oneself.

Murder can also be described in three ways: as killing an innocent human being, as killing the wrong person (or as killing a person that one should not), and as undue killing. The third description is formal, including a judgment of the evil of the action, the second description transfers this formal element to the material acted upon, but the first includes no formal element, although it implies a disorder in the action.[20] An innocent human being is

19. Kaczor (*Proportionalism*, 178–86) shows that Aquinas upholds some absolute norms that are nontautological.

20. The wrongful act that we call murder does not correspond entirely with

unfit material for the activity of killing, for killing implies use. Unlike a car or a computer, things directed to the good of being used,
human beings are meant themselves to be subjects of the good and
are fit material for the activity of sharing the good, not for the activity of bringing about evil. The act of killing an innocent human
being, therefore, is disordered, for it brings about the evil of death
in material that is meant to be the subject of good.

The Proportionalists' explanation of the moral species is not
entirely off the mark. Many moral actions do indeed incorporate
a measured term that includes a judgment of reason. Lust is indeed
an excessive desire for sexual pleasure; ambition is an excessive
desire for honors; and so on. The mistake of Proportionalism is to
suppose that every moral species must fit this pattern. Sometimes
the material is unfit through some attribute that does not incorporate an active judgment of reason.

God can command Abraham to kill Isaac because of a real attribute of Isaac, namely, original sin. God's command does not take
what was an evil action and make it good; rather, it transforms the
very nature of the action. It takes what would be an act of one individual harming another and transforms it into an act of a proper
authority instituting punishment. The former action is evil and can
never be made good; the latter action is good and permissible.

This point is clearer in Aquinas's explanation of Hosea's action,
who is commanded to take unto himself a prostitute.

> When Hosea took to himself a fornicating wife or an adulterous
> woman, he was neither a fornicator nor an adulterer, for he took
> the woman who belonged to him according to the mandate of God,
> who is the author of the institution of marriage.[21]

---

the act of killing an innocent human being, for murder is a broader concept, including within it other actions, such as a private individual killing someone who
is guilty; nevertheless, all acts of killing the innocent are acts of murder.

21. I-II, 100, 8, ad 3. "Osee accedens ad uxorem fornicariam vel mulierem
adulteram, non est moechatus nec fornicatus, quia accessit ad eam quae sua erat
secundum mandatum divinum, qui est auctor institutionis matrimonii."

God's command does not take an action of fornication and make it to be good; it takes an action of sexual intercourse, an action that would be fornication were it not for the command of God, and makes it a marital act. The material of the action is transformed, for this woman becomes Hosea's wife by God's mandate.

In a text of the *De malo* Aquinas appears to contradict his explicit treatments of dispensations from the Decalogue—in which he says the commandments cannot be dispensed[22]—and he follows, rather, the authority of Bernard, saying that God can dispense the commandments of the second tablet but not the first. Nevertheless, his explanation of Hosea follows the same pattern: "The divine command [to Hosea] makes it so that which otherwise would be a sin is no longer a sin."[23] Why say, in one instance, that God is not dispensing the commandment but is merely determining who is or who is not Hosea's wife, and then, in the other instance, say that God is dispensing from the commandment? Evidently, it depends upon how one views the commandment. Is it prohibiting sexual activity with one who is not one's wife in the most formal sense? Or, on the other hand, is it prohibiting sexual activity with one who, in the normal course of events, would not be one's wife?[24] If the former, then the commandment can have no dispensation, but only a determination. If the latter, then the commandment may be dispensed with. This reconciliation of the texts of Aquinas may become more evident in the next section (5.2), for Aquinas also treats dispensations from the Ten Commandments as instances of evil actions that become good.

Abraham's action of killing Isaac changes in a manner simi-

22. I-II, 100, 8; *III Sent.* d. 37, q. 1, a. 4 (Mandonnet, vol. 3, 1246–48).

23. *De malo,* 3, 1, ad 17 (Leonine ed., vol. 23, 68, 318–19). "set preceptum diuinum facit ut non sit peccatum quod aliter esset peccatum." *I Sent.,* d. 47, q. 1, a. 4 (Mandonnet, vol. 1, 1071–74), also maintains, contrary to Aquinas's other treatments, that God can dispense the commandments of the second tablet. This text should also be read as interpreting the second tablet to refer to the normal course of events rather than to the formality of justice.

24. See II-II, 154, 2, ad 2.

lar to Hosea's action. Isaac is innocent by human law but guilty of original sin by divine law. If Abraham were to kill Isaac of his own initiative, then his action would be one of using someone who is his equal, someone with whom he should wish to share the good. He could not claim to be punishing Isaac, for Abraham himself is not an authority of the divine law. Under the command of God, however, his action takes on another character. It is properly an act of punishment, for God has the authority to punish Isaac for original sin. It is more God's action than Abraham's.[25]

In short, God does not make evil actions to be good, but He does determine the precise nature of some particular actions.[26] His authority makes this act of killing into an act of punishment, for He is precisely the authority that can punish.[27] Thomas concludes his analysis of divine dispensations as follows:

> Therefore, the precepts of the decalogue are immutable with respect to the formality of justice they contain, but they are mutable with respect to the determination through an application to the sin-

25. II-II, 64, 3, ad 1.

26. Porter (*Nature as Reason*, 270) says that the act does not fall under the precept. In "Permanence of the Ten Commandments: St. Thomas and His Modern Commentators," *Theological Studies* 42 (1981): 422–43, at 429–43, Patrick Lee argues that a change in the moral value of an act requires a prior ontological change of the act itself. Surprisingly, Dedek ("Intrinsically Evil Acts 2," 225–26) cannot see in Aquinas the doctrine he finds in Durand, namely, that the act itself changes nature because God changes an attribute of the material. While paraphrasing certain texts of Aquinas Dedek often expresses this position, pointing out that God transfers ownership or changes a thing's nature; see, for instance, "Intrinsically Evil Acts: An Historical Study of the Mind of St. Thomas," *The Thomist* 43 (1979): 385–413, at 402, 404, and 406. Perhaps Dedek is blinded by the fact that he also finds in Aquinas what he supposes to be a contrary position, namely, that some acts are wrong because they formally contain an opposition to reason.

27. Contrary to Brugger's claim ("Capital Punishment," 369–71), Aquinas does say that even the normal authority of the state to execute derives from the authority of God; the state acts in the place of God. That human beings have the authority to determine that a killing is a punishment rather than murder ultimately derives from God.

gular act, for example, to determine whether or not this or that act is murder, theft, or adultery.[28]

Killing the innocent, then, is always wrong; killing the guilty is wrong unless carried out by the appropriate authority. The good and evil of these actions do not change. What changes is whether this particular act of killing is done with authority or not.

SECTION 5.2. *Evil Actions Becoming Good*

A similar analysis applies to the second set of challenging texts, those texts that seem to grant fluidity to the good and evil of killing.[29] Certain texts, for instance, claim that killing a man, while evil in itself, can become good with additional circumstances.[30]

> Something may be good or evil in its first consideration, insofar as it is absolutely considered, but with an additional consideration, matters may be reversed, for example, according to the absolute consideration it is good for a man to live and evil for him to be killed. But if concerning a certain man it is added that he is a murderer, or that he is a danger to the community, then it is good for him to be killed and evil for him to live.[31]

28. I-II, 100, 8, ad 3. "Praecepta ipsa decalogi, quantum ad rationem iustitiae quam continent, immutabilia sunt. Sed quantum ad aliquam determinationem per applicationem ad singulares actus, ut scilicet hoc vel illud sit homicidium, furtum vel adulterium, aut non, hoc quidem est mutabile."

29. Portions of this section are taken from my article, "When Evil Actions Become Good," *Nova et Vetera*, English ed. 5 (2007): 747–64.

30. For a Proportionalist interpretation of these texts see Janssens, "Norms," 232–33; "Question of Proportionality," 26–46; "A Moral Understanding of Some Arguments of St. Thomas," *Ephemerides Theologicae Lovanienses* 63 (1987): 354–60. For a cogent refutation of this view see Mark Johnson, "Proportionalism and a Text of the Young Aquinas: Quodlibetum IX, Q. 7, A. 2," *Theological Studies* 53 (1992): 683–99.

31. I, 19, 6, ad 1. "Aliquid autem potest esse in prima sui consideratione, secundum quod absolute consideratur, bonum vel malum, quod tamen, prout cum aliquo adiuncto consideratur, quae est consequens consideratio eius, e contrario

Aquinas's explicit treatment of these sorts of actions, actions that are evil in themselves but can become good, is within one of his early works,[32] but we should not suppose that he entirely abandoned the notion of evil actions becoming good. In the *De potentia* he mentions them in reference to dispensations from the Decalogue.[33] He mentions them in a late *Quodlibeta*,[34] and he even makes an offhand reference to them in the *Secunda secundae*. While discussing whether women can adorn themselves apart from mortal sin, he observes in an objection that it is a sin for women to wear men's clothing. Thomas does not doubt the supposition, but replies,

> Exterior clothing should correspond to the state of the person in accordance with common custom, so it is of itself sinful for women to wear men's clothing and vice versa, especially since this can cause lustful desires; therefore, it is specifically prohibited in the law, since the Gentiles used to exchange clothes for the purposes of idolatrous superstition. Nevertheless, this action can be done without sin because of some necessity, either for the purpose of hiding from the enemy, or because there is no other clothing available, or for other reasons of this sort.[35]

---

se habet. Sicut hominem vivere est bonum, et hominem occidi est malum, secundum absolutam considerationem; sed si addatur circa aliquem hominem, quod sit homicida, vel vivens in periculum multitudinis, sic bonum est eum occidi, et malum est eum vivere."

32. *Quodlibetum,* 9, 7, 2 (Leonine ed., vol. 25, 117–18, 77–141).

33. Questiones disputatae, vol. 2, *De potentia,* 1, 6, ad 4 (Taurini-Romae: Marietti, 1949), 22.

34. *Quodlibetum,* 5, 5, 3 (Leonine ed., vol. 25, 376, 17–27).

35. I-II, 169, 2, ad 3. "Cultus exterior debet competere conditioni personae secundum communem consuetudinem. Et ideo de se vitiosum est quod mulier utatur veste virili aut e converso, et praecipue quia hoc potest esse causa lasciviae. Et specialiter prohibetur in lege, quia gentiles tali mutatione habitus utebantur ad idololatriae superstitionem. Potest tamen quandoque hoc fieri sine peccato propter aliquam necessitatem, vel causa occultandi ab hostibus, vel propter defectum alterius vestimenti, vel propter aliquid aliud huiusmodi."

Evidently, then, we cannot simply ignore these references as irrelevant. Nevertheless, they are perplexing. On the face of it, they pose a logical conundrum. How can an attribute, such as being evil, apply to something considered in itself and yet disappear with further consideration? It seems that what belongs to something in itself must always belong to it. Therefore, if it is wrong to kill a man considered in itself, it must be wrong to kill a man in all situations. If the action of killing a man can sometimes be good, as in capital punishment, then why should we describe the action, when considered in itself, as evil?

5.2.1. Relative Qualities

Fortunately, we have a parallel: the attributes of being according to someone's will or against his will can apply to an action when considered in itself yet can be removed in the concrete. In general, for instance, a captain does not wish to throw his cargo overboard, so that the action of jettisoning cargo, considered in itself, is against his will. But in certain concrete situations, such as in a violent storm, he might want to throw the cargo overboard, so that the action now becomes voluntary or according to his will. What was against his will, when considered in itself, becomes according to his will, in the concrete.

How does the action lose its original attribute? If it is indeed against his will in itself, then must it not be against his will always? In the *Summa*, Aquinas poses an objection that expresses the difficulty well.

> What is in a certain way according to itself remains such given any additions, for example, what is hot according to itself is always hot whatever is added onto it. Since that which is done in fear is against the will in itself, then it must remain so even when the fear is added.[36]

36. I-II, 6, 6, objection 2. "Quod est secundum se tale, quolibet addito remanet tale, sicut quod secundum se est calidum, cuicumque coniungatur, nihilomi-

The key to overcoming this difficulty, Thomas says in his reply, is the relational character of the attributes.

> Those things that are said absolutely remain such given any additions, as being hot or being white, but those things that are said relatively change in comparison to diverse things. What is large in comparison to one thing is small in comparison to another. Being according to one's will, however, is said not only according to itself, as if absolutely, but also in relation to another, as if relatively; therefore, nothing prohibits that which is against the will in comparison to one thing to become according to the will in comparison to another.[37]

The earth is large when compared to the moon but small when compared to the sun. Similarly, an action might be voluntary in comparison to one person's will, but involuntary in comparison to another person's will, for the terms voluntary and involuntary express a relation between an action and the will. In the case of the cargo, of course, we have only one action and only one will, the captain's. We generate diverse relations only when we have at least three terms, such as the earth that relates both to the moon and to the sun. If we have only the earth and the moon, then the earth cannot be both larger and smaller. Similarly, it seems, if we have the single action of jettisoning cargo and only one will to which it relates, then it cannot be both according to the will and against the will.

Within the captain himself, however, we can find two wills to which the single action relates. The captain can have two diverse

---

nus est calidum, ipso manente. Sed illud quod per metum agitur, secundum se est involuntarium. ergo etiam adveniente metu est involuntarium."

37. II-II, 6, 6, ad 2. "Ea quae absolute dicuntur, quolibet addito remanent talia, sicut calidum et album, sed ea quae relative dicuntur, variantur secundum comparationem ad diversa; quod enim est magnum comparatum huic, est parvum comparatum alteri. Voluntarium autem dicitur aliquid non solum propter seipsum, quasi absolute, sed etiam propter aliud, quasi relative. Et ideo nihil prohibet aliquid quod non esset voluntarium alteri comparatum fieri voluntarium per comparationem ad aliud."

wills because, as Thomas says, what is voluntary is distinctive in that it is said not only relatively but also absolutely. The will, because it is a rational power, can relate to something considered absolutely or in itself.[38] In the concrete situation, the cargo is both something of value and a dangerous weight, so that the action of jettisoning is both an act of throwing out what is valuable and an act of eliminating a dangerous weight. With reason's ability to abstract, however, the captain can consider the action simply as an act of throwing away what is valuable, without considering what else it might be. His will responds to it as such by moving away from it, making it against his will. He might also consider the action simply as jettisoning a dangerous weight, without considering that the weight is also something of value, and then it is according to his will. In the concrete, of course, it is both valuable and dangerous, and he must relate to it in one way or the other.

The single action of jettisoning the cargo, then, can be both according to the will and against the will, insofar as it relates to diverse wills within the captain. He has these diverse wills because he can will something not only as it exists but also absolutely or in itself. Considered in itself, then, the action of jettisoning cargo is against the captain's will, but with additional consideration it loses this attribute and becomes according to the captain's will.

Similarly, the action of killing a man is evil considered in itself but becomes good with additional considerations. The parallel between the two cases is revealed in Aquinas's own treatment, for his discussion of evil actions becoming good is set, two out of five times, within the context of the discussion of willing something absolutely and willing in the concrete. Furthermore, just as the cargo has two aspects—it is both valuable and dangerous—so we have seen in Aquinas's treatment of capital punishment that the individual can be considered just as an individual or as part of the commu-

---

38. *Sententia libri Ethicorum*, book 3, lect. 5, (Leonine ed., vol. 47, 133, 144–54). See Brock, *Action and Conduct*, 151.

nity (section 4.3). The act of killing a man, then, can be both an action of bringing about the evil of that particular individual and also (in punishment) an action of bringing about the common good. If we consider the action simply in relation to the individual, then it is an act of bringing about evil, and as such it is disordered, but if we consider the action in relation to this man who is a threat to the common good, then it is an act of bringing about good, and as such it is well ordered. In the concrete instance, of course, the act of killing a man cannot be both disordered and ordered, but must be only one or the other.

Objects give species insofar as they relate *per se* to the primary cause, as a rock gives species to the act of seeing insofar as it is colored. Objects give moral species insofar as they relate *per se* to practical reason directing to some end. It follows that if reason itself is not singular but can sometimes direct to one end and sometimes to another, then a single object, materially considered, might give rise to diverse moral species. The captain's will is multiple, when considered in the abstract, so that the single action of jettisoning cargo can be both voluntary and involuntary, depending upon the will to which it is compared. Similarly, if the order of reason is multiple, at least when considered in the abstract, then a single object might give both an evil species and a good species.

For instance, Thomas says that the action of wearing clothing is ordered to the end of revealing one's state in society, so that a man should wear men's clothing and a woman wear women's. The action of wearing clothing, however, has many other ends, for example, protecting oneself from the environment or preventing sexual desires and temptations. Where there are diverse orders, we might find diverse moral species for a single material. The material of women's clothing when compared to the order of revealing a man's state is unfit and gives rise to an evil action. The same material when compared to the order of protecting oneself from the environment is not unfit, and so it gives rise to a morally indifferent action or even a morally good action.

If wearing clothing need not be ordered to the end of revealing one's state, then why should we say that the action of a man wearing women's clothing is disordered in itself? Because in the abstract we consider the action precisely under the formality of a certain order. "Wearing clothing" is ambiguous with regard to the order of reason, but when we consider "wearing women's clothing" we are focusing precisely upon the end of revealing one's state, just as when we consider "wearing warm clothing" we are considering the act of wearing clothing precisely insofar as it protects us from the environment. The very description "women's clothing" is a description of clothing insofar as it reveals a certain state. Therefore, a man wearing women's clothing, considered in itself, is directed to the end of revealing one's state. Since a man should reveal that he is a man, and women's clothing is not in potential to this revelation, it follows that the action bears upon unfitting material and is evil.

Likewise, the act of killing a human being can have diverse orders. It may be ordered to the individual's good and also to the common good. In some situations, however, the first order can be set aside, as when the individual is deserving of punishment. The same material, when compared to each of these orders, therefore, might give rise to diverse moral species. In comparison to the order of reason directing to the good of the individual, a human being is unfit material for killing, since the killing is opposed to his good. In comparison to the order of reason directing to the common good, a human being is sometimes fit material, namely, when he is a dangerous criminal. Why, then, should we say that killing is inherently disordered? Because when we consider the act of killing a human being, just in itself, we are considering the action insofar as it bears upon this individual, abstracting from any order to the common good. As such, it should be directed to the good of the individual but is not.

5.2.2. Multiple Actions

It seems that we are saying contradictory things about the same action. On the one hand, we say that the act of wearing women's clothing is ordered, of itself, to reveal the state of being a woman; on the other hand, we say that this order can sometimes be set aside. On the one hand, we say that the action of killing a man, in itself, is disordered because it lacks the order to the individual's good that it should have. On the other hand, we say that the action of killing a man need not always be ordered to the individual's good.

These contradictions arise because we are not dealing with a single action. In some manner, the action of jettisoning cargo is distinct from the action of throwing over a deadly weight; at least they may be described distinctly, although in this concrete instance they are realized in the same action. In a more profound manner, the action of killing an individual human being is distinct from the action of killing a dangerous criminal; they are distinct moral species, one good and the other evil, and as such, they are distinct actions. Clearly, however, they might also be one and the same action. How can this be? In a different context, Aquinas provides a possible explanation.

> Nothing prohibits something from being one insofar as it is in one genus and many insofar as it is referred to another genus, for example, a continuous surface is one insofar as it is considered in the genus of quantity but if it is partly white and partly black, then it is many insofar as it is referred to the genus of color. In this manner, nothing prohibits an act from being one insofar as it is referred to the genus of nature but not one as referred to the genus of morals, or vice versa, as was said. For example, an uninterrupted walk is one action in the genus of nature but it might happen to be many in the genus of morals, if the will of the one walking changes, since the will is the principle of moral actions.[39]

39. I-II, 20, 6. "Nihil prohibet aliquid esse unum, secundum quod est in uno genere; et esse multiplex, secundum quod refertur ad aliud genus. Sicut superficies continua est una, secundum quod consideratur in genere quantitatis, tamen est multiplex, secundum quod refertur ad genus coloris, si partim sit alba, et partim nigra. Et secundum hoc, nihil prohibet aliquem actum esse unum secundum quod refertur ad genus naturae, qui tamen non est unus secundum quod

Aquinas has in mind, no doubt, the standard example of a man walking to church with an intention of vainglory; midway in his walk he repents and turns his intention toward the glory of God. It is easy enough to separate out vainglory, the virtue of religion, and walking, the first two being moral species and the last a natural species. For a variety of reasons, the distinction is not as clear in the actions we are currently considering. For one thing, some of the species apply in the abstract but not in all concrete circumstances; for another, the natural action can be described in precisely the same way as the moral species.

Take the latter point. No one would confuse walking and vainglory, but it is easy enough to confuse the natural species of killing a man and the moral species of killing a man. They differ, we have seen, in their originating source (section 1.4.4). The action considered just insofar as it arises from the external power is the natural species; the action considered insofar as it arises from reason is the moral species. Whether we kill a man for revenge or for justified punishment we have the same natural species of killing, but we have diverse moral species.

> One kind of natural act can sometimes be ordered to diverse ends of the will, for example, killing a man, which is a single kind of act according to the natural species, can be ordered into the end of justice or to the end of satisfying one's anger. From these diverse ends there arise diverse acts according to the moral species, for one will be virtuous and the other vicious.[40]

---

refertur ad genus moris, sicut et e converso, ut dictum est. Ambulatio enim continua est unus actus secundum genus naturae, potest tamen contingere quod sint plures secundum genus moris, si mutetur ambulantis voluntas, quae est principium actuum moralium."

40. I-II, 1, 3, ad 3. "Possibile tamen est quod unus actus secundum speciem naturae, ordinetur ad diversos fines voluntatis; sicut hoc ipsum quod est occidere hominem, quod est idem secundum speciem naturae, potest ordinari sicut in finem ad conservationem iustitiae, et ad satisfaciendum irae. Et ex hoc erunt diversi actus secundum speciem moris, quia uno modo erit actus virtutis, alio modo erit actus vitii."

We are now suggesting that the same dichotomy can arise even while abstracting from diverse ends of the will. Indeed, it is precisely abstraction that allows this dichotomy. Killing a human being just insofar as he is a human being is one moral action; killing a human being who is a dangerous criminal can be another moral action; both actions, however, are the same natural species of killing a human being. The first of these is a moral species only because it is considered precisely under the characteristic of acting upon an individual human being, abstracting from his role within the common good. Likewise, a man wearing women's clothing is one moral action; a man wearing women's clothing out of necessity is another moral action; both actions are the same natural species. This example has the advantage that we might describe the action, naturally, simply as wearing clothing, leaving out the particular material of *women's* clothing. In any event, the first action is a moral species only because it abstracts from the possibility of wearing clothing apart from the purpose of revealing one's state. Describing the clothing as women's provides the action with the purpose of revealing one's state, even though this order can sometimes be lacking.

In all such actions the dichotomy is possible because the single natural action has an order of reason that may or may not be present. The order of reason directing our actions to the good of the individual is usually present, but as we have seen it is absent in the case of punishment (sections 4.4.3 and 4.4.4); the order of reason directing the wearing of clothing to reveal one's state is usually present, but it can be absent in certain constrained circumstances.

We have seen that in the cases of dispensations from the Decalogue God's command does not take an evil action and make it good; rather, God's command determines the precise nature of this action, for example, it determines whether an act of killing is a private action or an act of punishing under proper authority (section 5.1.3). In a similar manner, the additional considerations we are now discussing do not take what was an evil action and make it good. Rather, they determine the precise nature of this moral action.[41] If we consider the action from the perspective of its natural kind, viewing its moral characterizations as something like properties on the natural substance, then we can indeed say that the additional considerations take what was evil and make it good. They take the single natural action, which is evil by a kind of property, and make it to be good through a new property. On the other hand, if we consider the action from the perspective of its moral kind, then we have one moral species that does not *become* another. Rather, we have one moral species and another moral species, both of which are accidentally related to a single natural species.

It is worth noting that these actions differ dramatically from the hysterectomy case, in which we likewise find two actions that also might be described as one. The single action of the doctor might be described as removing a diseased organ, but it might also be described as killing the baby, since the death of the baby follows necessarily. In this case, however, there is not even a single natural species. The two descriptions are two natural species, one of which belongs to the substance of the act and the other being a mere circumstance or property. There is no single natural species that encompasses them both. In contrast, the single natural action of killing a man can belong both to the moral species of killing a man, that is, murder, and to the moral species of capital punishment.

5.2.3. Fitting Material

The claims of Proportionalism, then, are unfounded. Dispensations from the Decalogue and evil actions becoming good do not

---

41. *De potentia*, 1, 6, ad 4 (Marietti, vol. 2, 22) explicitly links evil actions becoming good and dispensations from the Decalogue. We can now say that when Aquinas says that the Decalogue has no dispensations, he takes the commandments to be referring to the moral species of the action, but in those two instances in which he says that God can dispense from the second tablet, he takes the commandments to be referring to the natural species that is usually, but not always, associated with the moral species.

indicate that moral species always incorporate a moral judgment of reason. Sometimes moral actions are characterized in such a manner, as murder might be characterized as "undue killing," or as "killing a person who should not be killed." But these "measured" characterizations are themselves founded upon features that reason does not actively constitute through its moral judgment. Just as the measured description "kicking at the wrong goal," is founded upon the description "kicking at one's own goal," so the measured description "undue killing" is founded upon certain passively apprehended attributes, such as the victim's humanity and innocence.

The moral species can often be identified simply by knowing the action and the material it bears upon. If the material is able to bear the form of reason implied in the action, then it is morally good; if the material is unable to bear the form, then it is evil. The material, then, sometimes provides this species of the action because, as Thomas says, it implies a defect: "Diversity of material [sometimes] has joined to it a formal diversity of the object, which arises according to diverse modes of repugnance to right reason."[42]

Although we have not heard the end of Proportionalism, we have reached the stage at which we might pass judgment upon the craniotomy case, even without further considerations.

SECTION 5.3. *Craniotomies and Other Conundrums*

5.3.1. Craniotomies and Hysterectomies

What the doctor does when she performs the craniotomy depends upon her intention. If she intends to kill the child, then her action is a killing; if she intends merely to resize the head, then her action is not a killing. We have seen, however, that intention itself is diffi-

42. II-II, 154, 1, ad 1. "Praedicta diversitas materiae habet annexam diversitatem formalem obiecti, quae accipitur secundum diversos modos repugnantiae ad rationem rectam."

cult to pin down; it must itself be specified by the exterior action (sections 2.2 and 2.3). How, then, can it give species to the very action that specifies it? Only because the exterior action is twofold: the exterior action conceived and the exterior action performed (section 3.1.2). As performed, the exterior action is specified by that which is intended, which gives rise to it; as conceived, the exterior action is the object that specifies intention.

How is the exterior action conceived specified? Through reason, which conceives the action in a certain manner. Just as the potter must conceive the items she is going to shape, so we must conceive the actions we are going to perform. Reason, however, is not free to conceive any action in any manner but is constrained in certain regards. First, reason must conceive an action that fits within the person's goals. If the doctor's goal is to end the labor, then she must consider actions that accomplish this goal. Second, reason is constrained by the causal realities in the world around us. In order to accomplish her goal the doctor must use the causes that present themselves. She cannot end the pregnancy by coaxing the baby out. Rather, she must causally change the shape of the baby's head, which needs be accomplished by crushing the baby's head.

The doctor, then, intends to crush the baby's head in order to reduce the size of the head in order to end the labor. The death of the baby does not causally produce the end of the labor; rather, it results from the crushing of the head, which does end the labor. The doctor, then, need not intend to kill the baby. Nevertheless, she must intend to crush the head, which is an act of harming the baby, even an act of lethally harming the baby.

Should the formality of harm be included within the moral species of the doctor's action? It need not be included within her intention, for the doctor can intend the harmful action not precisely insofar as it is harmful but insofar as it is useful for saving life. The doctor, then, must intend that which is harmful, a crushed skull, but she need not intend it under the formality of harm. Nevertheless, the moral species is not simply from the *formality* intended.

Rather, the species is taken from that which is intended. The moral character is derived more from reason than from intention. Intention provides a certain action upon a certain material. This action and this material take on moral character when compared to reason.

The mere formality of intention, or the mere formality under which the action contributes to the person's goal, does not itself exhaust the characterization of the action. Just as a potter actively conceives a shape but must passively recognize certain properties to the shape, even as a shape with no bottom will not hold water or a shape with a rounded bottom will not rest upright, so reason actively conceives an action in order to accomplish a certain goal, but it passively recognizes certain characteristics of that action. Certain properties or circumstances of the action of themselves imply a moral deformity that give species to the action, even as the sacredness of a chalice turns an act of theft into sacrilege, although the thief in no way intends to take the chalice insofar as it is holy and its holiness does not causally contribute to his goals. The doctor does not intend the crushing of the head precisely insofar as it harms the baby nor precisely insofar as it is lethal, but these characteristics might nevertheless give species to her action.

Of great significance for the moral species is the material acted upon. If the material is able to take on the form to which reason orders the action, then it is fitting, but if it is unable to take on the form, then it implies some defect. In the hysterectomy the doctor acts upon the womb. The womb is able to take on the form introduced by reason, namely, the removal of a danger, even though the child, who is not immediately acted upon, dies as a result. In the craniotomy, on the other hand, the doctor acts upon the unborn baby. Is the unborn baby able to bear the form introduced by reason?

Human beings are fitting material to share in the good but not fit material to be subordinated and used for some further goal. If a person commits some grave evil, thereby cutting himself off from the common good and making himself an offense that must be directed and ordered to the good, then he becomes a secondary part of the whole and may be used by the whole. Otherwise, if the person is innocent, he is fit material to share in the good.

Aquinas does describe murder as "undue killing," and he says that the command of God can make what otherwise would be wrong and undue into a good action. Further examination of his position, however, reveals that the command of God merely determines whether this action is a punishment or not. If it is not a punishment, then its morality is determined by passively observed characteristics of the person acted upon. Likewise, if it is a punishment, then its morality is still determined by characteristics of the material. God's command does not directly transform the good or evil of the action, but gives a certain order to the action, which in turn characterizes the action through the material.

What, then, is the moral species of the doctor's action? The natural species is an act of crushing a skull. The material acted upon is a human being and innocent. As such, he is not fit material to be used for some further goal.[43] The doctor does not escape this "using" by claiming that she does not intend the crushing insofar as it is a harm to the baby but only insofar as it is a resizing.[44] The thief cannot escape sacrilege by taking the chalice only insofar as it is valuable. More to the point, only the public official has the authority to distinguish between the harm done to an individual and the formality of some good. Even he can do so only in punishment or quasi-punishing activities.

43. Flannery argues that a craniotomy cannot be a proper procedure of good medical practice, since it does the object (the baby) no good (*Acts Amid Precepts*, 184), and it does not lead to a medical good (223). It is unclear, however, why we need bring in the medical practice. It is not only the medical practice that aims at the good of the subject or object; all human actions directed upon innocent human beings must do good, or at least not harm.

44. Sullivan and Atkinson conclude that "to intend a state of affairs that *recognizably* is an injury to another person, except where required by justice, is always and everywhere wrong" (*"Malum Vitandum,"* 108).

The morality of the action may be analyzed as follows: the doctor intends to crush the baby's skull. Since this crushing is a harm to the baby, the good she seeks to introduce in this material is the good of subordination or use for some further end. She cannot possibly seek to introduce the good of the subject itself, which is the good that the love of friendship would seek. Perhaps she does not seek to introduce the crushing precisely insofar as it is a harm, but actions take their species not solely from the formality of intention but from their relationship to reason. Since reason introduces the good of subordination or use, the material must be fit for this good; otherwise, the action will be evil. Since the unborn child is a human being, he is not fit material. He could be fit material only if some proper authority were to punish him. The doctor is no authority for any sort of punishment. Furthermore, the only offense for which the child could be punished is original sin, for which God is the only proper authority. Therefore, the craniotomy could be made good only under the direct command of God. Apart from this command, the moral species of the craniotomy falls broadly under murder. It may not be murder in the most precise sense, because the doctor does not intend to kill the baby, but it is murder in a common enough sense, for the doctor intentionally performs a lethal harm.[45]

5.3.2. Palliative Sedation

In part, we have used the material acted upon to distinguish between the hysterectomy case and the craniotomy case; in the latter, but not the former, the doctor acts upon the baby.[46] Only when we

---

45. In II-II, 64, 8, Aquinas notes that murder may be attributed to someone who does an evil action from which death follows, even as death follows upon crushing a skull, which is an evil action.

46. In the cases that follow, the primary concern will be the species of the action, whether good or evil. Often, other factors will come into play for a complete moral judgment. I should make another disclaimer as well: the analyses that follow are my best efforts at difficult cases.

act upon other human beings, seeking to bring about some change in them, do we use them. As such, in the hysterectomy case, the doctor does not use the baby. Christopher Kaczor has questioned this role of the material by way of a standard example in medical ethics.[47] A patient with intractable pain can be given barbiturates sufficient to render him unconscious, thereby eliminating his experience of pain. Unfortunately, the barbiturates can inhibit respiration, and conceivably this inhibition might shorten the life of the patient. Generally, such palliative sedation has been deemed acceptable, so long as the patient is already in such a critical condition that the shortening of the life is not that significant. The doctor has been judged not to be engaging in an act of killing the patient; rather, she is relieving pain, with a side effect that the patient dies. By the analysis given above, however, we should judge that the doctor seeks to bring about some change in the patient; as such, the effect of death should be a condition of the material, placing the action in the moral category of murder.

This case, however, is different from the craniotomy case. The doctor seeks to change the patient for his own good, namely, that he might be relieved of pain. Furthermore, she does so with his consent, or at least with his presumed consent. Previously, we have seen that the patient who requests the service of the doctor does not use the doctor, but merely finds her useful, for ultimately the doctor moves herself to act (section 4.1.4). Likewise, in this case, the doctor does not use the patient whose pain she relieves: first, because she seeks his good, not some further good; second, because he consents to it, so that he ultimately moves himself to this change.

The conclusion that the doctor does not use the patient, however, does not settle the issue, for it remains that the patient himself might use and subordinate the common good for his own benefit.

---

47. "Distinguishing," 82. In context, Kaczor is rightly opposing what might be called material-intention.

If a patient asks to be killed in order to relieve his pain (as in euthanasia), then the doctor who carries out the request does not use the patient, for she does so with his consent. Nevertheless, the patient himself subordinates the common good (and so, then, does the doctor) for his own sake, for the relief of his pain. Aquinas says,

> Damaging a healthy organ is not permitted to any private person, even with the consent of the one whose organ it is, because through this damage injury is done to the community, to which the individual and all his parts belong.[48]

On these grounds, Thomas argues that suicide is not justified, for the individual belongs to the community and does damage to the community through his suicide.[49]

The case of palliative sedation however, is different from euthanasia. The patient does not seek to bring about his own death; rather, he seeks relief of pain. Although the patient who asks for euthanasia might also want to be relieved of pain, he does so by means of death. In contrast, the patient in question seeks the relief of pain through sedation, foreseeing death as a possible result. The change he seeks to bring about in a chief part of the common good is not damage but pain relief.

5.3.3. Ectopic Pregnancy

In an ectopic pregnancy, the embryo implants somewhere outside the uterus, usually in a fallopian tube. If the embryo continues to develop, it will eventually rupture the fallopian tube, causing internal hemorrhaging, which if left untreated will kill the mother and child. In any event the child will die, but the mother can be saved. Christopher Kaczor analyzes the various available treatments using fundamentally the same principles as we have for the cranioto-

---

48. II-II, 65, 1. "Hoc autem non est licitum alicui privatae personae, etiam volente illo cuius est membrum, quia per hoc fit iniuria communitati, cuius est ipse homo et omnes partes eius."

49. II-II, 64, 5.

my and hysterectomy cases.[50] (1) Doctors might give no treatment, in hope of the likely probability of a miscarriage. This option involves no action upon the mother or upon the embryo, so we need not concern ourselves with using either of them. (2) Once the fallopian tube has ruptured, or when it is so inflamed to be in danger of rupturing, doctors might perform a salpingectomy, in which they remove the damaged fallopian tube. This option is like a hysterectomy, for the doctor acts upon the diseased organ of the fallopian tube, and not upon the unborn child. (3) Before the rupture of the tube, doctors might use methotrexate, a drug that inhibits the reproduction of cells in the embryo, primarily in the trophoblast. As William May points out, the trophoblast is an organ of the unborn child, if only a temporary organ, and as such the doctor acts directly upon the child.[51] The doctor reasons that she must bring about some change in the embryo in order to end the pregnancy. This change is in fact a kind of damage to an organ, even as crushing the skull is a kind damage. Therefore, the doctor uses the embryo to end the labor, but the human embryo is unfit material to be used. Finally, (4) doctors might perform a salpingotomy, in which the fallopian tube is slit open and the embryo is removed from it.

This last option poses the greatest difficulty. Certainly, the doctor plans to act upon the unborn child, for she removes him from the fallopian tube. The question, however, is whether the doctor plans to do damage. Kaczor argues that the doctor plans only to introduce a change of place, which is not of itself a damage, the way that a crushed skull is damage.[52] The change of place results in damage, but since the damage itself is not introduced, it is unclear whether it serves as a condition of the material, making it unfit for the form introduced. Contrary to Kaczor one might argue that the

50. Kaczor, "Ectopic Pregnancy"; Kaczor gives a thorough and clear explanation of the morality surrounding ectopic pregnancies; see also May, "Ectopic Pregnancies."

51. May, "Ectopic Pregnancies," 133.

52. Kaczor, "Ectopic Pregnancy," 68.

very removal is itself a damage to the placental organ, since the salpingotomy is sometimes described as "scraping" the embryo out.

Kaczor argues that the doctor would remove the embryo even
if she planned to transplant the embryo into the uterus, thereby
saving the life of the mother and baby. The very removal by itself,
therefore, cannot be a damage, since it might be a step in saving the
baby. The case of salpingotomy, then, is not clear. It hinges upon
whether the trophoblast is in anyway disengaged, and whether
such disengagement is a kind of damage. This question will be discussed further (section 5.3.4).

5.3.4. Blocking a Projectile

This next case parallels the trolley example and the rock climbing
example, both of which incorporated the notion of the negation
of a cause, or the inhibition or elimination of a cause (see section
3.3.4).[53] The change that the person seeks to introduce in the trolley is negative, that it not go down the left track where it is currently heading. She introduces this negative change by diverting the
trolley away from the left track, but she thereby introduces another
cause, namely, the trolley moving down the right track. Similarly,
the rock climber cuts the rope in order to introduce the negation
of a cause, namely, she wishes that the dangling climber cease pulling the other climbers down. By so doing, she also eliminates another cause, namely, that the climbers cease holding the dangling
climber up. Neither of these examples involve acting directly upon
the person who dies. Action is upon the trolley, which then in turn
acts upon the person on the right track; or action is upon the rope,
which thereby eliminates a cause holding up the dangling climber.
Now we must consider a case of the elimination of a cause in which
the person who dies is himself acted upon directly.

Vincent, who is resting upon the bridge, sees the soldier pointing his rifle at the walking child. Horrified, he screams, hoping to

53. I would like to thank Louis Jensen for help with this case.

divert the child from her path, and simultaneously he stands up in the line of fire. At that moment, the soldier fires the gun, and Vincent dies. Vincent has acted to divert the action of the bullet from the child, where it is currently directed, onto himself. Rather intuitively, we judge his action to be morally acceptable, at least in some circumstances.[54]

His action is like the trolley case, for he seeks to negate a cause, that is, to prevent the bullet from acting upon the child. Vincent is trying to prevent something, namely, the shooting of the child, and he must do so by eliminating the expected cause. Since he cannot stop the soldier from firing, he can only hope to stop the soldier's fire from acting upon the child. In the situation, this can be achieved by placing some interposing object, and the only object available is himself. That the bullet should then lodge itself within him is a consequence. Just as the trolley, by not going down the left track, must go somewhere else, so the bullet by being prevented from reaching the child must penetrate the intervening object. Vincent plans to act upon the bullet, that is, he plans to prevent its movement from reaching the child. He acts upon the bullet by providing an obstacle to it. Newton's third law of motion requires that when the obstacle acts upon the bullet, the bullet will also act upon it. In his plans, however, Vincent need aim only to act upon the bullet; the action of the bullet upon the obstacle is not a cause to which he need reduce his goal.

Just as we might say that the trolley does not go down the left track because it does go down the right track, so we might say that the bullet does not act upon the child because it lodges itself within Vincent. In Vincent's deliberations, however, the bullet fails to act upon the child because Vincent acts upon it, slowing and diverting its movement. That the bullet should then act upon Vincent, and

54. The case is parallel to that given by Finnis et al. ("Direct and Indirect," 20) of someone throwing himself upon a grenade in order to save innocent bystanders. Both cases are given by Long (*Teleological Grammar*, 73).

lodge itself within Vincent, is like the trolley going down the right track because it has been diverted from the left.

Vincent, of course, does act directly upon himself, by changing his place, but this change is not a kind of harm or damage, although some harm follows upon it.[55] The case, then, is unlike the hysterectomy, in which the doctor acts upon the womb and not upon the baby; she introduces no change into the baby as a means to save the mother. In contrast, Vincent does introduce a change into himself—a change of place—in order to save the child. At the same time, this case is unlike the craniotomy, in which the doctor acts directly upon the baby. Of course, Vincent does act directly upon himself. The two cases differ, however, because the doctor introduces a change that is harm or damage while Vincent introduces merely a change of place, upon which follows foreseen damage.

Vincent does place himself in harm's way. He himself does not place a bullet into his body, but he puts himself in the path of the bullet. Placing oneself in such dangerous circumstances is commonplace. Getting into the car and driving onto the busy freeway places oneself at risk. Likewise, Vincent places himself at greater risk, but even greater risk yet seems acceptable. A soldier might take up a position where he knows, with near certainty, that he will eventually be killed by the oncoming enemy. Nevertheless, as at Thermopylae, he accepts the danger because of the good he can do for the rest of his army by way of delaying the attack. Although the soldier acts upon himself, and places himself in great danger, nevertheless, he does not plan to bring about injury in himself. He changes his place, as does Vincent, and he performs other actions changing himself, but the harm that he foresees to himself is not a means of achieving his goals. He does not plan to do damage to himself in order to achieve some further end; rather, he places himself in danger in order to achieve some further end, and fore-

55. Similarly, in Bennett's quarantine example, the patients are acted upon, but are not harmed; rather, they are placed in a situation where they will not be helped (*Act Itself*, 212–13).

sees that others will harm him. As Long says of this case, "[I]t is not carelessness with respect to one's life to deliberately place it in hazard for the common good of justice, or truth, or for the lives of many others."[56]

The matter is complicated yet further by a similar case. Suppose Vincent does not move himself in the line of fire; rather, he shoves his son in the line of fire. Intuitively, his action is no longer acceptable. While he may sacrifice himself for the child, he may not sacrifice someone else. But why not? After all, he does not introduce damage into his son, but merely changes his son's place. The two cases are in all ways alike, except in the object interposed, whether Vincent himself or some other person.

It seems the difference depends in part upon the judgment of whether the danger is worth it. Although we might well find it morally acceptable for Vincent to place himself in danger, we certainly would not judge it a moral obligation for him to do so. If he wishes to do so, he may, but he is under no obligation. It is a noble and supererogatory action. Vincent, therefore, is in no position to demand such supererogation from someone else, such as his son. It is unacceptable, then, for him to forcibly move his son in the line of fire. While we can place ourselves in danger, we are not as free to place others in danger.

The distinction from the hysterectomy case must be kept in mind. In some sense, the doctor places the unborn child in danger. She does not, however, act upon the child himself; she introduces a change in the womb, which has a consequence for the unborn child. When Vincent places himself in danger, however, he acts upon himself. Similarly, if he puts his son in the line of fire, then he acts upon his son, presumably without his consent, aiming to bring about some change in his son that is useful to achieve some further goal, namely, protecting the girl walking across the bridge. Vincent, then, aims to place his son in a dangerous situation in or-

56. Long, *Teleological Grammar*, 75.

der to achieve some further goal. In the hysterectomy case, the doctor ends up placing the unborn child in a dangerous situation, but this change—of the child being in a dangerous situation—is not a means to achieve her goal; rather, it is a consequence of her action.

A parallel, then, might be drawn with the salpingotomy (section 5.3.3), which involves changing the place of the embryo, moving it outside the fallopian tube. Vincent brings about a change in his son, which places his son in danger. Similarly, the doctor brings about a change in the child, being removed from the fallopian tube, which is a danger to the child. If Vincent cannot force his son to sacrifice his life, then perhaps the doctor cannot force the unborn child to sacrifice his life.

Perhaps. Still, the two cases are not entirely alike. For one thing, the baby is already in a dangerous position even before being removed. Furthermore, the salpingotomy is like the captain throwing his cargo overboard. He does not actually directly aim that his cargo be in the sea; he merely aims at the negative state, that his cargo not be on his ship. Similarly, the doctor does not aim to put the unborn child in a place where he is endangered; she aims merely to remove him from a place where he is a danger to the mother. Just as the cargo, by being removed from the ship, must be in another place, such as the sea, so the embryo, by being removed from the fallopian tube, must be in another place. Vincent, on the other hand, does not seek to move his son from a place where he endangers the walking child; rather, he places his son in a dangerous position in order to save her. The doctor removes the child from a position where he threatens his mother; she thereby places the child in a dangerous situation. For Vincent, the dangerous position is a means to some further goal; for the doctor, the dangerous position is a consequence of removing the embryo from another dangerous situation, a danger both to the mother and to the unborn child.

Boyle plausibly considers this condition—of placing someone in danger—as relating to the morality of the action but being over and beyond the species of the action.[57] After all, it in part depends upon the authority of the person acting. Vincent has authority to place himself in such danger but not necessarily the authority to place his son in this danger. Nevertheless, I am inclined to think that the condition of placing someone in danger does enter into the species of the action; it ultimately changes the potential that the material has to take on the form introduced by reason. Vincent's son is material able to take on a good change or a neutral change, but the danger makes this neutral change into an evil, which he is not in potential to bear. Vincent himself, on the other hand, is in potential to be directed by himself into some danger as a means for the common good.

When all is said and done, this case is intuitively straightforward but intricate in its philosophical analysis. Let my suggestions be taken for what they are, considered philosophical reflections.

5.3.5. Self-Defense (see also sections 2.2 and 6.4)

It is presumptuous to suppose that Aquinas's explanation of self-defense is pellucid. The history of interpretation indicates otherwise. Furthermore, any account that conforms with our intuitions that we can fire a gun at our assailant is difficult to reconcile with Aquinas's own explanation and with other texts of Aquinas. Finally, an honest appraisal of Cajetan's plausible reading of Aquinas yields few real life applications.

For the most part, it would seem that the defender does act upon the assailant, seeking to bring about some change in him. Aquinas describes this change as repelling an attack.[58] Like the trolley case, it seems to be an act of diverting a dangerous cause or sequence (see section 3.3.4). The assailant is threatening the defender, whether he does so voluntarily or in ignorance, or even by

57. Boyle, "Embryotomy," 315.
58. It is his consistent manner of speaking; see, for example, in II-II, 64, 7, itself, and also in II-II, 41; II-II, 60, 6, ad 2; 1; II-II, 108, 2.

some accident. The defender seeks to divert this threat, by turning it away from herself. Just as the captain seeks to remove his cargo from the position where it threatens his life, so the defender seeks to divert the threat coming from the assailant, so that it no longer threatens her life. And just as the captain foresees that the cargo, by being removed from the ship, must be placed in the sea, where it will be lost, so the defender might foresee that by diverting the threat of the assailant, she might harm the assailant, or place him in a dangerous situation. To use Anscombe's example, the defender shoves her assailant off herself, foreseeing that he will be hurdled down a dangerous precipice.[59]

Unlike the hysterectomy case, the defender does act upon her assailant. Unlike the craniotomy case, she does not aim to introduce some harm into him; in the example given, she merely aims at a change in place. Unlike the case in which Vincent shoves his son into the line of fire, the defender does not aim to place the assailant in a dangerous situation as a means to save her life; rather, she aims to remove him from her, from the position in which he threatens her life, and she thereby foresees that he will be placed in a dangerous situation. Such defense, it seems, conforms most to the salpingotomy, at least if we follow Kaczor's judgment that the removal from the fallopian tube is not in itself a damage to the embryo. Such acceptable defense involves diverting a dangerous cause and foreseeing consequent harm to this cause.

Although instances of such defense are real enough, they are certainly few and far between, and they do not conform with contemporary intuitions regarding self-defense, for example, that it is legitimate to kill someone with a gun in order to defend oneself. Long concludes that this interpretation of Aquinas must be incor-

---

59. Anscombe, "War," 54. Long also gives the possible example of throwing someone down, causing lethal injury in the form of internal bleeding (*Teleological Grammar*, 50). Many plausible examples would seem to be available when the weapon of defense is something like a sword, the weapon Aquinas was likely to have had in mind.

rect, since it runs contrary "to moral common sense or even to the legal customs of Thomas's day."[60] Gregory Reichberg, however, has shown that the legal custom of Thomas's day was in part that of deputization,[61] a position that Long himself rejects. Furthermore, the laws of our own day concerning self-defense seem to operate upon the supposition of a deputized authority, that is, the state designates that in cases of emergency those who are otherwise private citizens are given the power to act with public authority. We have already seen that the idea of acting in emergency situations under the aegis of the state conforms wholly with Thomistic principles (section 2.2.5). Long is correct, however, that Aquinas does not provide this deputizing account when he explicitly addresses the question of self-defense.

What of "moral common sense"? Long has difficulty imagining someone who might deny parents the right to choose to kill someone assailing their child.[62] Elizabeth Anscombe, on the other hand, held a very restrictive view of what can be done in self-defense,[63] and she says that the doctrine of II-II, 64, 7 is "severe."[64] After all, Thomas says that one cannot defend one's life by lying or by committing adultery, two judgments far contrary to contemporary intuitions.[65] Why should it be so odd that he would also prohibit most instances of killing in self-defense? Furthermore, it is difficult to read St. Augustine without concluding that he also held perhaps an even more restrictive view on self-defense; indeed, Augustine allows public authorities to kill in self-defense and he also allows *per accidens* killings, but the only examples he gives of the latter are what we would call accidental, not involving reasonably

60. Long, *Teleological Grammar*, 36; see also "Response to Jensen," 108.
61. Reichberg, "Defensive Killing."
62. Long, *Teleological Grammar*, 54, 55.
63. Anscombe, "War," 54.
64. Anscombe, "Double Effect," 225. Cavanaugh takes a similarly restrictive view of what is permitted by 64, 7 (*Double-Effect*, 10–11).
65. II-II, 64, 7, ad 4, and II-II, 110, 3, ad 4.

foreseen deaths.[66] What, then, of moral common sense? The moral common sense of today would also find any prohibition against the craniotomy absurd. Why should we suppose, then, that Aquinas must have held Long's intuitions regarding self-defense rather than St. Augustine's?[67] Aquinas's intuitions certainly do not always conform with our own, for example, he maintained that killing heretics was an acceptable form of punishment.[68] Our own intuitions may well be influenced by centuries of deputized self-defense, in which we can indeed intend to kill in self-defense.

My own intuitions concerning self-defense certainly conform with Long,[69] yet I see no reason to suppose that Aquinas must have thought likewise, since alternatives such as Augustine were available to Thomas.[70] Nor do I see any reason to elevate Aquinas's treatment of self-defense to the status of a defining doctrine, without which Thomas cannot be understood. If Aquinas, in his very limited treatment of self-defense, failed to mention deputization, then it does not follow that he would have rejected such an account.

In his own rejection of deputization, Long supposes that the

66. Epistle 47, pt. 5 (Augustine, *Sancti Aurelii Augustini epistulae I–LV*. Corpus Christianorum 31, edited by Klaus-D. Daur [Turnhout: Brepols, 2004], at 135, ln. 1–136, ln. 7); also *De libero Arbitrio*, i, 5, (*Sancti Aurelii Augustini contra academicos, De beata via, De ordine, De magistro, De libero arbitrio*, Corpus Christianorum, Series Latina 29, edited by William M. Green [Turnholti: Brepols, 1970], 217–18) has Evodius questioning the laws which allow killing for various purposes, such as defending one's property; defending one's own life seems to be included in the purposes called into question.

67. Windass ("Double Think," 260) suggests that Aquinas's position was an attempt to balance Augustine's severity and the common practice of his own day.

68. II-II, 11, 3.

69. Although I am certainly open to views such as Anscombe's.

70. Since we live in an age in which the state has granted deputization, we take it for granted that we may intentionally kill in self-defense. The assumption may not have been as widespread in Aquinas's day. Furthermore, in 64, 7, Aquinas mentions the public official killing in self-defense (which could include deputized public officials), but he focuses upon the private individual precisely as a private individual, for whom self-defense is much more restricted.

deputization view would require some explicit recognition and deputization by public authorities, rather than an implicit granting of authority in necessity.[71] Yet Aquinas does not seem to require such an explicit recognition to permit taking possessions in need, for in necessity possessions are held in common. Any state that opposed such commonality of possessions would not have thereby prohibited what is just by natural law; it would have made no law at all. Furthermore, at least contemporary society seems explicitly to grant such deputization in its laws concerning self-defense, and if Reichberg is correct, Aquinas's Middle Ages were no different.[72]

Long himself, in his treatment of self-defense (see section 6.4), is silent as to whether the assailant must be in some manner guilty, but when he contrasts self-defense to the craniotomy case, then he brings in guilt. The two cases differ, it seems, in that the unborn child is innocent, while the assailant is at least performatively guilty.[73] I have no trouble with this use of guilt, although, as Flannery points out, Aquinas "gives no indication that the philosophical basis of his position has to do with the moral status of the attacker."[74] Furthermore, bringing in guilt seems to turn Long's account into a form of deputization, against which he argues so vigorously. Aquinas, as we have seen, says that harm may be done (even to the guilty) only in some form of quasi-punishment, which requires the activity not of a private individual but of the state (section 4.3.5).[75]

We are left with two alternatives. First, we can accept Aquinas's account of self-defense, thereby modifying our intuitions, recog-

71. Long, *Teleological Grammar*, 57.

72. Long seems to think otherwise; see *Teleological Grammar*, 57.

73. Long, *Teleological Grammar*, 104; "Brief Disquisition," 67–68; "Analytic Looking Glass," 288. Drawing the lines of "performative guilt" may not be a simple matter. Donagan, for instance, concludes that the unborn child in the craniotomy case can be deemed guilty insofar as he is a threat to the mother (*Theory of Morality*, 162). Cavanaugh argues against Donagan in *Double-Effect*, 49–50.

74. Flannery, *Acts Amid Precepts*, 174.

75. See II-II, 65, 2.

nizing that we are severely limited in our own defense. Second, we can turn to some other account, such as that account common in Aquinas's day as well as our own, that in the state of emergency provoked by the attack we are granted public authority; as such, we are able to intend injury upon our assailant. This account is not foreign to Aquinas; indeed it is based upon his own principles.

5.3.6. General Principles

In all of these cases an action is performed in which some people benefit but some people suffer, usually with death. In every case except that of palliative sedation, the person who benefits is separate from the person who suffers. The pertinent question in every case is whether the person who suffers is being used for some further end, that is, whether he is being subordinated as an instrument. For the case of palliative sedation, the subordination would not be of one person for another; it would be the subordination of a chief part of the common good—realized in the individual—for the sake of a private good—realized in the same individual. In that case, of course, we saw that no such subordination occurs.

In order to answer whether the person who suffers is being used, the first distinction is between those cases in which this person is acted upon and those cases in which someone or something else is acted upon. For the craniotomy, palliative sedation, the use of methotrexate, salpingotomy, blocking a projectile, and self-defense, the person who suffers was indeed acted upon. For the hysterectomy and salpingectomy the person who suffers was not acted upon. In these latter cases, the individual is not used for some further benefit. We should note that the action could still be wrong for other reasons, but these reasons need not concern us.

The former cases must be further analyzed. What change is being brought about in the person? This question is not over what change results, which is usually death, but what change the agent aims to bring about, in his deliberations, as a way to achieve his goals. In the craniotomy case, for instance, the doctor does not aim to bring about death, but she does aim to bring about some damage, namely, the crushing of the skull. The changes that are immediately brought about are of three sorts: they involve either benefit, damage, or they are neutral. The case of palliative sedation alone involved benefit to the person who suffers; the benefit of palliative sedation was sought with the recognition of a possible hastening of death. The craniotomy, methotrexate, possibly salpingotomy, and illicit forms of self-defense involved damage, and as such they were morally objectionable.

The last category, those that bring about a neutral change in the person who suffers, which include blocking a projectile, some forms of self-defense, and possibly salpingotomy, must be analyzed yet further. The case of blocking the projectile made it clear that the neutral change of place might nevertheless be a significant condition for the material acted upon, for Vincent cannot place his son in the line of fire. Although the change that he seeks to bring about is merely a change of place, which in itself is no damage to his son, nevertheless the action is objectionable. Why? Because the change of place puts his son in danger. The same might be said for all the neutral changes; in some manner, they all place the subject acted upon in some danger. Indeed, even the hysterectomy places the baby in some danger, although the baby is not directly acted upon.

A distinction must be made, therefore, between placing someone in danger as a means of achieving a good result and placing someone in danger as a result of achieving something good. Vincent places his son in danger as a means to save the girl crossing the bridge. In acceptable self-defense, however, the defender achieves the good result of deflecting the threatening cause, and consequently places the assailant in danger, as when the defender pushes her assailant from her—thereby deflecting the threatening cause—with the foreseen consequence that he will fall down a dangerous precipice. The latter case, of bringing about a good change with the result of placing someone in danger, is not an act of using the person, although we should note that the action could be evil for other reasons. The former case, of placing someone in danger in order to bring about a desired result, can be an act of using a person. The question of equality between individuals arises. While one has care over oneself, to the point of being able to place oneself in danger to achieve certain goals, such care is not always granted over others.

We have seen enough to understand what is involved in using another person: aiming to introduce some negative change in a person—either direct damage or at least placing the person in danger—in order to achieve some further result. In one's deliberations one must resolve the desired goal into this change in the individual. It remains, however, that we have not entirely explained what is wrong with using others. Furthermore, we have not considered actions, such as bestiality, that are wrong although they use or harm no one.

Long speaks of "that natural teleology [which] provides the grammar for the constitution of the species of the moral act."[76] So far, this grammar has remained hidden in the background; it is time to bring it to the fore. As we attempt to unfold the implications of chapter 4, we must ask how the order of reason, which directs us to love others with friendship and prohibits us from subordinating them to another good, relates to teleology.

76. Long, *Teleological Grammar*, 85.

6 | TELEOLOGY

The key to the moral species of human actions is the order to the good that reason aims to introduce in some material, which we have analyzed to some extent for the action of killing or harming more generally (chapter 4). The natural form introduced is death, but we have seen that this natural form implies using or subordinating the person for some further end. Human beings, however, are fit material for the act of using only if they are guilty of some offense, for the innocent are the chief parts of the common good, with whom the good must be shared. The basis for this order of reason, unfortunately, is unclear. Furthermore, certain actions have an order of reason unrelated to this order of love for others, for instance, sexual acts seem to depend upon an order to new life, so that the act of bestiality is evil through a failure in this order and not through any subordination of other human beings.

This chapter seeks to discover what basis the order of reason has within teleology. We will begin by examining, in the first two sections (6.1 and 6.2), how teleology relates to the morality of actions that do not fit entirely under the order of love discussed in chapter 4, actions such as sexual activity or telling a white lie. In the third section (6.3), we will see how teleology relates to the acts of justice and injustice, acts which have already been analyzed (chapter 4) in terms of the love of others. Finally, in the fourth section

(6.4), we will consider another sort of teleology currently being promoted by some contemporary interpreters of Aquinas.

SECTION 6.1. *Natural Error*

6.1.1. Beyond Harming Others

The analysis of the morality of homicide could be applied to many other actions performed on human beings. Any action of harm, whether it be killing, striking, taking possessions, backbiting, or many others, fit this pattern. The act of harm is an act of using the person, but the person, precisely as a human being, is not fit material to be used. It seems, however, that some actions, such as bestiality, do not fit this analysis. An animal is certainly not fit material for human sexual actions. Using the animal, however, has nothing to do with it, for animals need not be loved for their own sakes. Some order of reason besides "using" must be operative for such sexual sins. Certainly, the person does aim to use the animal, but it is not this use that makes the action evil. The animal must be unfit material for some other order that reason aims to introduce.

The standard analysis, which derives from certain texts of Aquinas, claims that sexual activity aims to introduce the order to new human life, for which an animal is certainly unfit material. This analysis, however, does not correspond with what we have seen so far concerning the specification of human actions. In particular, it relies upon an order, namely, the order to new life, that is neither intended nor falls within the patterns of deliberation examined earlier. We can say that a murderer does intend the order of using his victim. Furthermore, in his deliberations he must conceive his action as a using. In order to accomplish his goal he must introduce some change into this person. Since the change is a harm, it cannot be introduced as the good of the person himself. Therefore, it must be introduced as directed to bring about some other good. In other words, bringing about the change is an act of using. So must the murderer conceive his action, and so must the murderer intend his action. It remains, then, to recognize that an innocent human being is not fit material for this action.

That bestiality does not fit this pattern is evident. The person certainly does not intend to introduce new life, nor does this order seem necessary to accomplish his goals; indeed, it does not seem to be present at all, for how could sexual activity with an animal be ordered to new life? Certainly, it is not an order that deliberation introduces into the action for the sake of the goal. While deliberating, the soldier conceives his action of firing the gun as directed to killing the child and then to setting off the explosives, for he reasons backwards from the goal: setting off the explosives is accomplished by killing the child, which is accomplished by firing the gun. The same cannot be said of the one who performs bestiality. He does not reason backward from his goal of pleasure, thinking that it can be accomplished through new life, which can then be accomplished through sexual intercourse. New life, it seems, does not enter into his deliberations at all.

If anything, it seems, this order to new life is introduced not by deliberation but by nature. This physicalist approach, however, all the more highlights the difference between murder and bestiality. The order between firing the gun, killing the child, and setting off the explosives—the *per se* connection between these effects—is introduced by deliberation. For bestiality, the *per se* connection between the action and new life is introduced by nature.

Another action similar to bestiality can be recognized in a man wearing women's clothing. The action of wearing clothing is directed to reveal one's state in society. A man, therefore, wears clothing to reveal that he is a man, for which the material of women's clothing is clearly unfit. But from where does the order of the action arise? Presumably, people often do wear clothing with the intention of revealing their state in society, but they certainly need not. They might wear it simply for comfort or warmth or even as a sign of rebellion, that is, as a sign that they wish to reject their state in society. A man who has little regard for social conventions, for instance, might simply reason that he wants to wear something comfortable. From this goal he reasons back to what he considers the most comfortable means, which he supposes to be a woman's dress. He does not decide to wear the dress by reasoning back from a goal of revealing his state or even from a goal of revealing something contrary to his state. He simply reasons back from comfort and is led to a dress.

The order toward revealing his state as a man, however, remains in his action despite its absence within his deliberations. Surely, the mere absence of the intention of this order does not absolve someone of the responsibility of fulfilling it. True, we have seen that the order of revealing one's state is not absolutely necessary to the act of wearing clothing, and in certain situations it can be set aside (section 5.2.1). Nevertheless, it cannot be set aside simply upon a whim. This man cannot wear women's clothing simply because it is comfortable, and when confronted reply that he in no way directed his action to reveal anything about his state. Whether he directed it or not, it is so directed. Withholding this direction, either in intention or deliberation, does not remove the order from the action. Otherwise, the norm that we should wear clothing that befits our state would be impotent. The order, then, must arise from somewhere besides the agent's intentions and deliberations. The obvious candidate is not nature, as it was for bestiality, but human convention. It is the norm of society itself that clothing is directed to reveal one's state.

Lying is another such action. We have seen that according to Thomas the act of enunciating or speaking is ordered to the end of conveying the truth as one sees it (section 1.3.1). When someone lies, however, she clearly intends no such order but the opposite. Beginning with the goal of deceiving someone, she reasons back to the act of conveying falsehood, which she then sees as accomplished by saying certain words. Nowhere does she reason that she must convey the truth in order to accomplish her goal. Quite the contrary. From where, then, does the act of speaking derive its *per se* order towards conveying the truth? From nature or social convention, it would seem.

Bestiality, lying, and a man wearing women's clothing, then, have an order to an end that is introduced by something besides deliberation and intention. All three bear upon unfitting material. An animal is not in potential to the form of new human life, a false enunciation is not fitting material to convey the truth, and women's clothing is not in potential to reveal the state of being a man. The material is unfitting, however, from an order derived from something beyond deliberation. How, then, are we to account for these actions?

One way to deny the significance of these cases is simply to deny that any order can be found in the actions besides that which deliberation gives to them. If deliberation does not direct sexual activity to new life but rather to pleasure, then only the order to pleasure exists. If a man wears women's clothing in no way as an expression of his state in society, then it has no such order. If someone does not intend to direct his speech to the truth, but rather to falsity, then it has no order to truth.

This approach is certainly common enough in our times, in which the notion of a human nature that could direct actions to an end is largely rejected. We have already seen, however, that Thomas recognizes a human nature, and he thinks that it directs some of our actions, most notably sexual activity. Here is not the place to undertake the refutation of a mechanism that would deny any united human nature capable of directing ourselves and our activities to an end.

But even those who accept human nature, acknowledging for instance that sexual activity is naturally directed to reproduction, might nevertheless question its significance for ethics and the good or evil of human actions. Bestiality does run counter to the natural direction of sexual activity, they might argue, but such natural deficiency does not make it evil. Its evil arises from other causes, such as a psychological fixation upon pleasure. The good and evil of human actions, they will argue, arise from reason, not from nature. A mere natural failure does not make for moral evil, as if wearing earplugs, which inhibits the ear's natural order to hearing, were morally evil.[1]

Physicalism maintains that these actions are morally evil precisely because they oppose some higher order, such as the order of nature. Because this view is so contrary to our contemporary intuitions, however, it will take some development. We will begin by examining error, for it transpires that sin is a particular kind of error.

6.1.2. Evil, Error, and Sin

Aquinas says that moral evil is the evil of actions; more precisely, it is the evil of human or voluntary actions. Thomas portrays three categories of evil—evil, error, and sin—proceeding from the most general to the most specific.

> These three—evil, error, and sin—are related to one another as the more common to the less common. Evil is the most common, for the privation of due form, order, or measure in anything, whether in some subject or in some action, has the notion of evil. But error is some action lacking the owed order, form, or measure. One can say, therefore, that a curved tibia is a bad [malum] tibia, but one cannot say that it is an error (except in an extended way of speaking, in which the effect of error is called an error); rather, the limping is the error. Any act—whether of nature, art or morals—that lacks order may be called an error, but an error is not a sin unless it is voluntary, for an action lacking order is imputed to someone as fault only when it is in his power.[2]

---

1. See Grisez, *Contraception and the Natural Law* (Milwaukee: Bruce Publishing, 1964), 28.

2. *De malo*, 2, 2 (Leonine ed., vol. 23, 33, 123–39). "Quod hec tria, malum, peccatum et culpa, se habent ad inuicem ut communius et minus commune. Nam

The term *malum* (evil or bad) refers to any privation whatsoever, whether it be in sheep, in birds, in human beings, or in actions. But the word error refers only to the evil of actions. Blindness can be called evil or bad but it cannot be called an error, that is, an evil action, for blindness is not the privation of some action. A poor act of healing, on the other hand, can be called bad *(malum)*, and it can also be called an error.

Within the class of error we find sin. As odd as it may sound, then, Jones's act of murder is a certain kind of error. Although we often think of an error as involuntary, as a kind of mistake, what distinguishes sin from other errors is that it is voluntary. This statement, however, is prone to a rather simplistic misinterpretation. Someone might suppose a math teacher merely errs (and does not sin) when she miscalculates accidentally, but when she deliberately miscalculates (to make a point to the students) then she has sinned. Or one might suppose that a comic pianist has sinned when he deliberately misplays a note. Clearly, neither of these are instances of moral evil (or at least they need not be), yet they are voluntary errors. While this interpretation of Aquinas is plainly erroneous (but not sinfully so), it is not evident what is to be said in its place. Surely, a sin is not simply a mistake—of math, music, or whatever else—that someone does deliberately. But then what is it? In what sense is a sin a particular kind of error distinguished by the mark of being voluntary?

What Thomas means is not that a sin is a voluntary error, but rather that a sin is an erroneous voluntary action. "Voluntary" must

malum communius est; in quocumque enim, siue in subiecto siue in actu, priuatio forme aut ordinis aut mensure debite mali rationem habet. Set peccatum dicitur aliquis actus debito ordine aut forma siue mensura carens. Vnde potest dici, quod tibia curua sit mala tibia, non tamen potest dici quod sit peccatum, nisi forte eo modo loquendi quo peccatum dicitur effectus peccati; set ipsa claudicatio peccatum dicitur: quilibet enim actus inordinatus potest dici peccatum uel nature uel artis uel moris. Set rationem culpe non habet peccatum nisi ex eo quod est uoluntarium: nulli enim imputatur ad culpam aliquis inordinatus actus, nisi ex eo quod est in eius potestate." Also see I-II, 21, 2.

not be taken as a modifier of some error, but rather as a defining feature of some kind of action. There is not some kind of error, such as a mathematical error or a musical error, to which "voluntary" is added as an afterthought. Rather there is some kind of action—a voluntary action—that is erroneous. Just as there are medical actions, pedagogical actions, and mathematical actions, and each has its corresponding error, so there are voluntary actions, that is, human actions precisely as human, to which the corresponding error is sin.

Error is best understood in contrast to failure. Not every error is a failure, nor is every failure an error. Jones can aim poorly, performing an error of marksmanship, and yet by luck accomplish his goal of killing Smith, for example, if the bullet kills Smith after ricocheting off the wall. A math student might err in calculation and yet by luck land upon the correct answer. Conversely, a teacher might fail through no fault of her own—without error—because the student is ill prepared. And a doctor might fail to heal because the patient does not follow her directives.

Failure, it seems, is tied to the end product, for a failure is an action that does not attain its endpoint. A doctor fails, for instance, when she does not bring about health. The connection between a failure and its results, however, is clearly restricted by the end to which the action is directed. Not any and every result matters. An act of healing does not become a failure because it does not produce heat, but rather because it does not produce its endpoint of health. A failure, then, is an action that does not accomplish its endpoint, that effect toward which it is directed.[3]

Unlike a failure, an error need not be defective in its endpoint; rather, it is defective in its starting point. If Jones misfires, the problem is not so much the endpoint—for by luck he might attain the death of Smith—but that he does not properly aim the gun. He does not direct the gun, and hence the bullet, toward Smith. The

3. *Summa contra Gentiles* III, 2, no. 6 (Leonine ed., vol. 14, 6).

error, then, lies at the very beginning of the action, not in the endpoint. Indeed, if a failure may be defined as an action that does not accomplish its endpoint, then an error might be defined as an action that lacks the *direction* to the endpoint. Jones's misfire, even if it by luck should attain the endpoint, is actually directed elsewhere. Similarly, a teacher errs when she does not properly direct the subject matter toward the student's learning. When she does provide the appropriate direction but the student fails to learn nevertheless, then the teacher has failed but she has not erred; she provided the direction to the endpoint without attaining the endpoint. An error, then, does not necessarily lack the endpoint, but it does lack the direction to the endpoint. Thomas says, for instance, "Any act lacking direction, whether it be an act of nature, of art, or of morals, can be called an error [*peccatum*]."[4] And again, "Error [*peccatum*] properly consists in an act done for the sake of some end that does not have the required direction to that end."[5]

6.1.3. Agents and Orders

Aquinas's definition of error, "an act done for the sake of some end that does not have the required direction to that end," may seem paradoxical, for if an action is for the sake of some end, then in some manner it must be directed to that end; an error, then, is directed to an end and yet lacks the direction to that end. If Jones shoots and hits the wall rather than Smith, for instance, then his action is a misfire and error only because it is directed to hit Smith and yet not directed to hit Smith. It is directed to hit Smith because he intends to hit Smith, and had he intended to hit the wall, then it

4. *De malo,* 2, 2 (Leonine ed., vol. 23, 33, 134–36). "Quilibet enim actus inordinatus potest dici peccatum uel nature uel artis uel moris." The Latin word *peccatum* that Aquinas uses serves for both "failure" and "error," but here it seems to have more of the sense of "error."

5. I-II, 21, 1. "Quaelibet enim privatio boni in quocumque constituit rationem mali, sed peccatum proprie consistit in actu qui agitur propter finem aliquem, cum non habet debitum ordinem ad finem illum."

might have been an action well done; it is not directed to hit Smith, on the other hand, because Jones does not properly order the action toward the goal.

This conflict of directions arises from a discrepancy between a primary agent and the instrument it moves. The author, for instance, is the primary agent who directs the pen—the instrument—toward the endpoint of written words. Let us suppose that the pen streaks. The author intends to write "foundation," but on account of the streaking she writes only "ation." While she still directs the pen to write "foundation," the pen does not wholly succeed. The pen does not move completely toward the endpoint to which it is directed. The result is a duplicity of direction. On the one hand, the pen is directed to write "foundation," for such is the direction given by the author. On the other hand, the pen lacks the complete direction to "foundation," for on account of the streaking it does not faithfully execute the direction it receives from the author. The pen's action, then, is an error. It is directed toward a certain endpoint yet it lacks that direction.

A similar duality—between what moves toward the endpoint and what is moved to the endpoint—is found in Jones's misfire. On the one hand, he intends to kill Smith with the gun, thereby directing his action to the death of Smith. On the other hand, he does not fully carry out his intention, for he does not properly direct the gun toward Smith. Consequently, his action lacks the order to Smith's death. Jones's misfire, then, is both directed and not directed toward Smith's death. From his interior act of will it is directed to the endpoint, but from the execution of his exterior action it lacks the direction.

Thomas expresses this idea by stating that a defective action involves a failure to be moved by a primary agent.

> The perfection of any active principle depends on the power of the higher active principle, for an agent acts in virtue of a primary agent. Therefore, when an agent remains under the direction of the primary agent, its act is without defect, but if the agent diverts from

the direction of the primary agent then its act will be defective, as is plain in the case of an instrument that diverts from the movement of the agent.[6]

The author is the primary agent that directs to the endpoint; the pen is the instrument that diverts from the direction provided by the author. Similarly, Jones's intention is like a primary agent that directs to the endpoint, for it moves his bodily activity to the endpoint; Jones's external power (of marksmanship) is like the instrument that diverts from the direction provided by intention. In each case the action is directed to the endpoint by the primary agent, while it lacks the direction from the secondary cause or instrument. It follows that an error always arises from some defect in agency.

> Evil in actions [i.e., error] is caused on account of some defect in the principle of the action, either in the primary agent or in its instrument. For example, a defect in the movement of an animal may occur either because of some weakness in the moving power, as in an infant, or because of some defect of the instrument alone, as in limping.[7]

A child who cannot yet walk, or is just learning to walk, errs in his walking at least in part because of the weakness of his legs. Someone who has suffered polio limps (a kind of error in walking) because the instrument (the leg) is defective. In either event, the

6. *Summa contra Gentiles* III, 10, no. 14 (Leonine ed., vol. 14, 27). "Cuiuslibet siquidem activi principii perfectio virtutis ex superiori activo dependet: agens enim secundum agit per virtutem primi agentis. Cum igitur secundum agens manet sub ordine primi agentis, indeficienter agit: deficit autem in agendo, si contingat ipsum ab ordine primi agentis deflecti, sicut patet in instrumento, cum deficit a motu agentis."

7. I, 49, 1. "In actione quidem causatur malum propter defectum alicuius principiorum actionis, vel principalis agentis, vel instrumentalis; [sicut defectus in motu animalis potest contingere vel propter debilitatem virtutis motivae, ut in pueris, vel propter solam ineptitudinem instrumenti, ut in claudis." Also see *Summa contra Gentiles* III, 10, no. 7 (Leonine ed., vol. 14, 26).

error results from some defect in the agency. The primary agent that Aquinas speaks of in this passage—the moving power of the infant—is not primary in the fullest sense, for it is itself moved by another cause, namely, by the desire of the infant to walk. The moving power is called primary only insofar as it moves something else, namely, the leg, which is perceived as an instrument. Clearly, then, our previous examples may also be explained in terms of a defect in agency. Jones errs in shooting the gun because he has poorly developed his capacity to aim, and the pen errs in writing because of some defect in it; perhaps it is low on ink.

Likewise, the natural sexual power inclines to the end of new life and directs the male power of reproduction upon a woman. The action of bestiality deviates from this order, separating itself from the active principle of the power of reproduction; as such, it is a natural error. Similarly, the power of speech directs our speech acts to reveal what is on our minds. Since lying diverts from this order, it opposes the direction of the principal agent, and it is a natural error.

In what way does physicalism think that these natural errors are also sins? The connection is far from clear.

SECTION 6.2. *Voluntary Error*

Are certain natural errors sinful precisely because they are natural errors? So physicalism claims. Its position, however, is far removed from the contemporary worldview. We will begin (section 6.2.1), therefore, by examining the textual basis for physicalism within Aquinas. Second (section 6.2.2), the difficulty raised at the beginning of the last section (6.1.1), namely, that these sins involve some order that is independent of deliberation, will be scrutinized and found inaccurate. The order of nature is not entirely absent from deliberation. Finally (sections 6.2.3, 6.2.4, 6.2.5, 6.2.6, and 6.2.7), the rationale for such sins will be explored.

6.2.1. Textual Foundations

It is difficult to avoid the conclusion that the natural inclinations of our powers, such as the sexual inclination or the inclination behind speech, play a central role in Aquinas's understanding of certain sins. The trouble is in understanding why. Before we turn to this question, however, we should review some of the evidence that natural inclinations underlie the moral character of our actions, beginning with the most famous text, in which Thomas says,

> Because the good has the notion of an end while evil has the contrary notion, all those things to which man has a natural inclination he naturally grasps with his reason as good and consequently as an action to be pursued, while he grasps their contraries as evil and to be avoided. Therefore, the order of the precepts of the natural law follows the order of natural inclinations.[8]

The exact meaning of this text is hotly disputed. Does Thomas mean that we first know the natural inclinations, and thereby know what is good? Or does he mean that we naturally know what is good and thereby come to understand our natural inclinations?[9] In either event, it seems, all agree that at the level of being or ontology, as opposed to the level of our knowing or epistemology, our nature and our natural inclinations affect the character of the human good. As Rhonheimer says, "the moral virtues, nonetheless, are not defined without reference to anthropological truth, that

---

8. I-II, 94, 2. "Quia vero bonum habet rationem finis, malum autem rationem contrarii, inde est quod omnia illa ad quae homo habet naturalem inclinationem, ratio naturaliter apprehendit ut bona, et per consequens ut opere prosequenda, et contraria eorum ut mala et vitanda. Secundum igitur ordinem inclinationum naturalium, est ordo praeceptorum legis naturae."

9. This view is held by Rhonheimer, "Cognitive Structure," 5–6; see also Finnis, "Natural Inclinations and Natural Rights: Deriving 'Ought' from 'Is' According to Aquinas," *Lex et Libertas: Freedom and Law According to St. Thomas Aquinas,* Studi Tomistici 30, ed. Leo Elders and Klaus Hedwig (Rome, 1987), 43–55. For a response, see McInerny, *Aquinas on Human Action,* 184–92.

238 TELEOLOGY

is, to human nature, which is made known and imposes itself as a moral rule by means of reason."[10] Because human beings are not dogs, and they have a power to reason, knowing the truth is a good for them. Because they are not angels, and have a power of reproduction, having children is a good for them. As Thomas says,

> Virtue is a certain disposition of what is perfect. I call something perfect, however, when it is disposed according to nature, from which it is plain that the virtue of anything is said in order to some preexisting nature, namely, when everything is disposed insofar as it is fitting to its nature. Plainly, however, the virtues acquired through human actions, which were discussed above, are dispositions by which someone is fittingly disposed to the nature by which he is a human being.[11]

Another dispute, more central to our concerns, focuses upon the role these inclinations play within a larger picture of the human good. Perhaps, for instance, these natural inclinations are simply raw material that must be formed by the practical insights of reason.[12] Perhaps these inclinations are only secondary in relation to more fundamental inclinations of the will itself.[13] And perhaps

10. Rhonheimer, "Perspective," 501. He emphasizes the importance of "prerational aspects of human nature" for morality in "The Moral Significance of Prerational Nature in Aquinas: A Reply to Jean Porter (and Stanley Hauerwas)," *The American Journal of Jurisprudence* 48 (2003): 253–80.

11. I-II, 110, 3. "Virtus est quaedam dispositio perfecti, dico autem perfectum, quod est dispositum secundum naturam. Ex quo patet quod virtus uniuscuiusque rei dicitur in ordine ad aliquam naturam praeexistentem, quando scilicet unumquodque sic est dispositum, secundum quod congruit suae naturae. Manifestum est autem quod virtutes acquisitae per actus humanos, de quibus supra dictum est, sunt dispositiones quibus homo convenienter disponitur in ordine ad naturam qua homo est."

12. Porter says that prerational nature provides the starting points for practical reason; also, the realities of human sex are like raw materials to be shaped with rational judgments (*Nature as Reason*, 72, 77).

13. Rhonheimer thinks ("Perspective," 510) that natural goods affect moral good and evil insofar as they are goods and ends of *voluntas ut natura*, a position

these inclinations must be set within the context of overall human well-being.[14]

At any rate, it appears that at least sometimes natural inclinations provide the basis for moral species. We have already seen how Aquinas explains the sinfulness of unnatural sexual activity in terms of the order provided by the nature of the power of reproduction.

> Since the end of using the reproductive organs is the generation and education of offspring, every use of these organs that is not proportioned to the generation of offspring, and to their due education, is of itself disordered, for example, every act of these organs outside the union of male and female is manifestly unfit for the generation of children.[15]

> Every voluntary emission of semen is illicit unless it is suitable for the end intended by nature.[16]

Likewise, the sinfulness of lying depends upon the proper object of the power moved by the will.

> Moral acts take their species from two things, namely, from the object and from the end. The end is the object of the will, which is the first mover for moral actions; but the power moved by the will has

also held by Brock, "Natural Inclination and the Intelligibility of the Good in Thomistic Natural Law," *Vera Lex* VI, nos. 1–2 (2005): 57–78.

14. Porter, *Nature as Reason*, 33–82, especially 50.

15. *De malo*, 15, 1 (Leonine ed., vol. 23, 270, 133–41). "Finis autem usus genitalium membrorum est generatio et educatio prolis; et ideo omnis usus predictorum membrorum qui non est proportionatus generationi prolis et debitae eius educationi, est secundum se inordinatus. Quicumque autem actus predictorum membrorum preter commixtionem maris et feminae, manifestum est quod non est accommodus generationi prolis." For a discussion of the relationship between nature and natural law see Benedict Guevin, "Aquinas's Use of Ulpian and the Question of Physicalism Reexamined," *The Thomist* 63 (1999): 613–28.

16. *De malo*, 15, 1, ad 4 (Leonine ed., vol. 23, 271, 225–27). "Omnis uoluntaria emissio seminis est illicita nisi secundum conuenientiam ad finem a natura intentum."

its own object, which is the proximate object of voluntary acts and is related to the act of willing the end as material to form. The virtue of truth, and consequently the opposite vices, consists in manifestation, which is made through some sign. . . . But the proper object of a manifestation or enunciation is truth and falsity.[17]

It is plain, then, that Thomas thinks the sinfulness of at least some actions derives from a kind of natural error done voluntarily. The perplexing question that remains, however, is why this should be so. The evil of murder can be explained because the murderer aims to introduce an order in his actions—the order of subordinating or using another human being—that is opposed to the good of loving others. The person who commits bestiality, on the other hand, does not mean to introduce any order related to new offspring; he simply seeks pleasure. Why, then, should the order to new life have any bearing upon the good or evil of his action? Why should morality be derivative upon nature? Does not morality concern an error or disorder of the will rather than an error or disorder of some natural power? Rhonheimer expresses the sentiment: "'To act against nature' cannot be considered morally evil simply because it is contrary to something 'natural.'"[18]

6.2.2. Deliberation and the Order of Nature

We should remind ourselves that we do not deliberate about performing natural acts but about doing voluntary actions (sections 1.4.2 and 3.3.1). In other words, the sexual activity that concerns the moral life is voluntary sexual activity. It is not activity simply inso-

17. II-II, 110, 1. "Actus moralis ex duobus speciem sortitur, scilicet ex obiecto, et ex fine. Nam finis est obiectum voluntatis, quae est primum movens in moralibus actibus. Potentia autem a voluntate mota habet suum obiectum, quod est proximum obiectum voluntarii actus, et se habet in actu voluntatis ad finem sicut materiale ad formale, ut ex supra dictis patet. Dictum est autem quod virtus veritatis, et per consequens opposita vitia, in manifestatione consistit, quae fit per aliqua signa. . . . Obiectum autem proprium manifestationis sive enuntiationis est verum vel falsum."

18. Rhonheimer, "Perspective," 507. See Janssens, "Norms," 233.

far as it arises from the external power of reproduction; it is this activity insofar as it arises from the will. The will is not concerned to have well ordered biological sexual activity; it is concerned to have well ordered voluntary sexual activity. The error of physicalism to which many are adverse is the error of supposing that mere physical activity is morally good or evil. The exterior action, however, is not mere physical activity; it is physical activity insofar as it arises from the will.

To understand the significance of our natural powers let us return to the analysis of deliberation (sections 3.2 and 3.3). The soldier who wishes to stop the enemy must analyze this goal into its causes, first into the destruction of the bridge, then to the detonation of the bomb, and then to the killing of the child. A similar analysis takes place for bestiality. The person begins by seeking bodily pleasure and then recognizes that he can achieve this goal through engaging the power of reproduction. Of course, he has no interest in reproduction in itself, but he finds that engaging this power is in fact useful for his goal, just as the soldier finds killing the child useful. Rhonheimer makes the point as follows:

> To engage in sexual intercourse and pretend that this act has nothing to do with an act that is by nature procreative means to choose an act in an unreasonable manner. There exist natural teleologies that form a necessary presupposition for the reasonableness of any intentionality with which the corresponding acts are carried out.[19]

Similarly, the person who lies begins with some goal, for example, she wishes to steal money. She sees that this goal may be achieved by deceiving someone, which in turn involves engaging the power of speech, which is ordered to reveal the truth. The liar has no inherent interest in this direction, but she finds it useful; she even relies upon her interlocutor's belief that speech is ordered to truth.

With his reason, then, he who commits bestiality finds it use-

19. Rhonheimer, "Perspective," 505.

ful to direct himself towards new life, or he finds it useful to engage in an activity directed to new life, namely, the activity of using his reproductive organs. This direction does not arise from his own intention, but rather from nature; nevertheless, he seeks this order and this activity, merely as useful. Likewise, the liar finds it useful to direct herself toward the expression of truth, or she finds it useful to engage in an activity so directed, namely, the activity of speech. She herself does not introduce this order, but the nature of the act already has the order. Just as the soldier finds it useful to direct himself and his activity to the death of the child on the bridge, so he who commits bestiality finds it useful to direct himself and his activity to new life and the liar finds it useful to direct herself and her activity toward truth.

At the same time, however, the liar finds it useful to direct her activity to falsity and deception. Indeed, it was this very desire for falsity that led her to seek an action ordered to truth. Her position is not incoherent, for *she* directs her activity towards falsity, and *nature* directs her activity towards truth. Similarly, he who commits bestiality chooses an action directed toward new life—using his sexual organs—but he himself does not choose to direct it toward this end, for he chooses to direct the power of reproduction upon material that is in no way fit for the end. Once again, this decision is not incoherent, for it is nature that directs to new life and he with his intention that directs contrary to new life.

Both of these cases are clear instances of a deliberate and voluntary error. A lie is an error because it is an activity directed to an end that does not realize this direction. Just as the activity of writing is directed to written words, but when carried out with a streaking pen it does not realize this direction, so the activity of speaking is directed by nature to express the truth, but in a lie the activity does not realize this order. Similarly, bestiality is directed to new life by the primary agency of nature but is not directed to new life by the secondary agency of the person acting. The question before us, of course, is not whether these activities are natural errors, but why these natural errors should be morally wrong. Why are these natural errors also voluntary errors? Why are they errors of voluntary actions precisely as voluntary? We are now poised to answer this question.

6.2.3. Rejecting Order

An analogy may illuminate the cases. Suppose Louis seeks the medical assistance of Dr. Clare, who unbeknownst to him is his father's longtime nemesis. Dr. Clare sees her opportunity and prescribes a regimen far from beneficial to Louis; to the contrary, it leads to his deterioration. Does Clare commit an erroneous action of healing? In one sense, it may seem not, for she never intends to bring about Louis's health. An action must first be directed to the end of health before it can be an erroneous act of healing. We would not call a murder an erroneous act of healing, even though it is opposed to health and even if it were performed by a doctor. Like the murderer, Clare never directs her action toward health, so the lack of this order is no defect in her action.

Still, the situation demands further examination. After all, Clare is a doctor and Louis has come to her precisely for treatment, that is, precisely for an act of healing. Clare, then, uses her status as a doctor and Louis's status as a patient as a means to do him harm. The very context of her action, it seems, directs it towards health. When a doctor tells a patient what to do, her action is presumably directed towards his health. From where does it receive this direction? Not necessarily from the doctor, since Clare, for instance, seeks only harm. Rather, the direction seems to arise from the social context. One might say it arises from society or even perhaps from the state, since Clare is licensed by the state as a doctor. Whatever Clare herself intends, the social situation means that her action is directed towards health. To make the parallel with lying and bestiality more complete, we might say that Clare voluntarily chooses to engage her power to heal, a power given to her by the state. Her action, then, is a voluntary error: it is directed by the state towards health; by herself, who is a kind of secondary cause, it is directed towards harm.

When turning to the question of morality we should not let Clare's malicious intentions obscure the matter. Certainly, her action is evil because she seeks to harm. Similarly, a liar might intend to harm the person to whom she lies. But she need not. Indeed, with what we call a white lie, she might intend to help the person. The parallel we wish to draw, then, must exclude the malice of Clare's intention and focus simply upon her voluntary error. Suppose, for instance, in return for payment she writes a prescription for someone who plans to sell the medication on the black market. Her action will likely lead to harm for someone, but she in no way seeks to harm the person she acts upon. Nevertheless, her action appears to be a voluntary error. It is directed to the health of the person by the state, which has designated the activity of writing a prescription as an act directed to health, but it is directed by Clare to no such end.

When Clare gives directions for a treatment to Louis, she uses her power as a doctor, and so her action is directed toward health—by society, not necessarily by herself. If she intends to harm Louis, then she sees fit, in her deliberations, to do so by way of an act of healing, that is, by way of an action directed (by the state) toward health. As she deliberates, she plans to accomplish her goal of harm by way of an act of healing, and so she introduces the order to health. She herself, however, does not perceive the action as good through this order. Indeed, the order to health poses an obstacle to the good that she does seek, for if she realized the order to health, then she could not accomplish her goal. The realization of the order to health, then, is a perceived evil, an obstacle preventing her from achieving the good she desires. She must set aside this order and replace it with another. She must redirect the action, away from health, to some other end. Even if she is simply selling prescriptions for profit, she still sets aside the order to health for the sake of some other order that she prefers. The order to health is an obstacle, for if she were to institute it, then she could not give a prescription to this individual, who has no need for it.

Similarly, if Bruce lies to Bridget in order to deceive her, he chooses to accomplish his goal of deception through an action that is directed toward revealing the truth. The realization of this order to truth, however, is an obstacle to his goal; it is a kind of evil that must be set aside and replaced with another order, an order to falsity. Likewise, he who commits bestiality chooses to accomplish his goal of pleasure by means of an action—using his organs of reproduction—that is directed toward new life; it is so directed by nature, not by himself. In his deliberations, however, he does not perceive the action as good insofar as it is directed to life; rather, it is good insofar as it is directed to pleasure. Indeed, the order to new life is an obstacle to his own goal, for it demands that his action not be directed upon an animal. He chooses, therefore, to set aside the order to new life, as a kind of evil, and replace it with an order of his own. Finally, the man who wears women's clothing chooses to accomplish his goal, whatever it might be, by way of an action directed (by society) to reveal his state. In his own deliberations, however, the action is not good on account of this order but because of some other order. Indeed, the order to reveal his state is an obstacle—preventing him from wearing women's clothing—that must be put aside.

Given this analysis of a voluntary error, it becomes clear why Grisez's example of earplugs is irrelevant (section 6.1.1). We do not choose to engage the power of hearing as a means to achieve some goal. Rather, the power of hearing is passive, always receptive, and earplugs merely reduce this receptivity. There is no question of attempting to use the power of hearing for some contrary purpose that excludes the order to hearing. Indeed, the power of hearing is not voluntarily engaged at all, and the order to its end is in no way seen as useful under the circumstances. Not every instance of inhibiting some natural function, therefore, counts as a voluntary error. We must voluntarily use some power that directs to some end or some material, but we divert that power to some other end or material. We do not usually *choose* to hear (it merely happens), and by using earplugs we do not direct the power of hearing to some other end.[20]

In actions such as bestiality and lying, then, a person chooses an action that is directed—by nature or convention or some such thing—to some end. He does so not on account of this order but in spite of it. Indeed, he perceives this order as an obstacle to be removed. This removal amounts to a kind of error, because the person, as a secondary agent, diverts from the direction provided by the natural inclination. In these actions we find clearly laid out the two fundamental elements of Aquinas's account of the moral species of human action. Each action has two orders. First, the order that the action actually takes on; second, the order that the action should have. When these two orders agree, the action is good; when they conflict, the action is evil. The act of bestiality *should be* ordered to new human life; it *is actually* directed not to this end but to some other, such as pleasure. Since the actual direction does not live up to the direction the action should have, it is evil. The doctor's (Clare's) action should be directed to health; it is directed to harm or to profit or to some such end, to the exclusion of the order to health; as such, it is evil.

We have examined the source of the first order, the order that an action actually takes on, at some length. As executed, it arises from the agent's intention; as conceived, it arises from practical reason linking the real causes available to an agent in order to achieve some end. What of the second order, the order that an action should have? From where does it arise? In some manner from nature and sometimes perhaps from society. We have chosen not to address this problem directly, as it might be the subject of a much

20. For the same reasons, Rhonheimer's example of shavings one's beard is ineffectual ("Perspective," 307). Rhonheimer also seems to think that chewing gum, swimming, and flying are against nature, dubious suppositions at best.

lengthier study. Rather, we have chosen to show how this second order also arises in deliberation and becomes a certain object of intention. The liar deliberates about using a power ordered to conveying the truth. He who commits bestiality deliberates about using a power ordered to new life, and then he intends to use this power. In short, the second order enters into the first.

Nevertheless, in the order of agents—the order of one agent or cause moving another—the second order directs the first. The doctor chooses to engage her power to heal; this power, once engaged, directs her action toward health. The order that an action should have is precisely the order to which some primary agent directs the action. The author directs the pen to write, so that we might say the pen should have been ordered to written words; similarly, the power of healing directs the doctor to heal, so that we say her action should be ordered to health. Again, the power of reproduction directs the action of bestiality toward new life, so that it should be ordered to new life.

The order that the action does have, as opposed to that which it should have, is that to which the person directs his action. He who commits bestiality directs his power of reproduction upon an animal. Since the animal is not fit material for new life, this action cannot take on the order to new life. It might be ordered to pleasure or to some other end, but it cannot be ordered to new life. The order that the action should have, therefore, must be set aside; the agent prefers some other order, whatever it might be. It remains to see why this rejection of the order of nature is a moral evil. Aquinas provides two bases for explaining the evil of these actions. First, by rejecting the order of nature, the person himself becomes evil (section 6.2.4). More profoundly, by rejecting this order he turns from the good and directs himself to some false good or evil (section 6.2.5).

6.2.4. Becoming Evil

In our account of voluntary error, the order to the end that the action has from the primary agent is eliminated as a kind of obstacle, to be replaced with another order. The order from the directing power is rejected as a kind of evil. So what? Why should the rejection of a natural order matter to morality? Why can't we set aside a natural order when it prevents us from realizing some other? Ultimately, because by so doing we are rejecting a human good.

A doctor is good by healing well, a pen is good by writing well, and a good eye sees well. Each has its purpose or function, and each is good by performing its activity well. The activity, when done well, is the realization of the order of a thing to its end. Doctors are ordered to the end of health, and they realize this order by healing well; pens are ordered to written words, an order realized by writing well; and so on. The thing itself is good derivatively, by partaking in the good of the end. Because health is good, doctors are good, insofar as they are ordered to health, an order realized fully in the activity of healing well.

Likewise, human beings are good through an order to human goods. A person is good, for instance, through an order to new human life. This order is found first in the natural inclination to new life, but it is realized fully in activity. Human persons are ordered to the good not merely through natural inclinations; they are ordered through human actions, through acts of the will. Moreover, they are normally directed to the good not simply through interior acts of the will but through exterior actions, those acts of the will that belong directly to some external power and to the will through command, as a directing or primary cause. Someone is ordered to new human life not merely through bodily sexual activity but through voluntary sexual activity. Nor are they fully directed to new human life simply by wanting it or loving it—that is, through interior acts of will—but through the exterior action of engaging the power of reproduction.

He who commits bestiality also engages the power of reproduction. To realize the order to new life, however, the activity of this power must be directed upon material that is fitting, material that is able to bear the form of new life. But this order to new life, which is a human good and makes the person to be good, is seen as an obstacle to the act of bestiality, to the perverse pleasure that the person hopes to gain. He must remove this order, putting another in its place. In short, he sees the order of the human good as a kind of evil.

Once again, the analogy with the doctor is helpful. Precisely as a doctor, Clare is good by being ordered to health, even as a pen is good through an order to written words. This order is fully realized in acts of healing. When she engages the power to heal, either through the doctor and patient relationship or through the state's designation of actions that fall under her healing power, then she must yet direct her activity upon proper material: the correct regimen for Louis or someone truly needing the prescription.[21] If she wishes to direct her action elsewhere, then she must see the order to health, which is her good as a doctor, as an obstacle, since it requires that she direct her activity upon material that she spurns. By committing a voluntary error, then, she positively rejects the order to health, and thereby rejects the good of a doctor. Whatever good she seeks, it cannot be that of being a good doctor, for she has set aside that good as an obstacle, an evil to be supplanted.

Similarly, we direct ourselves to the good of revealing the truth through the activity of speech. When engaging the power of speech, then, we realize this order by directing our speech upon proper material, upon words that truly do reflect the truth. If, for whatever reason, we wish to direct our speech upon improper material, words that do not reflect the truth, then we must see the order to the truth as an obstacle, since it demands we direct our activity elsewhere. The human good of directing ourselves to the truth becomes an evil to be removed.

21. The material of her action, then, might be taken both as the patient acted upon and as the medications that she prescribes.

6.2.5. Turning from the Good

We have considered, to this point, what is effectively only constitutive harm; as usual, the harm of offense is more difficult to grasp (see section 4.3.4). How can we offend against a final cause? Some light might come from an analogy with a woman wronged by her husband. He does not actually damage her good constitutively, except that he takes himself away from her, which might be considered an element of her good. More profoundly, however, he harms her through offense. As his wife, she wishes to be loved by him, to be treated as a good. In effect, she longs that he should direct himself toward her as toward a good. Such also is the desire of love. A man who loves a woman wishes to give himself to her, wishes that she should be the one to whom he and his actions are directed. Adultery, then, is a particularly grievous offense, for the adulterer turns his love away from his wife to another. In contrast, if he should die, then she would lack his love, but she would not be offended against, for he would not have put aside his love for her and replaced it with some other. She would suffer only a constitutive harm and no offense.

She is offended against only by supposition of some prior direction to his love. If he spends time with his associates at work, or if he feeds the hungry in volunteer activity, she is not offended against, even though he has directed himself and his activity toward others. The offense comes only with romantic or sexual love. Why? Because he is her husband, and as such, he is directed toward her in this particularly intimate manner, to give himself bodily to her and to the raising of her children, a giving associated with a corresponding bodily affection. Just as a doctor is the sort of thing directed to the health of others, so a husband is directed to his wife through a bodily giving.

A doctor who plays golf or reads a novel does not offend against the end of health, although she does not order herself, in these activities, to the end of health. She offends against her end only by engaging the activity of healing but misdirecting this activity. She chooses an action directed toward health, but she rejects this order as a kind of obstacle. Similarly, a husband who reads a novel or feeds the hungry does not offend against his wife, although he does not direct himself toward her in these activities. He offends against her only by engaging in the activity that is properly directed to her, most particularly the activity of sexual relations. He chooses an action that is directed by itself to his wife, but he directs it elsewhere. The love of his wife, the giving of himself to his wife, which the order of his action demands, becomes a kind of obstacle, an evil to be rejected and replaced by some other good, namely, by the order to some other woman.

Of course, a husband could offend against his wife simply through neglect, for instance, he might devote himself too much to feeding the hungry, but such offense is much more difficult to pin down. It is offense through inaction rather than through action. Since the husband need not show his wife love at every waking moment, it is difficult to say precisely which failure to act on his part gives the offense. Indeed, the offense comes more from a pattern of inaction than from a single instance of failing to act. What concerns us at the moment is the rejection of his wife's good that is shown in his actions, in actions that are directed to his wife but which he directs elsewhere. Presupposed to this offense is that the husband himself and certain of his actions, are directed by their nature toward his wife and her good. Lacking this supposition, no offense can be given. His acts of sexual relations should be directed to his wife; he chooses to direct them elsewhere.

Likewise, actions such as bestiality or contraception offend against the good of new life only through some prior supposition of the order to new life. Someone who reads a novel does not offend against the good of new life, even though he does not thereby direct himself to it. Only when he engages in the activity that is directed to new life, namely, sexual activity, but rejects this order, finding it as a kind of evil to be replaced, does he offend against new life.

6.2.6. The Evil of Voluntary Error

The evil of voluntary error, then, is twofold. First, it makes the person himself to be evil, for it removes the order the person has to the good. A doctor is good by being ordered to health, but a doctor who rejects this order as a certain obstacle thereby makes herself to be evil, *as a doctor.* Similarly, we are good through the order of our actions—following upon natural inclinations—to various human goods. When we reject the order of an action as a certain evil, an obstacle to be removed, then we take away our own order to the good through which we ourselves become good.

Second, voluntary error is evil insofar as it harms through offense. It rejects the end and so offends against it. Just as a husband who commits adultery must turn away from his wife, rejecting her as a good to which he is directed and substituting some other good, so the doctor who deliberately heals poorly must turn away from health, rejecting this good for some other. He who commits bestiality must turn away from the end of new life, substituting some other good in its place.

When Aquinas wishes to identify the great evil that sets sin apart from all other evil, from mere physical evil or suffering, he turns to these two evils found in sin, that it makes the person himself to be evil and that it turns against God.

> Sin has a greater notion of evil than suffering . . . for two reasons. First, because from the evil of sin, but not from the evil of suffering, someone becomes evil. . . . Second, the evil of sin is properly opposed to the uncreated good itself, for it is opposed to the fulfillment of the divine will, and to the divine love by which the divine good is loved in itself and not only insofar as it is shared by creatures.[22]

22. I, 48, 6. "Culpa habet plus de ratione mali quam poena . . . Cuius est duplex ratio. Prima quidem est, quia ex malo culpae fit aliquis malus, non autem ex malo poenae. . . . Secunda ratio . . . malum vero culpae opponitur proprie ipsi

It is easier to see the harm of offense when it is against a person, such as God or the wronged wife. Nevertheless, we can offend against any good to which we are directed as to an end. Presumably, all such offenses ultimately reduce to offense against some person.

6.2.7. Order and Intention

In the next section (6.3) we wish to show how these sins of turning against nature relate to other sins, sins that follow the pattern of homicide, the evil of which arises not from the rejection of some natural order—or so it seems—but from the use or subordination of other human beings. Before we begin this task, however, one difficulty remains to be addressed. What is the relationship between the order of actions recently examined, such as the order of sexual activity to new life, and a person's intention?

The human good of order is realized not through the intention of the person but through carrying out the activity well. A doctor, for instance, does not have to intend to bring about health, although that may be the ideal. She and her activity are directed to health just so long as she carries out the act of healing upon proper material, as prescribed by her art or by the state's empowering of her. Similarly, someone might speak true words, hoping that the listener does not understand, that is, she might hope that she does not convey the truth (and not thereby intending to deceive). Nevertheless, her action is ordered to the truth.

Again, someone might engage in sexual activity hoping that no new life comes about, as would a fornicator even when he does not use contraception. Still, if he engages his power upon proper material, then he and his activity are directed to new life (although not to the education of new life).[23] This fornicator certainly does not

---

bono increato, contrariatur enim impletioni divinae voluntatis, et divino amori quo bonum divinum in seipso amatur; et non solum secundum quod participatur a creatura."

23. The material is "proper" in one respect, namely, it is a woman, and unfitting in another, namely, she is not the man's spouse.

see the order to new life as a good; it is not a feature of his action that makes it desirable to him. Nevertheless, if he does not contracept, then he does not actively oppose this order. He does not seek to remove this order, as if it were a kind of obstacle. He seeks only to remove the order to the education of new life.

Since sexual activity has other ends besides new life, such as the end of expressing fidelity within marriage, a married couple might engage in sexual activity, which is directed to new life, even though they do not intend to bring about new life but intend merely to express their love for one another. Indeed, they may be aware that their action will not lead to new life, for instance, if the woman is already pregnant or if she is sterile. Nevertheless, they do not reject the order to life as an obstacle to their good. While they do not positively direct themselves (through intention) to new life, neither do they reject this order. They direct themselves to another purpose of sexual activity—expressing their fidelity—while not opposing the order to new life.

There seems to be a difference, however, between the couple that has sexual relations but does not intend to conceive although they recognize the possibility of conception, and the couple that has relations knowing that the woman is sterile, with no possibility of conception. If she is sterile then it seems she cannot possibly be proper material for sexual activity, since she is not able to bear the form introduced by reason, namely, the order to new life.

Aquinas, however, thinks that a man's wife is fit material no matter her state of (involuntary) sterility. Why? Because nature, which is the primary agent directing to new life, directs the activity upon a woman. Nature disregards this or that contingent factor about a woman, such as sterility, for nature can concern itself only with types and not with contingent details. A woman is the type of thing directed to new life; her nature does not change through incidental sterility. But why should sexual activity be directed to the material according to its nature rather than according to its contingent realization in this woman? Because the power that directs to the end is itself a nature; it directs itself upon a corresponding nature. Nature cannot consider the contingent details; it must be directed upon a corresponding nature.

This correspondence between the power that directs and the material to which it is directed is well expressed by Thomas in response to another difficulty. While sexual activity as such is simply directed to the conception of new life, within a larger picture this new life is meant to attain maturity, not only physical maturity but emotional and spiritual as well.[24] According to Thomas, maturity is attained within the context of marriage, for the husband and wife together must bring up the child, each contributing various elements to the overall well-being of the child.[25] For this reason Thomas says that sexual relations must be reserved for marriage, the context suited for bringing the child to maturity.

Nevertheless, Aquinas recognizes that the combination of husband and wife is not absolutely necessary; it is simply the best and most consistent way to bring a child to maturity. Do sexual relations outside of marriage become acceptable, then, when one can see that the conditions are good for bringing the child to maturity, for instance, when a woman is sufficiently wealthy not to need the support of a husband? No, they do not. Aquinas's rationale depends upon the correspondence between the power that directs to the end and the material.

> The act of generation is ordered to the good of the species, which is a common good. While the private good is subject to the directive of each person, the common good must be ordered by law. Therefore, in an act of the nutritive power, which is ordered to the preservation of the individual, anyone can determine for himself what food is appropriate. But to determine in what way the act of generation is

---

24. II-II, 154, 2. The natural inclinations that direct human actions are inclinations of human beings, not of mere natural powers, so that they must be within a rational life (see Rhonheimer, "Cognitive Structure," 32–33).

25. *De malo*, 15, 1 (Leonine ed., vol. 23, 270–71, 142–66).

to be performed does not pertain to just anyone, but to the legislator, whose care it is to direct the begetting of children. Although in some cases of fornication it might happen that the intention of nature with respect to the generation and education of children is salvaged, nevertheless the act is of itself disordered and a mortal sin, for the law does not consider what might happen in some cases but what happens usually.[26]

Since the education of offspring is a common good, the individual couple engaging in intercourse are not sufficient of themselves to direct to this good; they must be directed by nature through the human community that makes matrimonial laws. It does not suffice, therefore, that they have privately agreed to stay together for the purpose of raising the child. They must be united in marriage by the community, which directs to the good of upbringing. Since the law is universal and does not descend to every contingent detail, it directs to the good of maturity by what works best and most consistently. Therefore, the woman, who on Aquinas's view is the material of the act of intercourse, must be married to the man. A

26. *De malo*, 15, 2, ad 12 (Leonine ed., vol. 23, 276, 320–37). "Actus generationis ordinatur ad bonum speciei, quod est bonum commune; bonum autem commune est ordinabile lege: set bonum priuatum subiacet ordinationi uniuscuiusque: et ideo quamuis in actu nutritiue uirtutis que ordinatur ad conseruationem indiuidui unusquisque possit sibi determinare cibum conuenientem sibi, tamen determinare qualis debeat esse generationis actus non pertinet ad unumquemque set ad legislatorem, cuius est ordinare de procreatione filiorum, et etiam Philosophus dicit in II Polit. Lex autem non considerat quid in aliquo casu accidere possit set quid communiter esse consueuit; et ideo licet in aliquo casu possit saluari intentio nature in actu fornicario quantum ad generationem prolis et educationis, nichilominus actus est secundum se inordinatus et peccatum mortale." See also II-II, 154, 2. In "Premarital Sex: The Theological Argument from Peter Lombard to Durand," *Theological Studies* 41 (1980): 643–67, at 654–60, John Dedek discusses the texts where Aquinas faces the objection that sometimes a child may be raised in virtue even outside of marriage. Dedek rejects the interpretation given by Milhaven ("Moral Absolutes," 177) that Aquinas is referring to a positive law that forbids fornication universally. Rather, says Dedek, the natural law is itself analogous to a positive law in that it prohibits what is harmful for the most part.

couple, then, raises a child to maturity not of their own primary agency. Just as a doctor is directed and given the power to heal by the state, so a couple is directed and given the power to raise children through marriage. It follows that a woman does not become fitting material based upon some contingent factors that would allow her to bring the child to maturity by herself. She is fitting material only by the universal and general feature of being married to the man. As law directs universally, so the material is fitting by a general feature.

Similarly, the nature that moves sexual activity to new life directs upon the sort of thing that is able to take on new life, namely, a woman. Unlike reason, nature cannot consider all the details that might make this or that woman fit or unfit for new life. Therefore, the action retains its order to new life as long as it is directed upon a woman, even if that woman happens to be sterile. When a woman is sterile, then, a couple need not set aside the order to new life. They can still have sexual relations for other good purposes, for which the order to new life is not an obstacle to be removed. That order remains even though they themselves do not seek it.

SECTION 6.3. *Universal Teleology*

Apparently, we find within Aquinas two diverse accounts of sin existing side-by-side. On the one hand, some actions are evil because they involve subordinating one person for the sake of some further end (chapter 4). On the other hand, some actions are evil because they oppose some higher order, such as the order of nature (sections 6.1 and 6.2). How do these two kinds of sins relate to one another? Can they be in any way united? On the face of it, it would seem not, but it is the telos of this section to see how they might be.

6.3.1. Indefinite Locomotion

We have seen that when we perform some exterior action, whether physical or merely mental, we engage some external power with our wills (sections 1.4.2 and 3.3.1). In sexual activity, for instance, we choose to use the power of reproduction. In lying, we choose to use the power of speech. In solving a math problem, we choose to use the power of the intellect. But when Jones kills Smith, what external power does he engage? There is no power of killing. Rather, Jones chooses to use what Aquinas calls the locomotive power, which is a kind of Jack-of-all-trades. It is simply the power to move about, the power to move our bodies. Usually, we thereby use certain instruments to accomplish our goals, even as Jones moves his finger in order to fire the gun in order to kill Smith. Indeed, when we engage other powers we often do so by way of the locomotive power. We engage the power of reproduction only by moving our body in certain ways, and we engage the power of speech by moving our mouths in certain ways.

Does the power of locomotion itself have some telos? Nothing more distinct, it seems, than bodily movement, which movement can be used to achieve a whole host of effects. Most of our powers have a definite end, as the intellect is directed toward understanding the truth, the power of speech is directed to reveal the truth, and the power of reproduction is directed to new life. The power to move about, however, is directed to nothing more definite than movement. It can involve a variety of bodily activities, and as we have seen, its action can be extended through a variety of effects (section 1.4.1). Of itself, however, it is not directed to any particular activities nor to any particular effects. When we engage the power of locomotion, then, we do not have to contend with some inherent order that we must respect. In contrast, when the doctor engages the power to heal, she must respect the order of the state that gave her the power; when an individual engages the power of reproduction, he must respect the order that nature has placed in the action, for this order is itself a human good. When Jones pulls the trigger, on the other hand, there is no inherent order of this particular bodily activity that directs it to any definite end.

Some have sought to supply this want of a definite end by way of human practices. Flannery, for instance, suggests that the craniotomy receives a telos from the human practice of medicine.[27] Indeed, we have used the practice of medicine as an analogy by which to understand sins against some inherent order. Still, it is rather odd to explain the evil of the craniotomy by way of the practice of medicine. Is there not something evil about the action of itself, whether practiced within the context of medicine or otherwise? Furthermore, it is difficult to imagine under what practice we will fit Jones's action of murder. Under the practice of marksmanship?

Yet without human practices must we say that some human actions—indeed, the vast majority of human actions—have no definite telos? When we engage some power such as the power of reproduction, or when we engage some social power of the community, such as the power inherent in wearing clothes to reveal one's state, then our actions have a definite end independent of our intention that we can choose to realize or to reject. But for other actions, it seems, no more definite telos presents itself than physical change. Is it for this reason that the account of sins against our neighbor appears so distinct from the account of sins against some inherent order?

A desire for unity and simplicity might send us in pursuit of some universal teleology. If we cannot use the teleology of human practices, then perhaps some other source might provide a definite end for actions that seem to have no direction beyond locomotion. In fact, we will discover this universal teleology much closer to home. We need not search in the diversity of the locomotive power, nor in human practices; the interior power of the will itself provides the telos.

6.3.2. Two Orders

A careful analysis of actions such as speech reveals a twofold order. On the one hand, there is an order from the power or capacity, di-

27. Flannery, *Acts Amid Precepts*, 183–85.

recting the action to some end; this is the order the action should have. On the other hand, there is an order from the agent's deliberations and intentions directing the action to some proximate end and material; this is the order the action takes on. The act of adultery, for instance, has an order directing the activity toward new life and the education of that life; it also has an order directing the power of reproduction upon this particular woman, who belongs to somebody else. The first order arises from nature, as if from a primary agent. The second order arises from the agent's own deliberation and intention, and is like a secondary agent that fails to be moved by the primary agent. The proper role of teleology in these actions, then, is to provide the order to the end that reason aims to introduce, the order that an action should have and the order toward which the material must relate *per se*.

6.3.3. The Teleology of Harm

Can we find this teleology in actions such as murder or the craniotomy? Can we, in short, explain all sin, murder as well as bestiality, by way of some normative teleology from which the action falls short? Yes, indeed. We should not look to any external power, however, but to the interior power of the will. Murder is wrong because we should love other people as subjects of the good, with a love of friendship, and not with the love of utility. But why? That is, why should we love others with friendship? What has set the standard, the telos, that we should love others with friendship? Since love is an act of the will, it should be no surprise that the telos derives from the will itself. We are directed by our nature to love others with a love of friendship. This teleology does not arise from the power of reproduction, the power of speech, or from any other external power; rather, it arises from the will itself, which is naturally inclined to love others with friendship. Our acts of will, then, are directed toward the good of others, but when we act upon others as useful, then we exclude the love of friendship.

Once again the action has two orders, one from a primary agent directing to an end and another from the agent's own deliberation and intention. The power of the will directs toward the love of others, acting as a kind of primary agent; the person himself, through his deliberations, directs to this or that end. In the act of killing, for instance, the natural inclination of the will directs the murderer to love his victim with friendship. In his own deliberations, however, he directs his action to his victim's death, seen as useful to achieve some further end. The structure parallels sexual sins.

The doctor, precisely as doctor, can reject her own good, the order to health. The order to public health is brought forward by her own use of her capacity as a licensed doctor, but she perceives it as an obstacle to be removed, thereby rejecting her own good, as doctor, and turning also from health as a common good. By turning from her direction to the good, she essentially attacks the value of this good. It does not cease being a common good simply because she has rejected it, for many besides her are directed toward it. Nevertheless, she ceases to partake in it, and it ceases to be a common good that includes her.

We can provide a parallel account of the evil of harming others. When one person harms another, he turns from her good because he rejects his own order to her good. We are naturally directed toward others as to a subject of the good, as toward one for whom we will to share the good. When we act upon others, then, directing our will upon them as upon some subject of action, our action is teleologically directed to their good. Nevertheless, we can refuse to realize this direction in our action. The order to their good can be seen as an obstacle, preventing us from achieving some other good. When we choose to harm, then we perceive some useful good in the act of harming, a useful good that turns us away from the good to which our will prompts us, namely, the love of others.

Recall that the offense of adultery presupposes a teleological order of a husband and his actions to the good of his wife (section 6.2.5). For this husband, actions of sexual intercourse are directed to an expression of giving himself bodily to his wife; when he chooses to direct his sexual activity upon another woman, he also chooses to reject the order to his wife. He sees the order to his wife as an obstacle, an evil to be removed. He offends against her because he rejects her good and substitutes some other.

Similarly, the offense involved in using another person presupposes a teleological order to share the good with her. Any time that we directly act upon another person, we intend to introduce some change in her. In our action, then, we must direct her to some good or other. If the change we introduce is in fact for her own good, or at least neutral, then we can seek to order her to the common good, that is, we can seek to share the good with her. If the change we introduce is her evil, then we must see this change as good for something besides her partaking in the common good; we must see her as in some manner useful for some other good besides the common good. From a natural inclination of our will, however, we are directed toward her as toward a part of the common good, to share the good with her. When we do evil to her, this order to her good becomes a kind of obstacle, an evil to be removed on the way to our goal. We must reject her good as a sharing in the common good and substitute some other good. As the husband offends against his wife, so we offend against those we harm.

The soldier who shoots the child seeks to introduce in her the change of death. Since this change is not her good, he cannot direct her, in his action, to partake in the common good. He must direct her to some other end. Consequently, the order to share the good with her poses a certain obstacle that would, if instituted, prevent him from using the child. He must reject the order to her good and substitute some other.

The other soldier destroys the bridge but does not aim to bring about any change in the child, although he foresees the change of death. He need not, then, seek to order her to any good, whether to partake in the common good or to use her for some further end. The order to share the good with her, that order presupposed to any offense, need not necessarily arise. Just as the husband who feeds the hungry does not offend against his wife, for the action that he chooses is not directed toward giving himself bodily to her, so the soldier does not necessarily offend against the child, for the action that he chooses is not directed to order her one way or the other. He need not choose to order her to some further end; he need not choose to reject the order of her sharing in the common good.

Both soldiers bring about constitutive harm to the child, for both bring about her death. The soldier who shoots the child, but not the other soldier, harms her by offense. He rejects her good, presented to him in the order of his action, and substitutes some other. Although the other soldier does not actually seek the good of the child, he need not turn from her good as if it were a certain evil to be overcome.

All human actions, then, even those that engage merely the power of locomotion, are good or evil in relation to some teleology. Sins such as murder do indeed fall short of some end to which they are directed, namely, the end of sharing the good with others, an end derived from the will. The very nature of the locomotive power is distant from a particular teleology. Nevertheless, the power underlying the locomotive power, namely, the will itself, has a definite direction to an end, namely, to the human good. When the will turns to act upon another human being, then it naturally seeks the good of that person; consequently, actions arising from the will and directed upon this person must realize this order. Since using another is opposed to the love of friendship, acts of using human beings are natural errors of the will, failures to realize the order implemented by reason.

The role of a natural teleology is to set a standard for our actions, to determine the order of reason, the order that an action should have. In all actions, this teleological order arises. In some actions, it arises through engaging some other power, such as the power of reproduction, which is ordered to new life. In other actions, it arises through the will itself, which is directed to the common good.

As we have seen, all actions have another order as well. Not only is there some order that an action should have; there is an order that an action does have. Teleology enters into the order that an action should have; does it enter into the other order as well? We have suggested otherwise. The order that an action actually takes on depends, in execution, upon intention and, as conceived, upon practical reason using the causes in the world around us for some end. Some thinkers, however, have attempted to insert teleology into the order that an action takes on. They have suggested that I-II, 18, 7 provides a teleology that serves what might be called a categorizing or logical role. We turn to this teleology in the final section (6.4) of this chapter.

SECTION 6.4. *Subordinate Species*

In I-II, 18, 7, Aquinas speaks of a *per se* order between an action— or, more precisely, its object—and the end intended by the agent, for instance, fighting well is *per se* ordered to the end of victory. The text implies an order to an end inherent to an action, perhaps a kind of teleology of the action. Does he use this order as we have seen him use it for sexual sins, as a standard that the action must live up to? It would seem not. Rather, this "teleology" plays what might be called a logical or categorizing role. It serves to place the species of an action within a more general category.

In the previous article, I-II, 18, 6, Aquinas distinguished between the species of the exterior action, taken from its object, that is, the *materia circa quam,* and the species of the interior act of will, taken from the further end intended. When someone steals in order to give to the poor, for instance, the exterior act of stealing has its species from the object taken, and the interior act of will takes its species from the further goal intended, namely, giving to the poor. Aquinas notes that the species taken from the end is more formal, so that someone who steals in order to commit adultery is more an adulterer than a thief. Having identified these two distinct

species, Aquinas proceeds in 18, 7, to investigate their logical relationship. He first makes what appears to be the teleological observation already noted above:

> The object of the exterior act can relate in two ways to the end of
> the will, either as *per se* ordered to the end, even as fighting well is
> *per se* ordered to victory, or as *per accidens* ordered, as taking what
> belongs to another is ordered *per accidens* to giving alms.[28]

These diverse orders, either *per se* or *per accidens*, give rise to two
distinct logical relationships. On the one hand, when the action relates *per accidens* to the end, then the species of the exterior action
is logically disparate from the species of the interior action. When
the two relate *per se*, on the other hand, then

> The specific difference which is from the end is more general while
> the difference which is from the object *per se* ordered to such an end
> is—in relation to the species from the end—[more] specific.[29]

In other words, it appears that this *per se* order between the object of the exterior action and the end of the will, serves to define a
genus/species relationship. The species from the end is generic,
while the species from the object falls under it as a more specific difference under a genus.

If I-II, 18, 7, truly expresses a natural teleology, then how important is this teleology in Aquinas's ethics?[30] Is it as central as the
normative teleology discussed in the last sections (6.2 and 6.3)?

---

28. I-II, 18, 7. "obiectum exterioris actus dupliciter potest se habere ad finem
voluntatis, uno modo, sicut per se ordinatum ad ipsum, sicut bene pugnare per se
ordinatur ad victoriam; alio modo, per accidens, sicut accipere rem alienam per
accidens ordinatur ad dandum eleemosynam."

29. "differentia specifica quae est ex fine, est magis generalis; et differentia
quae est ex obiecto per se ad talem finem ordinato, est specifica respectu eius."

30. Part of the difficulty posed by I-II, 18, 7, is identifying the precise nature
of the *per se* order. Unfortunately, Aquinas provides only the single example of
fighting well for victory. Long suggests implausibly that an action is *per se* ordered to the end when it is a necessary means; see Long, *Teleological Grammar*,

6.4.1. Self-Defense

Following Long, Jean Porter has suggested that the *per se* order elides the means into the end, so that the means no longer provides any independent moral characterization.[31]

> If the object is intrinsically related to the end, we may elide [the two] in describing and evaluating the overall action; otherwise, they represent two distinct components of one action, each of which carries an independent moral significance.[32]

Steven Long himself thinks that I-II, 18, 7, provides "a foundational teaching without which the other texts will be misunderstood."[33]

If this teaching of the means being subsumed and characterized by the further end is so central, then we should expect to find the analysis of 18, 7, permeating the moral thought of Aquinas, especially in the *Secunda secundae*. Do we? Long himself provides the

---

27; see also Porter, *Nature as Reason*, 301. Aquinas's single example in I-II, 18, 7, does not fit this interpretation, for fighting well is not a necessary means to victory, as when one army far outnumbers another. More plausibly, Rhonheimer suggests the *per se* order is connected to an action's proper effect ("Perspective," 484): "'to fight' itself is incomprehensible—it simply doesn't make sense—without a reference to 'victory' as its end." Fighting is defined as a struggle or an attempt. It is one of those rare verbs that seems to have "an attempt to" built into it. To fight is not to introduce some form, but to attempt to introduce some form, namely, the overcoming of one's opponent. Similarly, to investigate is not to discover something, but to attempt to discover something. We might say, then, that investigating well is ordered *per se* to discovering something. This minimalist interpretation also fits the only other example that I can find of Aquinas describing a *per se* order of a human action (in the order of execution) that is independent of intention, namely, the *per se* relation between publicly sinning and leading others into sin (see II-II, 43, 1, ad 4, and I-II, 73, 8). Insofar as a sin is public, it seems that its proper effect is that others are made aware of it. This awareness of a possible act of sin, says Aquinas, is one manner in which we can lead others to sin.

31. See Long, *Teleological Grammar*, 41–43, and Porter, *Nature as Reason*, 299–303.

32. Porter, *Nature as Reason*, 299.

33. Long, "Response to Jensen," 103. See also his *Teleological Grammar*, 25–31.

single example of self-defense.[34] This example, however, does not withstand scrutiny.

Porter and Long claim that the killing in justified self-defense is chosen as a means to the end of self-defense. Furthermore, sometimes this act of killing is *per se* ordered to the end, just as fighting well is *per se* ordered to victory. As such, the species of killing falls under the species of self-defense, as a difference under a genus. Since self-defense is inherently good, the killing that falls under it must also be good. At other times, the act of killing is not *per se* ordered to the end of self-defense, and as such it provides its own disparate species, which is evil. This interpretation depends upon end-intention, a view that has been discussed above both in general and for Aquinas's article on self-defense (sections 2.1.1 and 2.2.2). But even if we should grant end-intention, this reading faces difficulties.

6.4.2. Failure to Give Species

The primary difficulty is that Thomas himself does not state it. In the article on self-defense, he never mentions the principle that a means, when *per se* ordered to the end, falls under the species of the end. Indeed, he never says that killing is *per se* ordered to self-defense. To the contrary, the brunt of his argument is the polar opposite: he shows that killing is related *per accidens* to self-defense, and as such, it does not give species.[35]

---

34. Porter as well adopts this reading of Aquinas on self-defense (*Nature as Reason*, 301–2).

35. Long suggests that in the reply to the fourth objection Aquinas states that killing relates *per se* to self-defense ("Brief Disquisition," 61; *Teleological Grammar*, 49). See also Porter, *Nature as Reason*, 297; Flannery, *Acts Amid Precepts*, 187. Unfortunately, Aquinas never speaks of a *per se* order; rather, he speaks of something being "necessarily ordered." Aquinas himself does not link a necessary order with a *per se* order; he says, for instance, that an effect can follow accidentally upon a *per se* effect, "in one way, because it has a necessary order to the effect" (*Sententia Metaphysicae*, book 5, lect. 3, no. 789 [Taurini-Romae: Marietti, 1935], 260). "Uno modo, quia habet ordinem necessarium ad effectum.") Even if

Aquinas begins with the principle that what is outside intention does not give species, since it is *per accidens*. In the light of 18, 7, a novel meaning of species, and what falls outside of species, must be adopted. In 18, 7, Aquinas states that the species from the object falls under the species from the end, as the more specific under a genus. Both the object of the exterior action and the end of the will provide a species. The *per se* order between the two does not eliminate one of the species, but merely defines the logical relation between them. If killing is ordered *per se* to self-defense, for instance, then the complete action takes its genus—self-defense—from the end intended but still receives the narrower species—of killing—from the object of the exterior action, which serves as a means. In contrast, in 64, 7, the killing does not give species—whether narrower or broader—because it is *per accidens*.

Long claims that Aquinas refers to the manner in which a defining species is *per accidens* in relation to the genus.[36] The difference "rational," for instance, is accidental in relation to the genus "animal." Likewise, the difference of "killing" or "lethal" is accidental in relation to the genus of "self-defense." These defining differences do not give species to the genus. "Rational" is not part of the definition of "animal"; likewise, "killing" is not part of the genus of "self-defense." In this manner, then, we can say that the killing, which provides the narrower species, does not give species, since it is *per accidens* in relation to the more general species from the end.

The statement that the killing "does not give species," however, seems a bit strong. The means of killing does not give species to the genus, but it does provide some species; indeed, it provides the very species under consideration, namely, killing in self-defense.

we should grant that Aquinas, in this reply, identifies a necessary order with a *per se* order, the text still does not say that killing is necessarily ordered to self-defense; rather, it says that *the act from which killing follows* is necessarily ordered to self-defense. Aquinas seems at pains to distinguish the action that is necessarily ordered and the killing; the killing is not the action necessarily ordered, but follows upon it.

36. Long, *Teleological Grammar*, 43.

The difference of "rational," since it relates *per accidens* to the genus "animal," does not give species to "animal." It does, however, relate *per se* to "human being," thereby giving species.

> Not only that which belongs to something by reason of its genus, but also that which belongs to it by reason of its species applies to a thing *per se*, for example, rational and nonrational are in "animal" *per se* by reason of its [various] species, although not by reason of the genus "animal," for an animal, insofar as it is an animal, is neither rational nor nonrational.[37]

Similarly, the difference of "killing" or "lethal" relates *per accidens* to the genus "self-defense." As such, it does not give species to the more general act of self-defense, but certainly it does give species to the more particular act of "lethal self-defense," which is the very act Aquinas is discussing. Why, then, would Aquinas make the overly strong statement that the difference of lethality does not give species? Should he not have said, if he were applying the doctrine of 18, 7, that the killing provides the narrower species? In 18, 7, itself Aquinas never says that the narrower species does not give species. To the contrary, he says, "A difference that divides some genus, and *constitutes* the species of the genus, *per se* divides it [emphasis added]."[38]

Does Aquinas ever say that what is *per accidens* fails to give species because it merely gives the more determinate species? To the contrary, using words nearly identical to 64, 7, he denies the possibility: "That which is outside intention is *per accidens* so that it cannot be a specific difference."[39]

37. *De malo*, 2, 4 (Leonine ed., vol. 23, 39, 170–76). "Dicimus enim per se conuenire alicui non solum quod conuenit ei ratione sui generis, set etiam quod conuenit ei ratione sue speciei: sicut rationale et irrationale per se inest animalibus ratione suarum specierum, licet non ratione huius generis quod est animal; non enim animal in quantum est animal est rationale neque irrationale."

38. I-II, 18, 7. "Differentiae dividentes aliquod genus, et constituentes speciem illius generis, per se dividant illud."

39. II-II, 110, 1. "Id enim quod praeter intentionem est, per accidens est; unde non potest esse specifica differentia."

6.4.3. Per Accidens

Suppose we grant, contrary to Aquinas's typical manner of speaking, that the narrower species does not give species. It is still difficult to find I-II, 18, 7, within II-II, 64, 7. In 18, 7, Aquinas distinguishes two cases: first, the object relates *per se* to the end, in which case the species from the object falls under the species from the end (and so, we stipulate, does not give species); second, the object relates *per accidens* to the end, in which case the two species are entirely disparate, one not falling under the other. In the second case, there is no manner—even in some unusual extended sense—in which the species from the object fails to give species. If Aquinas were applying the teaching of 18, 7, to self-defense, then we should expect him to distinguish between these two cases, since the difference between the two determines whether or not the killing involved in self-defense gives species, a point on which Aquinas's justification of self-defense hinges.

Rather than distinguish between the two cases, Aquinas gives a universal principle, namely, that whatever is outside intention is *per accidens* and so fails to give species. Worse yet, his universal principle is consistent with neither of the two cases of 18, 7. In 64, 7, Aquinas's principle links what is *per accidens* with a failure to give species. In 18, 7, the first case links what is *per se* with a failure to give species (given our generous suppositions); the second case links what is *per accidens* with the giving of an independent species. The application of 18, 7, to 64, 7, appears far from manifest.

One might attempt to reconcile the two texts by way of a threefold ambiguity in the usage of *per accidens* in relation to the means. First, *per accidens* can refer to (PA1) all means insofar as they are all outside intention (granting end-intention); second, it can refer to (PA2) just some particular means, namely, those that are not *per se* ordered to the end, as stealing is not ordered to giving alms; finally, it can refer to (PA3) just some particular means, namely, those that are *per se* ordered to the end. The third meaning is most confusing,

Table 1. Uses of *per accidens* in Relation to the Means

Name	*How it arises*	*What it applies to*	*Implications for species*
PA1	From being outside intention	All means, since the means are never intended	None
PA2	Because it *is not* inherently ordered to end	A subset of means	Gives own independent species
PA3	Because it *is* inherently ordered to the end	A subset of means	Does not give species (i.e., species is subsumed)

since one and the same means is *per se* ordered to the end but *per accidens* related to the species from the end. Even when this confusion is cleared up, however, the potential confusion with PA2 is unavoidable. For PA2, the means give their own independent species, for instance, when someone commits adultery in order to steal, then the act of adultery gives its own species and is not subsumed under theft. In contrast, for PA3 the means do not give species, but rather their species is subsumed under the species from the end. If we want to know whether a means gives species, then, it is hardly illuminating to say that the means are *per accidens* in relation to the end intended, since that can mean either that they do give their own species (for PA2) or that they do not (for PA3).

If Aquinas wishes to make himself at all clear, then he must forestall this obvious confusion by (1) spelling out the diverse meanings of *per accidens* and then (2) indicating his particular usage in this argument. Does he? Certainly, he does not spell out the diverse meanings. He does, however, indicate which usage of *per accidens* he has in mind. If Porter and Long are correct, then Aquinas is using PA3 and he should tell us so by saying that the means are *per se* ordered to the end. But he does not. Rather, he indicates that by *per accidens* he means PA1, since only PA1 derives from being outside intention. Of course, on Long's reading all means are outside intention, and therefore all means are PA1. PA1, then, tells us nothing about whether or not the means gives species.

Long seems to think it mysterious that others have not grasped the "clear teaching of ST, II-II, q. 64, a. 7,"[40] and he searches for explanations of their failure.[41] Perhaps it is, as Long says, "difficult to break out of the *gestalt* of one's own reading."[42] But need we search that far? When Aquinas fails to mention the main principle that he wishes to use, when he instead begins with a principle that looks like its contradiction, it is little wonder that so few have grasped his meaning. Do we find, then, as Long would have it, an application of I-II, 18, 7, within Aquinas's account of self-defense? It seems unlikely.

6.4.4. Pilsner on Subordinate Species

Aquinas has dedicated an entire article to the genus and species relationship generated by this *per se* order. One might expect, then, that the notion of a *per se* order independent of intention would be fundamental in his account of the species of human actions. So one might expect. Nevertheless, one will search in vain for explicit applications of this doctrine in Aquinas's account of the species of various actions.[43] Indeed, at times he seems to disregard it. Adultery is surely not related *per se* to stealing, no more than it is to pre-

---

40. Long, *Teleological Grammar,* 63.

41. Long, *Teleological Grammar,* 51.

42. Long, *Teleological Grammar,* xv.

43. One might hope to find an explicit application in Aquinas's treatment of superstition, in II-II, 92, 2, for he does mention the dual specifying roles of object and end. Unfortunately, his application is entirely contrary to I-II, 18, 7; the object provides the genus and the end provides the species.

TELEOLOGY 273

serving one's own life, yet Thomas is willing to place one under the other, as a species under a genus.

> Vices have their species from the proximate end, while from the remote end they have their genus and cause. For example, when someone commits adultery so that he might steal, the species of adultery is taken from the proper end and object, but the ultimate end shows that adultery arises from theft and it is contained under theft as an effect under its cause or like a species under its genus.[44]

The Angelic Doctor might well be speaking loosely here, but his willingness to speak loosely, in one of the few instances where he discusses this genus and species relation, indicates that this doctrine may not be central to his account of this specification of human actions. Pilsner suggests that the genus and species relationship described here does not refer to a strict essential relationship of predication, as a dog is a species of animal, but rather to a relationship of general causality.[45] Aquinas himself makes this distinction in his treatment of legal justice as a general virtue.

> Something may be called general in two ways. In one way, by predication, even as animal is general with respect to human beings and horses and others of this kind. In this way, what is general must be essentially the same as that for which it is general, for the genus pertains to the essence of the species and falls in its definition. In another way, something is called general according to power, as a universal cause is general with regard to all its effects, for example, the sun is general to all bodies, which are illuminated or changed through its power. In this way, what is general need not be the same

44. II-II, 11, 1 ad 2. "Vitia habent speciem ex fine proximo, sed ex fine remoto habent genus et causam. Sicut cum aliquis moechatur ut furetur, est ibi quidem species moechiae ex proprio fine et obiecto, sed ex fine ultimo ostenditur quod moechia ex furto oritur, et sub eo continetur sicut effectus sub causa vel sicut species sub genere, ut patet ex his quae supra de actibus dicta sunt in communi." See also I-II, 75, 4.
45. Pilsner, Specification, 227–33.

in essence as those for which it is general, for a cause and its effect are not of the same essence. From what has been said, legal justice may be called general in this way, by a general power, insofar as it orders the acts of other virtues to its end, which is to move all the other virtues by way of command. Just as charity may be called a general virtue insofar as it orders the acts of all the virtues to the divine good, so legal justice is general insofar as it orders the acts of all virtues to the common good.[46]

As the text indicates, Thomas has the same doctrine, at the supernatural level, for the virtue of charity. Charity is the form of the other virtues, because it is like the primary agent that moves the others to act.[47] This same analysis might well apply to the remote end intended discussed in 18, 7: it acts as a kind of primary agency, directing the immediate action. As such, it plays a kind of generic role, at least when there exists a *per se* order between the two ends. In I-II, 18, 7, itself Aquinas justifies the genus and species relationship by way of the more universal agency associated with the remote end.

Pilsner also suggests that Aquinas does not intend this analysis to apply to action types in general but rather to actions as they are realized in the concrete.[48] If we consider theft by itself, or killing by

46. II-II, 58, 6. "Generale dicitur aliquid dupliciter. Uno modo, per praedicationem, sicut animal est generale ad hominem et equum et ad alia huiusmodi. Et hoc modo generale oportet quod sit idem essentialiter cum his ad quae est generale, quia genus pertinet ad essentiam speciei et cadit in definitione eius. Alio modo dicitur aliquid generale secundum virtutem, sicut causa universalis est generalis ad omnes effectus, ut sol ad omnia corpora, quae illuminantur vel immutantur per virtutem ipsius. Et hoc modo generale non oportet quod sit idem in essentia cum his ad quae est generale, quia non est eadem essentia causae et effectus. Hoc autem modo, secundum praedicta, iustitia legalis dicitur esse virtus generalis, inquantum scilicet ordinat actus aliarum virtutum ad suum finem, quod est movere per imperium omnes alias virtutes. Sicut enim caritas potest dici virtus generalis inquantum ordinat actus omnium virtutum ad bonum divinum, ita etiam iustitia legalis inquantum ordinat actus omnium virtutum ad bonum commune."

47. *De veritate*, 14, 5 (Leonine ed., vol. 22, 452–53, 131–66).

48. Pilsner, *Specification*, 234–38.

itself, then the remote end intended is accidental and does not belong to the species or essence of the action. If we consider these actions in concrete instances, as willed in particular situations, then
they take on an additional species from the remote end, and Aquinas is willing to consider this species as more general, insofar as it is
a cause that impresses its order and character in the proximate end.

6.4.5. The Role of Teleology

What role, then, does teleology play in the specification of human
actions? First, it sets a standard to which actions must conform
(section 6.3.2). The teleology of sexual activity, for instance, sets
the standard of an order to new life. One who voluntarily engages
the sexual power must direct his activity upon material able to bear
this order. If he directs his activity elsewhere, as in the act of bestiality, then he perceives the order to new life as an obstacle that must
be removed in his pursuit of his own goals (section 6.2.3). Properly speaking, teleology refers to the order that directs an activity to
an end. The realization or the failure of this order is not typically
called teleology. The act of bestiality, for instance, fails to realize
the order to new life. This actual order of the action, however, does
not express the telos of the action; it does not express that to which
the action is directed; indeed, it does not express an order at all,
but the falling short of an order. The marital act, on the other hand,
does realize the order to new life, but once again this actual order
does not express the telos of the action; it expresses the fulfillment
of this telos. In other words, teleology is primarily directive.

This directive teleology in some manner arises from nature, as
the order to new life arises from the nature of sexual activity and
the power of reproduction (section 6.2.1). The precise role that nature plays, whether it be through the will, through an overall fulfillment of human life, or some other means, has not been our concern; to recognize the good and evil of actions, it suffices to see
that actions are directed to some end from some source beyond the
agent's intention.

The teleological order of reason is like a primary cause moving the person and his actions, which are like secondary causes (section 6.1.3). The secondary cause is fulfilled and completed when it follows the movement and impulse of the primary cause; it is defective when it diverts from the primary cause. Our voluntary actions, then, are fulfilled by living up to the standard set by teleology; they are defective when we set aside the standard, seeing it as an obstacle to our own goals. This standard is the very measure of goodness, for we are good by being ordered to the end and evil by failing from this order (section 6.2.4). Indeed, we respect the good by ordering ourselves to it, and we harm the good through offense when we reject the order (section 6.2.5).

Teleology is universal in human actions. Even those actions analyzed previously, acts of justice and injustice, relate to some directing teleology (section 6.3.3). In this instance, however, the teleology is found in the will itself, which is a nature directed to love the good, directed in particular to love other human beings as the subject of the good, to love them as those who partake in the common good. When we act upon others, then we are directed toward their good, so that when we choose to subordinate them to some further good, we must reject the teleological direction towards their good as if it were a kind of obstacle, an evil to be removed. We must, in short, turn from them and harm them by offense.

The divide between transgression and omission depends upon this teleology. Why must we never do evil but we may sometimes fail to do good? Why must the second soldier refrain from killing the child, while the first soldier can fail to save the child from the danger of death, a danger that he himself has introduced? Because when we act upon another person, then we are already directed to his good by the teleology of our action. If we choose to do evil, then we reject the order to his good as an obstacle, an evil to be removed on our way to achieve our goals. On the other hand, if we do not act upon the other person, either by failing to act entirely or by acting upon something else, such as the bridge, then we are not directed—in this action—to share the good with the person. In some manner, we have a general telos to share the good, a telos not found in this particular action but in the overall purpose of our lives; consequently, we must not neglect the good of others entirely. This general telos, however, might be fulfilled in many ways, by helping a variety of people. It does not, usually, tie us down to help this particular person at this particular moment. By failing to do good to someone, we need not always reject the person's good as an obstacle to be removed.

Besides the normative teleology that plays so central a role in the ethics of Aquinas, we have also seen another "teleology," if we wish to call it that, an order that sets one action under another, as a species under a genus (section 6.4). This teleology does not define the good and evil of actions, but rather takes two actions that are already wholly defined in their moral species and relates one to another. This relationship is not a strict genus and species relationship, but rather expresses the relationship of a general cause to a more particular cause (section 6.4.4).

A misapplication of this teleology leads to a harmful form of physicalism, in which actions, by means of this teleology, are placed within their proper species (sections 6.4.1, 6.4.2, and 6.4.3). On this account, teleology provides a kind of inherent nature to the physical act. This view combines some of the worst features of both Abelardianism and physicalism. It relies on end-intention to provide the genus of actions, thereby freeing up the species of some actions from real causes, for example, killing in self-defense is not really killing, but only self-defense. To prevent the same reduction for actions such as adultery, this view attempts, by way of this inherent "teleology," to tie down certain actions to an independent species, thereby approaching actions with a forward movement rather than with the backward movement of resolution.

We have now uncovered the contours of the two pieces of Thomas's account of moral species. Every action has two orders, the order that an action should have and the order that an action does take on. The first order arises from teleology, from some higher agency directing the action to some end. The sexual act, for instance, is directed to new life by the power of reproduction. This order remains, even if the person does not desire it, even if he intends to oppose it. This teleological order does have a link with intention, for it comes into play when the person intends to engage the power or activity. When someone intends to use his sexual organs, for instance, then he intends an action that is ordered to new life. He may not want the new life, he may not intend the new life, but he does intend an action directed to new life. Perhaps he intends it for some other purpose, such as pleasure, but nevertheless he finds it useful to intend this action with such an order. He can choose to fulfill this order; on the other hand, he can also disregard it, directing his action upon material that cannot possibly fulfill this teleological order. Then he must see the teleological order as a kind of evil to be removed from the action. As a human being, however, he finds his good in the order of his actions; therefore, by rejecting the teleological order of his actions he also rejects his own good.

The second order, the order that an action takes on, does not depend upon teleology. Rather, it either conforms to the order the action should have or it falls short of this order. If the agent directs his action, through deliberation and intention, upon material fit to bear the teleological order, then his action is good, for it realizes the order it should have; if he directs his action upon unfit material, then his action is evil. How does the agent direct his action upon fitting or unfitting material? For the exterior action performed, through intention; for the exterior action conceived, through deliberation. In order to achieve his goals he must aim to bring about some change in some material.

It remains to see, in the final chapter, in what way Aquinas says that moral actions are good and evil in their very species.

7 | MORAL SPECIES

Aquinas teaches that human actions alone are good and evil in their very species. Other things are good or evil, but their good or evil does not define what they are. If we are fully to understand Aquinas's doctrine of the specification of human actions, then, we must see why human actions have their good or evil in their very species. We must first see in what manner an action evil in species must always be evil, no matter the circumstances (section 7.1). These actions, called moral absolutes in the contemporary discussion, are the realization of negative moral rules without exception, for example, the rule "Do not kill an innocent human being." Proportionalism wishes to say that no such rules exist, unless they are mere tautologies, such as, "Do not kill whom you should not kill." All other rules, Proportionalism claims, have exceptions.

After we examine moral absolutes, we will see what is distinctive of human actions, such that they are good or evil in their very essence (section 7.2). Finally, we will revisit the journey we have taken (section 7.3).

SECTION 7.1. *Moral Absolutes*

7.1.1. Evil from any Single Defect

In an early text, Aquinas divides human actions into four sorts, those that are indifferent, those that are good in species, those that are evil but can become good, and those that are always evil.[1] In later writings he tends to ignore the third possibility. In fact, he repeatedly says that an action evil in species can never be made good. In contrast, an action good in species can sometimes become evil by circumstance or intention. Why the asymmetry? Because, says Thomas, what is good requires that everything essential be in place, while evil arises from any single essential defect. A good action must be good in species, have all the proper circumstances, and the proper end intended; an action is evil if it lacks any one of these. When an action is evil in species, then, nothing can make it good, since it already lacks an essential element.

The fourth category of actions, then, those actions that are always evil—which in later writings seems to encompass every action evil in species—appears to correspond with moral absolutes. We must take care, however. Aquinas's standard example of the third category, actions that are evil but can become good, is the act of killing a man. Yet Aquinas's dictum, that an action evil in species can never become good, might easily apply to the *moral species* of killing a human being precisely as a human being. We have seen previously (section 5.2.2) that this moral species does not become good. Rather, the natural action with which it is associated can sometimes belong to a different moral species, such as capital punishment. In short, killing a human being—as a moral species—is always wrong, since evil is found in any single defect, but this very moral species can itself disappear in certain concrete circumstances, to be replaced with a morally good species. Since actions occur in the concrete, moral absolutes must be found in an evil species that cannot be removed. Moral absolutes must apply to every singular instance of the natural kind.

The question arises whether Aquinas's fourth category of actions exist, whether any moral absolutes exist, or whether every single evil action fits the pattern of killing a man, which as a moral

1. *Quodlibetum*, 9, 7, 2 (Leonine ed., vol. 25, 117, 77–119).

species can be removed from the corresponding natural species. In short, does every negative precept have some exception, or is there such a thing as a moral absolute, an exceptionless moral norm? To take an example from the contemporary discussion, can the act of contracepting within marriage ever become good? Of itself, it opposes the natural order to new life, but can this order be set aside in need? Perhaps the life of the woman would be threatened through pregnancy. Could the couple, then, intend to have contraceptive sexual relations in order to express their fidelity, setting aside the order to new life?

Evil actions that can become good involve a natural action that can relate to two distinct orders of reason, at least one of which can sometimes be removed. The natural act of killing a human being, for instance, relates both to the order for the good of the individual as an individual and to the order for the common good. In circumstances such as capital punishment, however, the latter order can remove the former. Moral absolutes, therefore, require some order that cannot be removed, some order that is always associated with the natural species.

We have already seen that the act of killing an innocent human being can never become good (chapter 4 and section 5.1.2). This action at least, then, is without exception. Why? Because the condition of being "innocent" relates *per se* to the order for the common good. An innocent person is a chief part of the common good, and therefore must be ordered to the common good through sharing in that good. This order to the common good, however, cannot be removed from actions in which we bring about some change upon another human being.

Not even God's dispensation from the Ten Commandments opposes this moral absolute. God does not make the act of killing an innocent human being to be a good action. Rather, He determines that this action of Abraham is in fact an act of punishing someone who is guilty, for even Isaac is guilty of original sin, which is punishable under the authority of God (section 5.1.3). Killing the innocent, then, provides the type of what we are looking for. First, it involves a natural action that has some teleological order of reason always associated with it: the act of killing a man, or any action upon any person for that matter, must always be ordered to the common good. Second, its material has a feature that relates *per se* to this order: an "innocent" person must be ordered to the common good through sharing in it.

In order to better understand these actions that are always evil we will begin with the much misunderstood case of theft (section 7.1.2). Careful examination will reveal that theft, like killing the innocent, has these two features: it has some order of reason that cannot be removed and it has some feature that relates *per se* to this order. We will then turn to other actions (section 7.1.3), such as lying and certain sexual sins, that also fit this pattern.

7.1.2. Theft

Aquinas's treatment of theft is intriguing. Although we should not take what belongs to someone else, Aquinas grants that in need it might be permissible to take something, for example, if Barb needs Bob's boat in order to save a drowning swimmer, then she can take it. Aquinas's explanation, however, does not fit the pattern of evil actions that become good. He does not say, as he does for wearing women's clothing, that taking what belongs to another is evil in itself but it can become good in necessity. To the contrary, he says that taking what belongs to another is evil and can never be good.[2] How does he explain taking Bob's boat? As we have already seen (section 2.2.5), he says that in necessity all things are held in common, so this act of taking in need is not in fact an act of theft.[3] Since ownership is itself not a physical feature of an item, like its

---

2. More completely, theft is taking what belongs to another in secret. See Pilsner, *Specification*, 116–17. The secrecy of theft and the force of robbery assure that these actions are truly "takings," that is, they are not done with the consent of the owner.

3. II-II, 66, 7, ad 2; II-II, 32, 7, ad 3; II-II, 110, 3 ad 4.

color, but rather a social construction, it is an aspect that is readily changed by circumstances.

Why would Thomas choose this seemingly casuistic approach when he had another alternative available? Why did he not say, simply, that taking what belongs to another, considered absolutely, is wrong, but it can become good with the additional circumstance of necessity? To compound the perplexity, Aquinas treats the seemingly parallel case of failing to return a deposit as a wrong action that sometimes becomes good. Although we should generally return items held in deposit, in some circumstances, such as when the common good is threatened, then we should not. Plato's story of a madman who wants his weapon back provides Aquinas's typical example of an exception.

Aquinas's treatment of theft is often confused with his treatment of returning deposits, as if he were saying fundamentally the same thing in both instances.[4] He is not. Theft has no exceptions; it can never become good. In contrast, returning deposits is Aquinas's standard example of a norm that has exceptions. Failing to return a deposit is usually evil but sometimes good. Theft is always evil; seeming exceptions are actually instances of taking what belongs to us, for in need everything is held in common. Barb does not take Bob's boat; she takes a boat that belongs to anyone who needs it, which includes herself. Why did not Aquinas treat returning deposits in the same way? Why didn't he say that the madman's weapon no longer belongs to him? Presumably, the two cases must truly differ.

4. See, for instance, Rhonheimer, "Perspective," 506; see also R. A. Armstrong, *Primary and Secondary Precepts in Thomistic Natural Law Teaching* (The Hague: Martinus Nijhoff, 1966), 164, who ultimately supposes that both are exceptionless. John Boler, however, in "Aquinas on Exceptions in Natural Law," in *Aquinas's Moral Theory: Essays in Honor of Norman Kretzman*, ed. Scott McDonald (Ithaca, N.Y.: Cornell University Press, 1998), 161–204, at 185–87, provides a good division of exceptions, in which theft, and actions like it, do not truly involve exceptions; rather, the nature of the action itself changes. Returning deposits, on the other hand, is truly a norm that has exceptions.

In Aquinas, returning deposits closely parallels killing a human being. Both are allowed on account of an order to the common good; both are justified because of some deficiency in the individual.[5] Theft, on the other hand, is different from both of these actions. The permission to take what normally belongs to someone else does not depend upon any deficiency in the owner. Bob need not be in some way harmful or guilty in order for Barb to take his boat.

The Proportionalists will claim that theft is defined in moral terms—it means "taking what one should not take"—and as such it cannot possibly have exceptions. Even if they were correct, they would not have explained why returning deposits is any different; why didn't Aquinas define returning deposits in moral terms? We have seen that Thomas does sometimes define moral species in a formal manner, including a judgment upon its fittingness, even as murder might be defined as undue killing; at other times, he defines the moral species apart from any moral judgment (section 5.1.3). Should we suppose, then, that theft falls in the first category while returning deposits falls in the second?

It would seem not. Theft is readily analyzed apart from any tautological moral terms. Taking an object is an action directed towards its use, for the taking itself is a minimal use. Therefore, it must bear upon material fit to be used. Things possessed, unlike human beings, are generally speaking material fit to be used. The notion of possession, however, reserves the use, or at lease the procurement for use, to a particular individual. Bob's boat is a boat that is reserved for his use, or at least for him to decide who can use it. Therefore, if Barb were to take Bob's boat, her action would necessarily be evil, for it is an action directed to the use of the boat, but the boat, insofar as it belongs to Bob, is not material ordered to her use. The material cannot bear the order introduced by reason.

---

5. Aquinas says that the norm for returning deposits fails only when there is some defect in the person who owns the item, in II-II, 57, 2, ad 1.

We need not suppose, as Bennett does, that to say an object belongs to Bob is to say that it is morally wrong for others to use it.[6] The analogy with soccer is apropos. The goal that belongs to team A (goal A) does not mean "the goal that it is wrong for team A to kick at." It means "the goal by which team B scores." That it is "wrong" for team A to aim at its own goal follows from the end that team A seeks, namely, that it score and that team B does not. Goal A is not in potential for this end; it is not ordered toward this end. The "wrongness" is not defined into the very meaning of goal A. Rather, it follows from the incompatibility of goal A with the end at which team A aims in its activity. Given another activity, such as protecting the goal, then goal A is appropriate material, for now the goal is in potential to the end of the activity (which is to prevent something bad).

Similarly, "women's clothing" does not mean "clothing that it is wrong for men to wear"; rather, it means "clothing that reveals to others that one is a woman." That it is wrong for a man to wear women's clothing follows because of the goal at which a man aims (or should aim), namely, to reveal to others his true identity as a man. Or rather, since his activity of wearing clothing is directed to this goal, whether he wants it or not, then if he chooses unfit material, he must reject this goal.

Material possessions pose a greater difficulty because in some sense they are all in potential to be used by anyone. Barb finds herself quite able to use Bob's boat as well as her own. Why should we say, then, that "another's possession" cannot bear the form of "using" at which the action of the thief aims? Because the order to the end of use is ambiguous. It might refer to the order that the thief herself seeks to gain, such as making money, and then the material is proportioned to the form. The jewelry she steals truly is able to

<hr/>

6. Bennett, *Act Itself*, 221. See also Rhonheimer ("Perspective," 506) who thinks that the taking must be described as unjust; Milhaven, "Moral Absolutes," 170; Janssens, "Question of Proportionality," 40.

make her money. On the other hand, the order of use might refer to using something for the common good. Then the material is proportioned to the use of some people but not of others.

According to Aquinas, the common good demands private possessions for the smooth running of society.[7] This boat is reserved for Bob's use, therefore, in order that the common good is served. Since society as a whole—and not just a single individual—most properly directs to the good of the whole, it follows that society can designate which items may be used, and in what way, for the common good. The manner in which some particular item can be used for the common good, then, depends upon the designation of the whole community. Consequently, "Bob's boat" does not mean "the boat that it is right for Bob to use and wrong for others to use"; it means "the boat that Bob is able to use for the common good." This potential arises ultimately from the community that directs to the common good.

That it is wrong for Barb to use the boat follows from the goal at which she aims (or should aim) in using, namely, the common good. Or rather, since her activity is directed to this goal by the natural inclination of her will, whether she wants it or not, then if she chooses unfit material, she must reject the goal. In other words, the order of using for the common good is the teleological order that serves as a measure of the action; it is the order that the action should have. It does not arise from the agent's own personal goals but from a natural inclination, in this instance an inclination of the will. Barb may wish to use the boat for her own personal goals, but she chooses to engage a power directed to the common good. The act of using for the common good, however, demands certain conditions—or due circumstances—for example, that the object be designated, by the community, for Barb's use. If she chooses to act upon other material, such as Bob's boat, then she must see the order to the common good as an obstacle to be removed. The evil of

7. II-II, 66, 2.

theft, then, follows immediately upon the goal of the act of using, together with the potential of the material. Moral terms need not be incorporated into its definition.

If Barb is allowed to take Bob's boat, then something must give. Either the boat must cease to be Bob's, that is, it must no longer be reserved for his use, or Barb's action of taking must cease to be ordered to using for the common good. Thomas takes the first alternative, but taking the second alternative would place theft in the category with killing a human being. It would be an evil action that becomes good because the order of reason to the end is set aside in necessity. We can readily see, then, why Aquinas takes the first alternative, for any act of taking is a use of some sort, and all activity of the will must be directed to the common good.

Refraining from returning a deposited item is not ordered to its use. One does not aim to use the madman's weapon; one simply does not let the madman himself use it. Considered in itself, failing to return a deposit has a formality of not giving someone what is his due; as such, it is an evil action. We have already seen, however, that the order to an individual's good can be set aside when that individual opposes the common good. Since the person is in some manner harmful to the common good, for he intends to use the weapon against the common good, it follows that the order to his good may be set aside in preference to the order for the common good.

The difference between the two cases is to some degree a matter of terminology, but it is a terminology demanded by the nature of the actions. That an act of taking should also be an act of using is unavoidable. The order to the end of using, then, cannot be set aside. What must change, when the common good demands it, is the ownership of the item. In contrast, that an act of withholding an item should oppose the order to the individual's good is not necessary, for this order can be set aside for the sake of the order to the common good.

Theft, then, is always evil because the nature of the action is unavoidably connected with a certain order of reason to the end, namely, the order to the common good; furthermore, the material relates *per se* to this order, for "another's" is precisely that which someone else must direct to the common good. The same cannot be said of wearing clothing or of killing a human being. Wearing clothing typically is ordered to reveal one's state, and if we describe the clothing as women's, then we are considering it precisely with this order, but it need not be so ordered. Nothing about the very nature of wearing clothing demands it, as the nature of taking demands use for the common good. Similarly, although killing is ordered to death, and death is a certain kind of harm to the individual, the act of killing need not be directed by reason—with the order that an action should have—to the good of the individual; it can sometimes be directed to the common good alone, as in capital punishment.

We have seen that sometimes a single natural action, or a single action as picked out by intention or deliberation, can have diverse orders of reason to the end (section 5.2.1). The single action of wearing clothing can be directed to the end of revealing one's state or to the end of protecting oneself from the environment. From these diverse orders arise multiple moral species, even when there is only one natural species. Failing to return a deposit, it seems, fits within this pattern. The order to the good of the individual would make the action evil; the order to the common good would sometimes make the action good. The single natural action, then, is sometimes good and sometimes evil.[8]

Theft must be different. It must have only one order of reason, one order to the end. Or at least, it must have one order to the end that cannot be set aside, whatever other orders might accrue to it. The act of taking, of course, has one natural order, arising from in-

8. Flannery says that norms such as that concerning deposits have exceptions because they are not exact in their formulation (*Acts Amid Precepts*, 83). Rather, they are exact, but diverse orders to the end can apply to them, with one order sometimes being set aside.

tention and deliberation, which is the use of the object. The teleological order of reason invariably attached to this, it seems, is the order of using for the common good. Since this order cannot be set aside, and since something that belongs to another is unfit material for the person's use, it follows that theft must always be evil. Let us now examine other actions that fit this pattern.

7.1.3. Orders Linked to the Nature of an Action

From our analysis of the order of sexual actions (sections 6.1 and 6.2), it becomes clear that contraception belongs with theft and not with returning deposits. The order that sexual activity has toward new life arises from the natural power of reproduction, which power must invariably be engaged with sexual activity. Diverse conditions or necessities cannot remove this order that comes from nature; it cannot be set aside. The sexual sins, such as contraception, bestiality, and masturbation, can never be made good. Not only is the order to the end irremovable, but the nature of the material itself is unchanging. While the ownership of an item can be easily transferred, so that what was Bob's comes to be possessed by those in need, the nature of the animal used in bestiality cannot be transformed. As we have seen, the power of reproduction is directed upon a certain material according to its nature, that is, it is directed upon a woman, who has the nature of being ordered to new life, even if she happens to be sterile (section 6.2.7).

On the end of the material, we find a little flexibility for the other sexual sins, such as fornication or adultery. The order to the end is still necessary, for the further order of reason toward the education of the child follows upon the purpose of bringing about new life. Just as taking is unavoidably a using that must be directed to the common good, so actions that engage the power of reproduction are unavoidably directed by reason to the full maturity of any new life. The order cannot be set aside. The material for these actions, however, are not determined by nature: this or that woman does not belong to this or that man by nature. Rather, the social institution of marriage designates some individuals as "belonging to" others, that is, fit for their sexual "use." Nevertheless, Thomas gives little leeway for change in the material, since he thinks that the need for marriage arises from the common good of the species, so that only He who has care over this good can make changes regarding who belongs to whom. In short, only God has the authority. Aquinas claims, therefore, that God can allow polygamy and that He can designate a woman of His choice to belong to Hosea.[9]

Aquinas has a similarly restrictive view of our use of speech, which by its nature is directed to reveal the truth. The nature of the action is unavoidably connected with the order to the end, which therefore can never be set aside. Consequently, Thomas does not allow even so-called jocose lies, that is, lies told in jest, with no intention to deceive. Although these lies do not actually deceive, they still fail to realize the direction provided by the nature of the action, for they bear upon material not fit to reveal the truth. Irony, hyperbole, and similar features of speech, might allow some flexibility in the material (the words spoken), but the order towards truth must always be present.[10]

9. See *IV Sent.*, d. 33, q. 1, a. 2; I-II, 94, 5, ad 2; I-II, 100, 8, ad 3.

10. See *Super evangelium S. Ioannis*, cap. 21, lect. 6 (in *Opera omnia*, vol. 10 [Parmae: Typis Petri Fiaccadóri, 1855], 645). Such flexibility does not seem to extend so far as Alexander Pruss supposes, so that one can deny, without lying, that one is hiding Jews on the grounds that to a Nazi the word "Jew" means "a subhuman, cold-hearted, shameless, calculating trafficker in vices." See "Lying and Speaking Your Interlocutor's Language," *The Thomist* 63 (1999): 439–53, at 445–46. Perhaps Pruss is correct, to the Nazi the word "Jew" includes this extension. The intension of the word, however, or its *res significata*, is simply a member of a certain race or religious group. Nor can we suppose, as does Benedict Guevin, that the denial falls short of a lie because the exchange with the Nazis does not even count as communication, since it does not foster trust; see "When a Lie Is Not a Lie: The Importance of Ethical Context," *The Thomist* 66 (2002): 267–74, at 273. Given this standard, I fear that in politics lying would be well nigh impossible. Despite the lack of trust generated by war Aquinas says, "Someone might be deceived by the deeds or words of another in two ways. First, because something false is said to him or a promise is not kept, and this is always unlawful, so

It becomes clear that when the order of an action to the end arises from its very nature, then we find exceptionless norms or moral absolutes, for the end cannot be set aside. Sometimes these exceptionless norms are quite flexible, since although the order of the action is fixed, the nature of the material is itself changeable, as the possession of an item might be changed. Sometimes both the order of the action and the material are unchanging, leaving no room for flexibility.

Those actions that receive their order to the end from some power besides the power of locomotion, such as the power of speech or the power of reproduction, will have at least one fixed order to the end that reason aims to realize. Among these actions are included the emotions, which can be seen as kinds of external action insofar as they arise from reason and will.[11] The emotion of anger, for instance, is directed to vengeance, and it is morally good when this vengeance is perceived by reason as truly just. Even as taking must always be ordered to use for the common good, so anger must always be ordered to just retribution.

The emotions, however, are difficult to pin down to a clearly defined material. Which acts of vengeance are just and which not? Guidelines can be given, but ultimately reason must pass the judgment, and the emotion responds to the good of retribution as judged by reason. Similarly, the emotional desire for food is directed to acts of eating that reason has judged appropriate. We have seen that the material "what belongs to another," has a flexibility

---

that no one should deceive the enemy in this way, for there are certain rights of war and agreements that must be kept even between enemies." (II-II, 40, 3. "Dupliciter autem aliquis potest falli ex facto vel dicto alterius uno modo, ex eo quod ei dicitur falsum, vel non servatur promissum. Et istud semper est illicitum. Et hoc modo nullus debet hostes fallere, sunt enim quaedam iura bellorum et foedera etiam inter ipsos hostes servanda.") For diverse defenses of a more restrictive account of lying see Lawrence Dewan, "St. Thomas, Lying, and Venial Sin," *The Thomist* 61 (1997): 279–300, and Christopher Tollefsen, "Lying: The Integrity Approach," *The American Journal of Jurisprudence* 52 (2007): 273–91.

11. Much of Aquinas's discussions of the virtues concern these activities.

dependent upon circumstances (section 7.1.2). Even more do the materials of the emotions have flexibility, often building the judgment of reason into the very material.

Sexual desire is a clear exception. It bears upon sexual activity, which itself is an action with a definite order and definite material. The morality of the physical activity of sexual intercourse is itself placed under the morality of the sexual desire. In contrast, the external actions to which other emotions are directed are usually placed under some other virtue, as the activities of buying, selling, and using possessions are placed under justice rather than generosity, which is the virtue of the emotions that concerns such actions.[12] The order of sexual activity, however, does not clearly fit within justice, since we are dealing with life not yet realized, to which one cannot have justice. The physical activity, then, is placed under the desire for it, although sometimes the activity may have nothing to do with the desire, as when a prostitute performs immoral actions merely for money.

Closely related to this first set of actions, actions that have an order arising from their very nature, are those actions ordered by some human convention, such as the convention of using clothes to reveal one's state, the conventions of buying and selling, and the conventions of promise making. Human convention is more flexible than nature, so these orders probably have conditions under which they may be set aside. The purpose of using clothing to reveal one's state, for instance, is not of necessity connected to the activity of wearing clothes.

Actions evil in their species, then, may never be done. Some natural actions underlying the evil species have an order of reason necessarily attached to them, as do lying and bestiality, so that in no way can the action be good. Other evil actions, considered according to their natural species, may or may not have a particular order of reason, even as an action upon another human being may

12. See II-II, 118, 2; II-II, 118, 3, ad 2.

sometimes have the order to her good set aside. Moral absolutes apply only to the first kind of action, to natural actions necessarily associated with a moral species. The natural act of bestiality is always joined to the moral act of bestiality; as such, it may never be done. In contrast, the natural act of killing a human being is not always joined to the moral act of killing a human being; sometimes, it is joined to the moral act of killing a criminal in punishment. Therefore, no moral absolute applies to it. It is the union of a natural species with a morally evil species that makes for moral absolutes.

SECTION 7.2. *Evil in Species*

The good is found in order, and order is realized in action (sections 4.3.2, 6.2.4, and 6.2.5). A doctor is good through acts of healing, for thereby she is ordered to health. A pen is good through an order to written words, which is realized in the act of writing. The good of these things is derivative upon an order to something beyond themselves, something that has its own good. Health is good even apart from doctors, as are written words without pens. A doctor and a pen, then, partake in another good through an order to it. Not only are these things good by way of order; more profoundly, they exist for the sake of this further good. The very reason for doctors is to be for the sake of health, and the very purpose of pens is written words. Health is a doctor's good, which means not only that a doctor is good by being ordered to health but also that the doctor is for the sake of health. Health is a particular kind of good—a doctor's good—because the doctor exists for it.

Evil or badness is found in disorder, or at least in the lack of order. A pen is bad when it lacks the order to written words, for example, when it streaks. A doctor is bad when she lacks the order to health; worse yet, when she is ordered to its opposite, such as sickness and death. Although order is found in action, mere inactivity does not make something to be bad, at least not usually. A pen that is not currently writing is not necessarily a bad pen; rather, it is bad when someone uses it to write but it fails to do so. Similarly, a doctor who is currently playing golf is not thereby a bad doctor, although at the moment she is not ordering herself to health; rather, a doctor is bad when she performs an act of healing but fails in that act.

In these instances the agent diverts from the direction of some higher agency (section 6.1.3). The pen is moved to write by the author, but it diverts from the movement of the author, failing to dispense ink as she directs. The doctor chooses to engage her power to heal so that now she is moved by some higher agency, by the state that gave her the power to heal or by society. When she fails to heal well, then she diverts from the direction of this higher agency.

Likewise, human beings are good through an order to the good that is realized in actions. Each person is a part within the greater whole of the human community (section 4.3.1). A part is good by being ordered to the whole, as a hand is good through its order to the whole person. As members of the human community we are ordered to the whole through our actions, most generally through actions of sharing the good with others (sections 4.3.2). We also realize particular orders to particular goods through diverse activities, as through speaking we direct ourselves toward truth or through sexual intercourse we direct ourselves to continue the species with new human life (section 6.2.2). The complex of human life, then, is an ordering of actions that directs the person to a good beyond herself, thereby making her to be good. Just as a doctor is not good in isolation but only by relating to a good beyond herself, so an individual human being is not a self-contained good. God alone is good in and of Himself. Human beings must be good through an order beyond themselves.

> A thing is perfected in its proper relation to all those things beyond
> itself only by way of properties in addition to its essence, for the ac-
> tions by which one thing is in a manner joined to another arise from
> its essence by way of powers beyond the essence. Therefore, abso-
> lute goodness is attained only through completion both in a thing's

substance and in a thing's properties. What perfection creatures have from the combination of their essence and properties, however, God has united and simple in His being.[13]

Not only are human beings good by being directed to the good; more profoundly, they exist for the sake of the good (section 6.2.5). Just as a pen is for the purpose of writing and a doctor for the sake of health, so human beings exist for something beyond themselves. The good of the doctor is health because the doctor exists for health. Similarly, God is the good of human beings because human beings exist for the sake of God. Likewise, the common good is the good of the individual because the individual exists for the sake of the shared good.

Human evil is found in disorder, the disorder of voluntary actions, which we call sin (section 6.1.2). In these sins something new appears. Not only is there lack of order; now we find the rejection of the proper order. Not only is there constitutive harm; now we find the harm of offense. Imagine some secondary agent that not only lacked the order to the end but also provided another order, a substitute order that replaced the proper order. What if a pen, for instance, not only had some defect by which it lacked the order to written words; what if it directed itself to some other end, an end inconsistent with written words? No pen, of course, has the power to do so. But what if? Would not the evil of its action take on a special character? Its evil would not merely be the lack of the order to the end; its evil would be a positive order, an order to another end, substituting for the proper order. It would imply not only some de-

---

13. *De veritate*, 21, 5 (Leonine ed., vol. 22, 606, ln. 107–19). "Ut debito modo se habeat ad omnia quae sunt extra ipsum, non perficitur nisi mediantibus accidentibus superadditis essentiae, quia operationes quibus unum alteri quodam modo coniungitur, ab essentia mediantibus virtutibus essentiae superadditis progrediuntur; unde absolute bonitatem non obtinet nisi quod completum est et secundum substantialia et secundum accidentalia principia. Quidquid autem creatura perfectionis habet ex essentialibus principiis et accidentalibus simul coniunctis, hoc totum Deus habet per unum suum esse simplex."

fect; it would imply some positive assertion of a contrary order. Such is the evil of human sin, and human sin alone.[14]

When she lies, a person not only lacks the order to truth; she positively asserts another order in its place, an order to falsity, which she sees as good for some reason or another.[15] He who commits bestiality not only lacks the order to life; he positively asserts a new order toward pleasure that requires the removal of the proper order. A murderer lacks the order to the good of his victim, but he also asserts another order, the usefulness of his victim for some other good. Human sin prefers some other order in place of the proper order, in place of the order for the human good.

No other evil is greater. Any damage to the completion of the good, such as sickness or even death, is not so great as the rejection of the good. A streaking pen does not reject the order to written words; it merely lacks it. In a sinful action, on the other hand, the sinner not only lacks the order to the human good; he rejects it for some other. The soldier who destroys the bridge, thereby killing the child, does damage to the common good, but he does not reject it; he does not subordinate the common good to some other. In contrast, the soldier who kills the child in order to destroy the bridge not only damages the common good; he also rejects it. The sharing of the good with the child is an obstacle, an evil to be eliminated.

God has graciously shared His good with us. We partake in His

14. Angelic sin would also fit this pattern, but our discussion has focused on human actions. Comparisons to other actions have inevitably been to natural actions, while angels have been omitted from the discussion. Any reference to exceptional character of human actions, then, should be taken in reference to the natural physical world, ignoring any parallels that might be found in the purely spiritual realm of angels.

15. Ultimately, matters are more complicated than presented here, for Aquinas distinguishes between mortal and venial sins. Only the former truly assert a contrary order that excludes the order to God. The latter assert an order that has nothing to do with God but does not exclude the order to God. Many lies are merely venial sins; see Dewan, "Lying."

good by being ordered to Him in our actions. We find in our actions the order to the good, the order toward partaking in the divine good. Yet, at times, we reject this good. We view it as an obstacle to some other good that we desire. We remove the order to the divine good so that we can have our own order. In all that is, no evil can compare.

Such evil is possible in human affairs but in no other because the human will is not determined to one but may turn to this or that thing under the broad formality of its being good in some manner or other.[16] It may happen, then, that a person turns to some good of a part of himself to the exclusion of his overall good. He might turn, for instance, to the good of satisfying his emotional desire for pleasure but do so to the exclusion of the order to new life found in sexual activity.

The upshot, says Thomas, is that human actions, and human actions alone, can be evil in their very species.[17] Human sins are not simply actions that have a kind but are defective in that kind, as the act of the pen still has the kind of writing but fails to realize the completion of this kind. Rather, human sins are a new kind. They are a new action, with a new order to a new end. Nevertheless, they are evil, for this new order is not the order of the human being. Sin asserts a new order, replacing the order to the true human good. This new order, then, with its new species, is not good but evil.

> Just as in nature a privation follows some form, for example, upon the form of water follows the privation of the form of fire, so in morals when some mode, species, or order is posited, there follows the privation of the owed mode, species, or order. From what is found

16. I-II, 10, 2; I-II, 13, 6.

17. I-II, 18, 5; *De malo*, 2, 4 (Leonine ed., vol. 23, 37–42); a good account of the basic elements of Aquinas's teaching on actions as good and evil in species can be found in Pilsner, *Specification*, 61–69. Dermot Mulligan, "Moral Evil: St. Thomas and the Thomists," *Philosophical Studies* (Ireland) 9 (1959): 3–26, shows in what manner sin is evil through a privation and yet evil in species.

positively in the act, the act receives its species, but from the consequent privation it is called evil. And just as it applies *per se* to water that it is not fire, so it *per se*, and in its species, applies to such an act to be evil.[18]

Sin has something good about it, for it turns toward some new good; nevertheless, it is ultimately evil, for it turns from the true good.

Although the end contrary to reason eliminates the end of reason, it is nevertheless some sort of good, for example, it might be pleasing to the senses or something of this sort. These sorts of ends are good in some animals, and even in human beings when they are moderated by reason, so what is evil for one thing might happen to be good for another. Therefore, not even the evil that is a specific difference in morals implies something that is evil according to its essence. Rather, it implies something that is good by itself but evil for human beings, insofar as it deprives them of the order of reason, which is the human good.[19]

18. *De malo*, 2, 4, ad 8 (Leonine ed., vol. 23, 41, 324–34). "Sicut in naturalibus priuatio consequitur aliquam formam, sicut ad formam aque consequitur priuatio forme ignis; ita in moralibus ad positionem alicuius modi uel speciei uel ordinis sequitur priuatio debiti modi aut speciei uel ordinis. Et ita ex eo quod positiue in actu inuenitur, recipit actus speciem; set ex priuatione consequente dicitur malus. Et sicut per se conuenit aque non esse ignem, ita per se conuenit tali actui et secundum suam speciem esse malum." *Summa contra Gentiles* III, 9, no. 3 (Leonine ed., vol. 14, 21); *De potentia*, 3, 6, ad 11 and 12 (Marietti, vol. 2, 54).

19. *Summa contra Gentiles* III, 9, 1 (Leonine ed., vol. 14, 21). "Finis autem ille, etsi tollat finem rationis, est tamen aliquod bonum: sicut delectabile secundum sensum, vel aliquid huiusmodi. Unde et in aliquibus animalibus sunt bona; et homini etiam cum sunt secundum rationem moderata; et contingit quod est malum uni, esse bonum alteri. Et ideo nec malum, secundum quod est differentia specifica in genere moralium, importat aliquid quod sit secundum essentiam suam malum: sed aliquid quod secundum se est bonum, malum autem homini, inquantum privat ordinem rationis, quod est hominis bonum."

SECTION 7.3. *Conclusion: The Species of Actions*

Since the good is found in order, and order is realized in actions, it follows that the order of our actions is of the utmost importance. Do our actions direct us to the good or do they direct us to some other end that excludes the human good? In an act of killing, it is not only the upshot of death that matters but the very order toward death realized in the action. Both the craniotomy and the hysterectomy result in the death of the child and the saving of the life of the mother. Nevertheless, the two have diverse orders. The hysterectomy is directed upon the womb of the mother, and seeks to remove a diseased organ; as such, it is ordered to the good of the mother, an order that completes the natural inclination to treat others with a love of friendship. The craniotomy is directed upon the child and aims to introduce damage into the child; as such, it uses the child to the exclusion of the good of the child. The natural inclination to treat the child as a subject of the good is seen as an obstacle; the good of the child is viewed as an evil to be overcome, so that a new order is instituted, an order of subordinating the child to some other end. What order the action takes, then, is not merely a matter of scrupulous casuistry; it is a matter of good and evil. It follows that the species or kinds of actions are at the heart of ethical consideration. Any ethics worthy of the name will dwell upon the nature of actions, seeking to know their essential order.

Sorting out an action from its effects, however, is no simple matter. The first hint of how to sort them points us toward intention (section 1.2), for, it is said, actions are specified by intention. This dictum, however, proves to be an overstatement. Intention does not give species to action, although the species is taken from that which is intended (section 3.5.4). Unfortunately, the overstatement is often tacitly accepted in efforts to discover the species of actions. As a result, the focus shifts to the precise formality under which something is intended. Is the death intended as an "end," whatever precisely that indicates, or as a means? Is the death intended only under the formality of some good? Does the thief intend to take the chalice insofar as it is holy or only insofar as it is valuable?

The upshot of such distractions is that the species of actions are drained of all content (sections 2.2 and 2.3). Formalities turn out to have a thousand subtleties and nuances. The spelunkers intend to disperse their compatriot's bodily parts but not to kill him. The defender intends to stop the attack by shooting him, but she does not intend to harm him. The physical nature of the action becomes all but irrelevant, and the strength of the agent's imagination becomes a force by which she can redescribe her action in innocuous terms.

The true weakness of intention as a specifying principle is revealed when we recognize that intention itself is most properly specified by exterior actions (section 2.3.4). We are seeking the source by which actions receive their direction, and we are told to turn to intention. But when we try to discover the source from which intention itself receives its direction, we run straight into exterior actions, concerning which we began our inquiry. The intention to kill is specified by the act of killing. The perplexity is not paralyzing because it turns out that the exterior action is itself two-fold: the action conceived and the action performed (section 3.1). Intention is specified by the exterior action conceived, which serves as its object. The exterior action performed, however, takes its species from that which is intended. Jones first deliberates about killing, then he intends to kill, basing his intention upon the action he has conceived; finally, impelled by his intention, he actually kills.

From where does the exterior action conceived receive its character (section 3.2)? Not from intention itself, at least not from the intention in question, for otherwise we will have a vicious circle. Does the exterior action conceived, then, have a direction of its own, from its very nature? In a sense, yes; at least sometimes. Sexual activity, for instance, is directed to new life, and speech is directed to reveal the truth (section 1.3). Upon reflection, however, we come to see that this inherent direction, although indispensable for understanding the species of human actions, is not the direction that we seek.

Every action has two orders or directions: a teleological direction arising from its nature and a concrete direction arising from the will or deliberation (section 6.3.2). The act of bestiality, for instance, is directed by nature to the good of new life; by the individual's will it is directed upon this animal, a material of which nature knows nothing. The moral species of an action incorporates both these orders. The teleological order informs the order of reason, the order that reason aims to introduce in the action; the individual's order becomes the order of the action that must be compared to reason. For instance, the order to new life is the standard to which all sexual acts must be compared; the order to this or that material, provided by deliberation and will, is the order that either lives up to the standard or falls short of it. The contemporary discussion rarely adverts to this distinction between orders. It either ignores one or the other, or it blends the two into one, trying to make a single ordering do both jobs. Without doubt, however, the focus has been upon the order that derives from intention and deliberation.

The concrete order of the exterior action conceived can derive neither from intention nor from nature. Rather, it derives from the agent's deliberations (section 3.2). With his reason, the person conceives his action as directed to this or that effect and to this or that end. The soldier, for instance, conceives the action type of killing a child, which he orders to the end of destroying the bridge. This ordering is possible because deliberation does not move forward, inspecting the characteristics of a physical activity, looking for some clue of an end to which it is directed. Rather, deliberation moves backward, beginning with an end to be achieved and then tracing backward to various actions that might achieve it. The soldier begins with the goal of destroying the bridge. He then recognizes that he can destroy the bridge by blowing it up, so he conceives the act of blowing up the bridge *in order to* destroy it. And so it goes. In each instance the "in order to" link does not exist in the nature of things but is forged by reason.

Since deliberation forges certain links and conceives of certain action types, it appears that reason is actively involved in the order of actions. Nevertheless, reason is not free to fabricate any actions and orders it pleases. To the contrary, reason is tightly bound by the nature of things. Reason must conceive of actions that truly do lead to the proposed goal (sections 3.2.4, 3.2.5, and 3.2.6). The soldier cannot suppose that snapping his fingers will destroy the bridge. Furthermore, as reason moves backward, it cannot skip causal connections. The soldier cannot imagine that he fires the gun in order to destroy the bridge, leaving out the middle step of killing the child. The shooting makes sense only insofar as it includes injuring the child.

Reason is also bound by another reality of the action, namely, once an action type has been conceived, then its properties or attributes must be passively recognized (sections 3.4 and 3.5). The potter is free to imagine various shapes for her clay, but if she settles upon a shape, then she must recognize its various properties. Similarly, if the thief conceives the action of taking the chalice, then he must recognize that he is taking a holy object. He cannot eliminate this feature of his action simply because it is not the primary or direct aim that he seeks.

In particular, having conceived of a given action with its proper effect, reason then passively apprehends whether this action upon this material relates *per se* to the teleological order to the end, the order that an action should have. In other words, reason perceives the clash or the harmony between the two orders. All actions have some concrete order of bringing about some form in some material. At the same time, they have a teleological order, an order arising from the power engaged, whether it be the will itself, the power of reproduction, or some other power. In a good action, these two orders conform with one another; in an evil action the concrete order turns away from the teleological order, eliminating it as a kind of obstacle.

> Human acts, which are called moral, have their species from the object in relation to the principle of human acts, which is reason. If the object of the act includes what conforms to the order of reason, it will be a good act in its species, for example, giving alms to those in need. If the object includes something repugnant to the order of reason, then the act will be evil in its species, for example, stealing, which is taking what belongs to another. When the object of the act does not include something pertaining to the order of reason, for example, to pick up sticks from the ground, to walk through a field, and so on, then these acts are indifferent in their species.[20]

He who commits bestiality directs his action upon material fit to give him pleasure (given the perversity of his desires), but not upon material fit for new life, which is the teleological end of the power of reproduction.

What elements, then, enter into the species of human actions? According to Aquinas, human actions take their species precisely insofar as they are good or evil (section 7.2). Any feature of an action can give species, then, not simply those features that are formally intended; any feature gives species insofar as it makes the action good or evil. The thief might not intend to take the chalice insofar as it is holy, but this holiness determines the nature of the material, such that it is not fit material to be used by the thief. Therefore, the action is specified as sacrilegious theft.

What role does intention play? Has it become otiose, since cir-

20. I-II, 18, 8. "Actus humanus, qui dicitur moralis, habet speciem ab obiecto relato ad principium actuum humanorum, quod est ratio. Unde si obiectum actus includat aliquid quod conveniat ordini rationis, erit actus bonus secundum suam speciem, sicut dare eleemosynam indigenti. Si autem includat aliquid quod repugnet ordini rationis, erit malus actus secundum speciem, sicut furari, quod est tollere aliena. Contingit autem quod obiectum actus non includit aliquid pertinens ad ordinem rationis, sicut levare festucam de terra, ire ad campum, et huiusmodi, et tales actus secundum speciem suam sunt indifferentes."

cumstances specify not in relation to intention but in relation to the teleological end of the action?[21] Not at all. Without intention, there is no action at all, nor any material (section 3.5.4). The action of adultery is itself an act of sexual intercourse precisely because the adulterer has intended to use the power of procreation. It bears upon this woman, rather than some other, because the adulterer directs it so. He does so, perhaps, because he finds her fit material for pleasure. Nevertheless, his action is not specified simply through this formality. The woman must be fit material not for his pleasure but for the teleological order to new life.

Likewise, identifying what falls outside intention is crucial for understanding the species of actions. Four related but distinct cases will clarify this point. First, in the hysterectomy case, the doctor intends no harm but rather the good of removing a diseased organ; the foreseen harm to the baby falls outside the species of the action. Second, in the typical case of murder, the murderer intends some harm, usually the harm of death, but he does not intend it precisely as an evil; rather, he seeks it as some useful good, perhaps even a noble good, such as saving others' lives. Third, in capital punishment, the judge also intends to bring about the harm of death but not insofar as it is harm; rather, he intends it under the formality of justice, as restoring the order of the common good. Fourth, in what might be called malicious capital punishment, the judge or other public authority intends to bring about the harm of death precisely because he hates the criminal, that is, he intends the criminal's evil under the formality of evil. Malicious murder, in which the murderer, out of envy or hatred, seeks the death of his victim precisely insofar as it is evil for his victim, also fits in this fourth category.

We must distinguish between intending that which is evil and

21. Flannery notes ("Field of Moral Action") that the category of the moral extends not merely to what is intended but to the entire extent of voluntary actions, taken very loosely. He correctly concludes that intention and *praeter intentionem* are not the whole of ethics, but he implies, too strongly, that these two are not central to the specification of actions.

intending it under the formality of evil. Only in the fourth case does the agent intend the evil under the formality of evil. In the second two cases—the typical case of murder and non-malicious capital punishment—that which is evil for the person killed is intended, namely, his death, but it is intended under some good formality. The first case differs from all the rest, for the doctor does not intend even that which is evil for the baby. She does not intend to bring about the death of the baby, for as she reduces her goal into its causes, she is not led to the death of the baby, or to any harm for the baby, as a cause of achieving her goal. Rather, she is led to the removal of the womb, which has as a consequence some harm to the baby.

Malice is always evil, whether carried out by a private individual or by a public official, whether done to the innocent or to the guilty, so that we may never intend to bring about evil under the formality of evil.[22] This intention does not so much indicate an evil of the exterior action in itself, but rather an evil interior act of will, namely, hatred of another. Such malice, therefore, carries all actions into the species of vice.[23] It does not, however, carry the exterior action in itself toward this evil species; rather, it carries the whole human act, interior and exterior, into the species of vice. Malicious capital punishment, when it is performed upon someone who has been determined to be truly guilty by way of proper judicial procedures, is—considered in itself—a good exterior action. The action as a whole, however, is evil through the evil of the interior act of will. The fourth case, then, steps beyond what has been our primary focus, namely, exterior human actions. Sorting out the remaining three cases, on the other hand, has occupied much of our effort.

Actions take their species from their order to some end or object, as the act of heating is specified by the heat to which it is di-

22. II-II, 34, 3.
23. I-II, 1, 3, ad 3.

rected. In the first case, the action is directed to the good of the person acted upon, even if it then has *per accidens* evil consequences for others, or even if, as in the case of palliative sedation, it has negative consequences for the very person acted upon. In contrast, the second and third cases are directed to the evil of the person acted upon, although they are not directed to this harm precisely as evil. These actions are *per se* ordered to some harm, so that they in some manner take their species from this harmful thing. Both murder and capital punishment, for instance, have the species of killing—as a kind of natural species—while the hysterectomy case is not a killing even in its natural species, for it is not *per se* directed to the death of the baby.

Human actions take their species from the order to the end, but this order must be considered in relation to reason, that is, in relation to the teleological order to the end that reason aims to introduce. When we intend to act upon some subject, then we aim to direct it to some good, either to some useful good or toward a participation or sharing in the good. At the same time, reason teleologically directs the action to some human good. When we eat food, for instance, reason introduces the order of usefulness for nutrition. Now the order of individual human beings to the good is found, apart from some deficiency, through sharing in the good. When we act upon other human beings, then, reason usually aims at the teleological end of their sharing in the good. The second and third cases are opposed to this order of reason. They involve an action directed to the individual's evil, which is thereby opposed to his sharing in the good. Although the agent does not intend this evil precisely as evil, nevertheless, the action is directed to that which is evil, and as such it is opposed to the order toward the person's good.

The first case, however, is not opposed to sharing the good with the individual. In the hysterectomy case, for instance, the doctor does not intend to act upon the baby, so she in no way aims to direct the baby to some good. The hysterectomy case is not opposed to sharing the good with the baby because the action does not aim to order the baby in any way. It neither orders the baby to share in the good nor orders the baby as subordinated to the good. The case of palliative sedation is slightly different, for the doctor does intend to act upon the patient, so that she seeks to introduce into him some order. What she seeks, however, is his good, namely, the relief of pain, and she foresees some proportionately lesser harm, the shortening of his life. The first sort of case, then, can conform to the order that reason aims to introduce, namely, the sharing of the good with others.

Neither the second nor the third case, however, is consistent with this order of reason. Nevertheless, the two cases differ by way of another order that reason seeks to introduce, namely, the order to the common good. In the case of capital punishment, the subject acted upon need no longer share in the good. On account of some defect, that is, on account of an evil deed through which he has separated himself from the common good—thereby making himself a secondary part—he is now ordered to the common good not through sharing but through subordination. The first order, the order of sharing the good with the subject, is set aside for another, a higher order, the order of being directed to the common good. This direction can arise only from the community and its representatives, for while anyone can share the good with others, and so promote the common good, no private individual can direct another equal individual to the common good.

The second and third cases, then, are separated through two distinct orders of reason. In each, the action is ordered to the evil of the individual, but this single order must be compared to two diverse orders of reason, the order of sharing the good with another individual and the order of directing a secondary part to the common good. Malice in all events must be excluded, so that the evil cannot be intended under the formality of evil. Nevertheless, exterior actions take their species not from the formality of intention but from comparison to the order of reason. Intention provides us with some order, for both cases the same order, namely, the order to the death of the individual. This single order, however, is compared to diverse teleological orders of reason. It is opposed to the order of sharing the good, which is the only order that a private individual can aim to introduce when acting upon his equal. The same order towards death, however, is not always opposed to the subordination sought in punishment.

For the species of exterior actions, then, intention provides an order, the introduction of some form into some subject. The precise species of the action does not depend upon the formality of intention. It depends upon a comparison to reason. This order intended—this introduction of some form into some subject, such as death into a fellow human being—must be compared to another order, the teleological order to the human good that reason aims to introduce, the order that the action should have. The first case differs from the other two based upon intention, for the order that intention introduces—even before it is compared to reason—is distinct. In the first case, the action is directed, by intention, to the good of the subject acted upon, or at least not to his harm. As such, this order does not oppose the teleological order of reason, namely, that we share the good with others. In the second and third cases, the action is directed by intention to the harm of the person acted upon. As such, it is opposed to the order of sharing the good with others, although it is not always opposed to the order of subordination realized in punishment. Since the order to the good of an individual can sometimes be set aside, as in punishment, the act of harming another is not always evil, at least when carried about by some public authority for the common good. In other words, the second and third cases do not differ through intention. In both, death is intended; in neither is death intended precisely as evil. They differ, rather, in that they are compared to two diverse teleological orders. The relation of these two orders, one from intention and the other from reason, supplies the moral species.

The consequent moral species are not tautological, incorporating a moral judgment in their very definition; at least they need not be (section 5.1). Certainly, one could describe unfit material precisely as unfit, as one might describe murder as an act of killing the wrong person or of killing someone for whom it is not due. Indeed, when the unfitting material has many factors and aspects, such moral descriptions are perhaps best, for instance, ambition is most easily described as seeking inordinate honors. Often, however, the material can be described without including its unfittingness, as the material of theft is what belongs to another. Such a description does not mean "what is wrong to take" but "what is reserved for the use or procurement of another." It is not difficult to see that using what is for another's use is an action bearing upon inappropriate material. The simplicity of discovery, however, does not imply tautology; it is easy to see that the whole is greater than the part, but no tautology makes it so.

The order of our human actions, then, fits within the human good. Indeed, it largely constitutes the human good. Our actions are directed to some good beyond ourselves. If we realize this order, by moving to the end according to the direction of reason, then we ourselves become good, sharing in the good of the end. Indeed, we realize or institute the good, which is not found simply in an end state but in order. At times, however, we reject the order to the end, seeking our own order instead. We turn from the good, and so become evil.

We have come full circle. The species of actions *is* the good and evil of actions, and the good and evil of actions *is* our good or our evil. Let us, then, like the wise man, put order into our actions.

BIBLIOGRAPHY

Works of Aquinas

Aquinas, Thomas. *Super evangelium S. Ioannis,* cap. 21, lectio 6. In *Opera omnia,* vol. 10. Parmae: Typis Petri Fiaccadori, 1855.

———. *Reportatio: In decem praeceptis, praeceptum v.* In *Opera omnia,* vol. 7, pt. 2. Parmae: Typis Petri Fiaccadori, 1865.

———. *Scriptum super Sententiis magistri Petri Lombardi,* edited by P. Mandonnet and M. F. Moos. Paris: P. Lethielleux, 1929–1947.

———. *In duodecim libros Metaphysicorum Aristotelis expositio,* edited by M. R. Cathala and R. M. Spiazzi. Taurini-Romae: Marietti, 1935.

———. *Quaestio disputata de caritate.* Taurini-Romae: Marietti, 1942.

———. *Quaestiones disputatae de potentia,* vol. 2. Taurini-Romae: Marietti, 1949.

———. *Opera omnia iussu Leonis XIII P. M.* Rome: Editori di San Tommaso, 1982–1996.

Other Works

Anscombe, G. E. M. "Modern Moral Philosophy." *Philosophy* 33 (1958): 1–19.

———. *Intention.* 2nd ed. Ithaca, N.Y.: Cornell University Press, 1963.

———. "Two Kinds of Error in Action." In *Ethics, Religion and Politics,* 3–9. Minneapolis: University of Minnesota Press, 1981.

———. "War and Murder." In *Ethics, Religion and Politics,* 51–61. Minneapolis: University of Minnesota Press, 1981.

———. "Action, Intention and 'Double Effect.'" In *Human Life, Action and*

Ethics, edited by Mary Geach and Luke Gormally, 207–26. Charlottesville, Va.: Imprint Academic, 2005.

Aristotle. "*Physica.*" In *The Basic Works of Aristotle*, edited by Richard McKeon, 218–394. New York: Random House, 1941.

Armstrong, R. A. *Primary and Secondary Precepts in Thomistic Natural Law Teaching.* The Hague: Martinus Nijhoff, 1966.

Augustine. *Sancti Aurelii Augustini contra academicos, De beata via, De ordine, De magistro, De libero arbitrio.* Corpus Christianorum. Series Latina 29, edited by William M. Green. Turnhout: Brepols, 1970.

———. *Sancti Aurelii Augustini epistulae I–LV.* Corpus Christianorum 31, edited by Klaus-D. Daur. Turnhout: Brepols, 2004.

Austriaco, Nicanor Pier Giorgio. "On Reshaping Skulls and Unintelligible Intentions." *Nova et Vetera* 3 (2005): 81–100.

Belmans, Theo G. *Le sens objectif de l'agir humain: pour relire la moral conjugale de Saint Thomas.* Vatican City: Libreria Editrice Vaticana, 1980.

Bennett, Jonathan. "Morality and Consequences." In *The Tanner Lectures on Human Values*, vol. 2, edited by Sterling McMurrin, 45–116. Salt Lake City: University of Utah Press, 1981.

———. *The Act Itself.* Oxford: Clarendon Press, 1995.

Boler, John. "Aquinas on Exceptions in Natural Law." In *Aquinas's Moral Theory: Essays in Honor of Norman Kretzman*, edited by Scott McDonald, 161–204. Ithaca, N.Y.: Cornell University Press, 1998.

Boyle, Joseph M. "Double Effect and a Certain Type of Embryotomy." *Irish Theological Quarterly* 44 (1977): 303–18.

———. "*Praeter Intentionem* in Aquinas." *The Thomist* 42 (1978): 649–65.

Bradley, Gerard V. "No Intentional Killing Whatsoever: The Case of Capital Punishment." In *Natural Law and Moral Inquiry: Ethics, Metaphysics, and Politics in the Work of Germain Grisez*, edited by Robert P. George, 155–73. Washington, D.C.: Georgetown University Press, 1998.

Bratman, Michael. *Intentions, Plans, and Practical Reason.* Cambridge, Mass.: Harvard University Press, 1987.

Brock, Stephen L. *Action and Conduct: Thomas Aquinas and the Theory of Action.* Edinburgh: T. & T. Clark, 1998.

———. "Natural Inclination and the Intelligibility of the Good in Thomistic Natural Law." *Vera Lex* VI, nos. 1–2 (2005): 57–78.

———. "*Veritatis Splendor* ¶ 78, St. Thomas, and (Not Merely) Physical Objects of Moral Acts." *Nova et Vetera.* English edition 6 (2008): 1–62.

Brugger, Christian. "Aquinas and Capital Punishment: The Plausibility of the Traditional Argument." *Notre Dame Journal of Law, Ethics & Public Policy* 18 (2004): 357–72.

Cajetan, Thomas de Vio. *Commentaria in Summam theologicam s. Thomas Aquinatis.* In *Opera omnia iussu Leonis XIII P. M.,* vol 7. Rome: Editori di San Tommaso, 1892.

Cavanaugh, Thomas A. "Aquinas's Account of Double Effect." *The Thomist* 61 (1997): 107–21.

———. "Double Effect and the End-Not-Means Principle: A Response to Bennett." *Journal of Applied Philosophy* 16 (1999): 181–85.

———. *Double-Effect Reasoning: Doing Good and Avoiding Evil.* Oxford: Clarendon Press, 2006.

Connell, Richard J. *Nature's Causes.* Revisioning Philosophy, vol. 21. New York: P. Lang, 1995.

Davidson, Donald. *Essays on Actions and Events.* Oxford: Clarendon Press, 1980.

Dedek, John F. "Intrinsically Evil Acts: An Historical Study of the Mind of St. Thomas." *The Thomist* 43 (1979): 385–413.

———. "Premarital Sex: The Theological Argument from Peter Lombard to Durand." *Theological Studies* 41 (1980): 643–67.

———. "Intrinsically Evil Acts: The Emergence of a Doctrine." *Recherches de theologie ancienne et medievale* 50 (1983): 191–226.

Delaney, Neil. "To Double Business Bound: Reflections on the Doctrine of Double Effect." *American Philosophical Quarterly* 75 (2001): 561–83.

Dewan, Lawrence. "St. Thomas, Lying, and Venial Sin." *The Thomist* 61 (1997): 279–300.

———. "St. Thomas, John Finnis, and the Political Good." *The Thomist* 64 (2000): 337–74.

———. "Thomas Aquinas, Gerard Bradley, and the Death Penalty: Some Observations." *Gregorianum* 82 (2001): 149–65.

———. "St. Thomas, Rhonheimer, and the object of the human act." *Nova et Vetera.* English edition 6 (2008) 63–112.

Donagan, Alan. *The Theory of Morality.* Chicago: University of Chicago Press, 1977.

Finnis, John. *Natural Law and Natural Rights.* 2nd ed. Oxford: Clarendon Press, 1980.

———. "Natural Inclinations and Natural Rights: Deriving 'Ought' from 'Is' According to Aquinas." In *Lex et Libertas: Freedom and Law*

According to St. Thomas Aquinas. Studi Tomistici 30, edited by Leo Elders and Klaus Hedwig, 43–55. Rome, 1987.

———. "Intention and Side-Effects." In *Liability and Responsibility: Essays in Law and Morals,* edited by R. G. Frey and Christopher W. Morris, 32–64. New York: Cambridge University Press, 1991.

———. *Moral Absolutes: Tradition, Revision, and Truth.* Washington, D.C.: The Catholic University of America Press, 1991.

———. "Object and Intention in Moral Judgments according to Aquinas." *The Thomist* 55 (1991): 1–27.

———. *Aquinas: Moral, Legal, and Political Theory.* Oxford: Oxford University Press, 1998.

———. "Public Good: The Specifically Political Common Good in Aquinas." In *Natural Law and Moral Inquiry: Ethics, Metaphysics, and Politics in the Work of Germain Grisez,* edited by Robert P. George, 174–209. Washington, D.C.: Georgetown University Press, 1998.

Finnis, John, Germain Grisez, and Joseph Boyle. "'Direct' and 'Indirect': A Reply to Critics of Our Action Theory." *The Thomist* 65 (2001): 1–44.

Flannery, Kevin L. "What Is Included in a Means to an End?" *Gregorianum* 74 (1993): 499–513.

———. "More on Abortion." *Gregorianum* 79 (1998): 163–67.

———. *Acts Amid Precepts: The Aristotelian Logical Structure of Thomas Aquinas's Moral Theory.* Washington, D.C.: The Catholic University of America Press, 2001.

———. "The Multifarious Moral Objects of Thomas Aquinas." *The Thomist* 67 (2003): 95–118.

———. "The Field of Moral Action According to Thomas Aquinas." *The Thomist* 69 (2005): 1–30.

Foot, Philippa. "Killing and Letting Die." In *Killing and Letting Die,* edited by Bonnie Steinbock, 280–89. New York: Fordham University Press, 1994.

———. "The Problem of Abortion and the Doctrine of Double Effect." In *Killing and Letting Die,* edited by Bonnie Steinbock, 266–79. New York: Fordham University Press, 1994.

Frey, R. G. "Some Aspects of the Doctrine of Double Effect." *Canadian Journal of Philosophy* 5 (1975): 263–64.

Gaffney, James. "The Pope on Proportionalism." In *Veritatis Splendor: American Responses,* edited by Michael E. Allsopp and John J. O'Keefe, 60–71. Kansas City, Mo.: Sheed and Ward, 1995.

Grisez, Germain. *Contraception and the Natural Law*. Milwaukee: Bruce
    Publishing, 1964.
————. "A New Formulation of the Natural-Law Argument Against Con-
    traception." *The Thomist* 30 (1966): 343–61.
————. "Toward a Consistent Natural Law Ethics of Killing." *American
    Journal of Jurisprudence* 15 (1970): 64–96.
————. *The Way of the Lord Jesus 1: Christian Moral Principles*. Chicago:
    Fransiscan Herald Press, 1983.
————. *The Way of the Lord Jesus 2: Living a Christian Life*. Quincy, Ill.:
    Franciscan Press, 1993.
Grisez, Germain, Joseph Boyle, John Finnis, and William E. May. "Every
    Marital Act Ought to Be Open to New Life: Toward a Clearer Under-
    standing." *The Thomist* 52 (1988): 365–426.
Guevin, Benedict M. "Aquinas's Use of Ulpian and the Question of Physi-
    calism Reexamined." *The Thomist* 63 (1999): 613–28.
————. "When a Lie Is Not a Lie: The Importance of Ethical Context."
    The Thomist 66 (2002): 267–74.
Hart, H. L. A. "Intention and Punishment." *Oxford Review* 5 (1967): 5–22.
Janssens, Louis. "Norms and Priorities in a Love Ethics." *Louvain Studies* 6
    (1977): 207–38.
————. "Ontic Evil and Moral Evil." In *Readings in Moral Theology No. 1*,
    edited by Charles E. Curran and Richard A. McCormick, 40–93. New
    York: Paulist Press, 1979.
————. "St. Thomas Aquinas and the Question of Proportionality." *Lou-
    vain Studies* 9 (1982): 26–46.
————. "A Moral Understanding of Some Arguments of St. Thomas." *Eph-
    emerides Theologicae Lovanienses* 63 (1987): 354–60.
Jensen, Steven J. "A Defense of Physicalism." *The Thomist* 61 (1997): 377–
    404.
————. "A Long Discussion Regarding Steven A. Long's Interpretation of
    the Moral Species." *The Thomist* 67 (2003): 623–43.
————. "Do Circumstances Give Species?" *The Thomist* 70 (2006): 1–26.
————. "The Trouble with Secunda Secundae, 64, 7: Self-Defense." *The
    Modern Schoolman* 83 (2006): 143–62.
————. "When Evil Actions Become Good." *Nova et Vetera*. English edi-
    tion 5 (2007): 747–64.
Johnson, Mark. "Proportionalism and a Text of the Young Aquinas: Quod-
    libetum IX, Q. 7, A. 2." *Theological Studies* 53 (1992): 683–99.

Johnstone, Brian V. "The Meaning of Proportionate Reason in Contemporary Moral Theology." *The Thomist* 49 (1985): 223–47.

Kaczor, Christopher. "Moral Absolutism and Ectopic Pregnancy." *Journal
of Medicine and Philosophy* 26 (2001): 61–74.

———. "Distinguishing Intention from Foresight: What is Included in
a Means to an End?" *International Philosophical Quarterly* 41 (2001):
77–89.

———. *Proportionalism and the Natural Law Tradition.* Washington, D.C.:
The Catholic University of America Press, 2002.

Knauer, Peter. "The Hermeneutic Function of the Principle of Double Effect." In *Readings in Moral Theology No. 1,* edited by Charles E. Curran
and Richard A. McCormick, 1–39. New York: Paulist Press, 1979.

Lee, Patrick. "Permanence of the Ten Commandments: St. Thomas and
His Modern Commentators." *Theological Studies* 42 (1981): 422–43.

Long, Steven A. "Evangelium Vitae, St. Thomas Aquinas, and the Death
Penalty." *The Thomist* 63 (1999): 511–52.

———. "St. Thomas Aquinas through the Analytic Looking Glass." *The
Thomist* 65 (2001): 259–300.

———. "A Brief Disquisition Regarding the Nature of the Object of the
Moral Act according to St. Thomas Aquinas." *The Thomist* 67 (2003):
45–71.

———. "A Response to Jensen on the Moral Object." *Nova at Vetera* 3
(2005): 101–8.

———. *The Teleological Grammar of the Moral Act.* Naples, Fla.: Sapientia
Press, 2007.

———. "Veritatis Splendor ¶ 78 and the Teleological Grammar of the
Moral Act." *Nova et Vetera.* English edition 6 (2008): 139–56.

Mangan, J. T. "A Historical Analysis of the Principle of Double Effect."
Theological Studies 10 (1949): 41–61.

May, William E. "The Management of Ectopic Pregnancies: A Moral Anal-
ysis." In *The Fetal Tissue Issue: Medical and Ethical Aspects,* edited by
Peter J. Cataldo and Albert S. Moraczewski, O.P., 121–47. Braintree,
Mass.: Pope John Center, 1994.

McInerny, Ralph M. *Aquinas on Human Action: A Theory of Practice.*
Washington, D.C.: The Catholic University of America Press, 1992.

McMahan, Jeff. "Revising the Doctrine of Double Effect." *Journal of Applied Philosophy* 11 (1994): 201–12.

Milhaven, John G. "Moral Absolutes and Thomas Aquinas." In *Absolutes in Moral Theology?*, edited by Charles E. Curran, 154–85. Washington: Corpus Books, 1968.

Mulligan, Dermot. "Moral Evil: St. Thomas and *The Thomists.*" *Philosophical Studies* (Ireland), 9 (1959): 3–26.

Murphy, Mark. "The Common Good." *Review of Metaphysics* 59 (2005): 133–64.

Osborne, Thomas M. *Love of God and Love of Self in Thirteenth Century Ethics.* Notre Dame, Ind.: University of Notre Dame Press, 2005.

Pakaluk, Michael. "Is the Common Good of Political Society Limited and Instrumental?" *Review of Metaphysics* 55 (2001): 57–94.

Pilsner, Joseph. *The Specification of Human Actions in St. Thomas Aquinas.* Oxford: Oxford University Press, 2006.

Porter, Jean. "The Moral Act in Veritatis Splendor and in Aquinas's Summa Theologiae: A Comparative Analysis." In *Veritatis Splendor: American Responses,* edited by Michael E. Allsopp and John J. O'Keefe, 278–95. Kansas City, Mo.: Sheed and Ward, 1995.

———. "'Direct' and 'Indirect' in Grisez's Moral Theory." *Theological Studies* 57 (1996): 611–32.

———. *Nature as Reason: A Thomistic Theory of the Natural Law.* Grand Rapids, Mich.: Eerdmans, 2005.

Pruss, Alexander R. "Lying and Speaking Your Interlocutor's Language." *The Thomist* 63 (1999): 439–53.

Reichberg, Gregory M. "Aquinas on Defensive Killing: A Case of Double Effect?" *The Thomist* 69 (2005): 341–70.

Rhonheimer, Martin. *Natural Law and Practical Reason: A Thomist View of Moral Autonomy.* New York: Fordham University Press, 2000.

———. "The Cognitive Structure of the Natural Law and the Truth of Subjectivity." *The Thomist* 67 (2003): 1–44.

———. "The Moral Significance of Pre-rational Nature in Aquinas: A Reply to Jean Porter (And Stanley Hauerwas)." *The American Journal of Jurisprudence* 48 (2003): 253–80.

———. "The Perspective of the Acting Person and the Nature of Practical Reason: The 'Object of the Human Act' in Thomistic Anthropology of Action." *Nova et Vetera.* English edition 2 (2004): 461–516.

Scholz, Franz. "Problems on Norms Raised by Ethical Borderline Situations: Beginnings of a Solution in Thomas Aquinas and Bonaventure." In *Readings in Moral Theology No. 1,* edited by Charles E. Curran and Richard A. McCormick, 158–83. New York: Paulist Press, 1979.

Sen, Amartya. *Inequality Re-examined*. Cambridge, Mass.: Harvard University Press, 1992.

Smith, Janet. "Moral Terminology and Proportionalism." In *Recovering Nature: Essays in Natural Philosophy, Ethics, and Metaphysics in Honor of Ralph McInerny*, edited by Thomas Hibbs and John O'Callaghan, 127–46. Notre Dame, Ind.: University of Notre Dame Press, 1999.

Staley, Kevin. "Metaphysics and the Good Life: Some Reflections on the Further Point of Morality." *American Catholic Philosophical Quarterly* 65 (1991): 215–34.

Sullivan, Thomas D., and Gary Atkinson. "Benevolence and Absolute Prohibitions." *International Philosophical Quarterly* 97 (1985): 247–59.

———. "*Malum Vitandum*: The Role of Intentions in First-Order Morality." *International Journal of Philosophical Studies* 1 (1993): 99–110.

Tollefsen, Christopher. "Lying: The Integrity Approach." *The American Journal of Jurisprudence* 52 (2007): 273–91.

Windass, Stanley. "Double Think and Double Effect." *Blackfriars* 44 (1963): 257–66.

INDEX